Surfing into life on a Bathboard

A Gaeilgeoir Republican's Pathway to an Imperfect Peace

Surfing into life on a Bathboard

A Gaeilgeoir Republican's Pathway to an Imperfect Peace

Jake MacSiacais

Beyond the Pale Books

First published June 2022

BTP Books Ltd
Teach Basil
2 Hannahstown Hill
Belfast BT17 0LT

www.beyondthepalebooks.com

© 2022 Jake MacSiacais has asserted his right under the Copyright, Designs and Patents Act 1988 to be identified as the author of this work.

All rights reserved. No part of this work may be reproduced in any form or by any means, electronic or mechanical, including photocopy, without permission from the publisher.

ISBN 978-1-914318-17-7 (Pbk)

Printed in Belfast

Cover illustration from a painting by Amos Nattini (1892-1985). Dante and Virgil leave the seventh circle of hell on the back of a winged monster, from Canto XVII of 'Inferno' from 'The Divine Comedy' by Dante Alighieri, 1923. By kind permission of Bridgeman Images.

Seanfhocail: The Irish proverbs used in this work are used with the kind permission of Jim Herron from his book of Irish proverbs, *An Griangraf Gáfa*.

Contents

Dedication		vi
Foreword		vii
Prologue		xi
1	Thirty years growing	1
2	In the eye of the storm and the midst of conflict	21
3	H-Blocks: 'The Breaker's Yard'	63
4	Via Dolorosa – The road of suffering	85
5	Back in the world, back in the struggle	103
6	Things are not always what they seem	115
7	'Fere libenter homines id quod volunt credunt'	129
8	A new era, an unsettling era	153
9	The first decade of the new millenium	187
10	Toward the three score and beyond	195
11	Differing discourses	205
12	Life beyond the nightmare	214

Dedication

This memoir is dedicated, with heartfelt thanks, to Jarlath Benson who guided me safely through Dante Alighieri's hell and purgatory, setting me back on the road to recovery and the path towards whatever paradise I could find. I also dedicate it to Chrissie Keenan, my wife and my principal hero, and to my deceased sister, Volunteer Pauline Brady, a constant source of pride and inspiration.

Foreword
Barry McCaffrey

This book is Jake MacSiacas's own story. Whether or not you agree with his beliefs or his decision to become an active member of the Republican Movement for nearly three decades, few would disagree that he has led an unorthodox and eventful life. Only he can tell his story of the tumultuous events of the conflict that he lived through. Critics may dispute his version; that is their right, as it is his right to give his personal account of experiences as he saw it.

While this is the story of an unapologetic republican activist, he does not shy away from addressing mistakes that were made by the IRA which cost the lives of civilians. He recounts the row which erupted with his father who lambasted the actions of the IRA on Bloody Friday when nine people were killed and 130 injured.

This book is at times brutally honest. In his effort to provide power to truth MacSiacas recounts many personal and harrowing experiences, including being the victim of child abuse, family disputes and his own personal struggle with mental health issues.

Many republicans, loyalists and former members of the RUC and British army have chosen to tell their own stories in print. Each is unique and comes from the author's own point of view. Jake's story is arguably unique due to the senior roles he held within the Republican Movement at critical points in the conflict over nearly 30 years. Having joined the youth wing of the Republican Movement as a 10 year-old in 1968 he would remain active until his resignation in 1997 on the cusp of the Good Friday Agreement. It is ironic that he chose to leave the organisation, which he had dedicated his life to, at the very moment when it was being brought in from the cold by the political establishment. In the pages that follow he sets out his reasons for taking the momentous decisions which shaped his life.

This book reveals his first experience of incarceration which came as a 17-year-old teenager in 1975 when he was jailed in the Cages of Long Kesh. Released in April 1977, within seven weeks he had been re-arrested and was back in prison, charged with a gun attack on a British Army patrol. He is among the few people to have survived being shot at by loyalists, fellow republicans and the British Army. Court papers later revealed that he had cheated death by the narrowest of margins when an undercover soldier, hidden in a roof above him, was repeatedly refused permission by a commanding officer to shoot MacSiacas as he prepared to mount an attack on British soldiers. While he escaped with his life that day, he was to spend the next five years behind bars, much of it on the Blanket protest in the notorious H-Blocks.

This book gives a telling insight into the strategic and political differences which went on within the Republican Movement during the conflict which few outsiders knew was happening. Republicans may have had a collective goal of securing a united Ireland through armed struggle but within the movement divisions between the ideologies of nationalism, communism, socialism, internationalism and Catholicism battled constantly for supremacy. MacSiacas would witness first hand and play a leading role in the prison struggle between Margaret Thatcher and the IRA.

This book takes the reader through many shocking and traumatising experiences during that struggle, starting with the Blanket and No Wash protests and culminating with the death of ten of his comrades on hunger strike in 1981. The reader is left in no doubt that, 40 years on, the memories of those deaths remain a constant in his thoughts.

Within a year of the hunger strike having ended MacSiacas was released from the H-Blocks and found himself back at the very heart of the Republican Movement. He would play a key role in helping to build the electoral success of Sinn Féin, although never actually becoming a party member. Readers are given an inside account of the protracted efforts by Martin McGuinness and Gerry Adams to gradually move the Republican Movement away from armed struggle during the late 1980s and early 1990s. We learn of the bitter opposition which developed within the IRA from those who were opposed to Sinn Féin's entry into mainstream politics. MacSiacas provides a perceptive time-line of the internal politicking which went on within the higher echelons of the IRA throughout this period as to whether politics or militancy would hold the upper hand. While this process would ultimately lead to the IRA's August 1994 ceasefire, it also caused a bitter split with those determined to carry on the 'armed struggle'.

He reveals how, after spending most of his adult life at the very centre of the Republican Movement, he took the momentous decision to resign from the organisation in 1997 over his firmly held belief that Sinn Féin's decision to join the Stormont Assembly was politically flawed as it re-enforced partition. However despite his disagreement with Sinn Féin's Stormont strategy he refused to join former comrades determined to carry on the 'armed struggle', believing that such actions were ultimately futile and bound to end in failure. This book is Jake MacSiacas's story, which he has tried to tell honestly and openly. History will judge.

Belfast, June 2022

Prologue

In 1968, at 10 years-of-age, I was to learn a lesson I'd never forget. It coloured my view of people for a long time. Friends from my street were always around Tornaroy and Hannahstown, where my uncle John had a farm, on which we often spent time. It was a beautiful summer's day in that seminal year. One of my friends cajoled me into going with him to St Joseph's Church. He told me that there was a man at St Joseph's who was kind and generous. We entered the church. I distinctly remember the rays of the sun shining brightly through the church windows, speckled with dust like shimmery curtains of dancing midges. A stair led upwards to a choir loft. My 'friend' told me to go up the stairs and left.

In the loft, a man sat alone on a chair. I can only say that he looked like an old man. I knew he was a neighbour of my uncle John. He wore a cap on his head, which surprised me, given the heat of the day. He was puffing on a pipe which he set aside when I appeared. The smell of the pipe was wonderful and redolent of my own grandfather. I was unsettled, for reasons I didn't fully understand, but the smell of the pipe and the associations it conjured of my grandfather settled me somewhat. I still felt uneasy, something wasn't quite right. I couldn't explain my uneasiness, but I knew something was strange and amiss. I was both curious and a little frightened. He broke the silence and asked me to come and sit on his knee. He began singing the hymn 'Amazing Grace'. Gradually he began fumbling about in my trousers with one hand and doing the same with his other hand in his own trousers. I was terrified but strangely excited. I began to feel a sensation I'd never experienced before and one which made me both afraid and ashamed. More than anything I was confused and couldn't quite understand what was happening.

Suddenly he stopped singing and began mumbling in a strange fashion. My heart was in my mouth. He roughly grabbed my hand and thrust it down his trousers. I was shocked. I jumped from his knee and sprang back. He instantly became angry and threatening. In seconds he changed and became cajoling and threatening by turns. He stood up and told me not to be afraid. He pressed a florin – a coin worth two old shillings and big money for a lad in those days – into my hand and told me I was a good boy, but added that I would be in very big trouble if I ever told anyone about what had happened. He then told me I was a filthy, dirty boy and if I ever told anyone everyone would know.

I rushed from the church and over the next few days I spent the florin. I had just started my first job mixing the sausage meat in Arthur Webb's butcher's shop on Slievegallion Drive. I gave my earnings to my mother, who would give me back a shilling. We were, like all those around us, extremely poor. By this stage there were eight children in our house. Throughout that summer I would return to St Joseph's Church six or seven times. Greed had taken hold of me and had overcome the shame of a 10 year-old boy. I would allow this pervert to abuse me; all the while he mumbled and softly cried. I also touched him, as he insisted I do. Thank God the abuse went no further than touching. I don't know how I would have coped had it gone further. I was always in a state where fear, pleasure, and shame beset me. I was so innocent at that time that I didn't fully understand what was happening. I was troubled by it all, but the money and the greed were to bring me back, even though I knew it was wrong. His threats were always there, but I was the one going back. I was unable to tell anyone about this for another 49 years. I am happy it never scarred me. In adulthood I understand that it is the power and control of the abuser which causes damage to children and young people facing such horrors. I reclaimed control and ended the abuse. That effectively denied control to my abuser and meant he couldn't rent space in my head.

If 1968 was a seminal year for me, it was even more so for the north of Ireland. 1966 had witnessed the renewed rise of Orange violence with murders and bombings directed against the Catholic people of the North. By 1968 the Orange response against the ongoing demand for basic civil rights was to see the RUC take centre stage in front of the world's television cameras. On October 5th, the RUC brutally

Prologue

attacked a civil rights' march in Derry.[1] They batoned and bludgeoned members of the English parliament and hundreds of civil rights marchers in Duke Street, setting the tone for things to come. The days of innocence were over.

Even the best memory is not without fault; therefore, before you read on, I would like to make this disclaimer: it's how I and I alone remember it. I'm not sure that any of us can wholly rely on another's recall of events, and indeed, at times, even on our own recall. So treat these following pages as my honest attempt at giving you a flavour, which is as reliable as I can make it, of my journey through life. This is my short account of some of those things which left their mark on me as I made my way through life and the little bit of the world which I had travelled. I have left lots out, forgive me that. This is also an account of the road travelled by the Republican Movement which I joined with an honest heart and fervent hope. We haven't achieved, so far, the vision that I had – Ireland is not yet free, nor socialist, nor are her people sovereign. Neither is she Gaelicised, yet. Remember, however, that the only time we'll be beaten is when we're not on the field.

I was persuaded to commit this memoir to paper following the darkest period of my life. On January 21st 2016, a black dog came visiting out of the blue, as it seemed to me at the time. I now realise that the black dog had been nibbling away at me for some time. I was in a serious depression. That day I suffered a complete breakdown and a long crisis, with which I was to struggle for several years. I would not have been able to cope with my mental health crisis without the love and support of my hero and life-partner, Chrissie Keenan, and my children, Orliath, Conchuir, Eimear, Fionnghuala and Tiarnán. I remember a moment, in the middle of my darkest hours, when a friend, Noel McGuigan, called to see me at home. I was unable to even have a worthwhile conversation with him but his act of solidarity and caring left an impression on me. He showed me yet again that there was always kindness in the world despite the darkness.

---

1 The Derry Housing Action Committee, DHAC, a militant direct action group, proposed a march for October. The march was endorsed by the Northern Ireland Civil Rights Association, NICRA, who withdrew their support when the Stormont government banned it. DHAC said they would go ahead. NICRA caved in to public pressure and agreed to rejoin the planned march. As it reached the edge of the city centre the march was viciously attacked and scenes of RUC men batoning peaceful marchers, including politicians and MPs, were broadcast around the world, revealing the ugly and violent face of the Stormont regime to the world.

I'm eternally grateful to my late parents Gerry and Rosie, and to my sisters Pauline (RIP) Carol, Collette, Theresa and Martine, also my brothers Rab, Mick and Eamonn. I am also deeply indebted to my stalwart friend, Pat Rice, and am particularly indebted to Seán Mistéil and Pilib Ó Ruanaidh; I often wonder what might have happened had it not been for their support and friendship and that of many others. I am not going to dispense advice, you'll be glad to hear. I am at one with Oscar Wilde who said: 'I always pass on good advice. It is the only thing to do with it. It is never of any use to oneself.'

Jake MacSiacais, June 2022

Chapter 1

Thirty years growing

'In war truth is always the first casualty.' Aeschylus (525–456 BCE)

Surfing into life on a bathboard

I surfed into life on a bathboard, if the story my mother told me is true.[1] Surfing into life on a wooden board, above the holy waters drawn by the merciless Sisters of Mercy. Not the most auspicious beginning, nor the worst. It was my start and we only ever get the one. It was a new start for my parents as well. My first day was like any other day before or since: the world spun merrily on its axis, oblivious to my existence. The day marked the arrival of a tiny, innocent, little child, if you don't buy into the original sin myth. I was ordinary, unremarkable, no better or no worse than any other.

Rosie McNally was approaching her time. She and my father, Gerry Jackson, decided that morning they would leave my elder siblings with their granny, and head-off for a day's shopping. They set out along the Crumlin Road, destined for the Shankill Road, a habit of Ardoyne and Falls Road Catholics in those days, before the loyalist violence re-emerged in the late 1960s. The memory of the 1920s and the sectarian slaughter of hundreds of innocent Catholics was the burden of their parents.

Young Rosie and Gerry had a spring in their step as they set off. But as the Greek proverb translated to Latin by the Dutch scholar Erasmus says: 'Multa cadunt inter calicem suprema que labra' – there is many

---

1 A wooden safety cover for baths, used until the 1970s in hospitals and institutions.

a slip twixt cup and lip. They didn't reach the shops, heading instead to the Mater Maternity Hospital. My mother had announced her 'time had arrived'. Gerry was happy to observe the traditions of the day, when they suited his own agenda, therefore he escorted Rosie, a girl in her 20s, and deposited her at the Mater. Sure wasn't it the custom of the day! His duty was done. Besides he would need to head to the pub to celebrate the child's anticipated arrival with friends. My father was always fond of a drink, even though he was a hard and diligent worker. He never stopped working until health failed him in his 70s. Unfortunately with his working life over, he developed an even greater fondness for the drink.

At the doors of the Mater, at the height of a bright summer's day, my mother waited nervously. She drew a deep breath, and marched confidently through the doors. Rosie was more than capable of being strong when needed, but she was a very gentle soul. She introduced herself, explained her situation and turned herself over to the ministrations of the Sisters of Mercy. However she got little mercy from those rigid Brides of Christ. The Sisters were severe traditionalists. They didn't do mercy. Theirs was a calling to the work of God, which needed done according to the rules. It was a habit they perhaps formed on the battlefields of the Crimea, where they worked with Florence Nightingale. My mother explained that she was about to give birth. The only answer she received was: 'In there with you, girl, to the bathroom. You will bathe first and then we will see about the baby. Don't you know well that "cleanliness is next to godliness".' Poor Rosie, I'm certain she hadn't a clue as to why a Catholic nun would be quoting the English Methodist John Wesley. My mother had no choice but to do as she was bid.

Rosie gave me unremitting and unconditional love. I returned that until the end of her days. She never passed judgement on others. One of her constant refrains was: 'Don't judge until you've walked a mile in their shoes.' She also had great respect for all shades of clergy and respected authority – at least those authorities which warranted respect. She was, like many of her working-class contemporaries, without much formal education. She had left school at 14 to find work in the mills.

My mother was left in the locked bathroom alone. According to her account, she had barely been able to pull the heavy wooden bathboard into place before I made my entry into the world. I was unceremoniously launched on life's journey. I was born on August 7th 1958, a Thursday, the day between the two Catholic fasts. I weighed in a fine, healthy 7lbs 8oz baby. If the old rhyme was true, I 'had far to go'. My mother fed me herself and, if family myth is true, continued to do so until I was two years-of-age, with a fine set of teeth in my head.

I was Gerry's first son, therefore I would inherit his name. My mother had a great fondness for Gerard Majella, the patron saint of expectant mothers. By the age of five I had been given the nickname 'Jake', which has stuck with me ever since. My mother often mentioned Gerard Majella and asked me to pray to him. 'He never let me down,' she said. She had nine healthy children, all of whom lived into adulthood. When anyone asked how many children she had, Rosie replied: 'Myself and Gerry had eight, but we'd an extra one thanks to Arthur Guinness.' That was baby Eamonn, born just after Operation Motorman[2] in 1972, when the British Army smashed through the barricades which had surrounded nationalist districts since the internment swoops of August 1971.[3] Eight of us still live in Belfast, except baby Eamonn, who moved to Gortahork following the death of our parents.

I'd only arrived, but the wheels of life ground on. Máiréad Ní Gaoithín (Peig Sayers), and historian Dorothy McArdle, author of the *Tragedies of Kerry*, bowed out. They were among thousands of authors I would get to know. I always had a great love and respect for books. My red-headed father implanted this love in me. His red hair earned him the nickname 'Ginger'. Red heads are a big feature in our family; my first grandson Séadhna sports a wonderful head of curly red hair. Gerry, like my mother, left school at 14. He always had a good book in his hand. He had beautiful, even classical handwriting – a gift I missed out on. He was ambidextrous, thanks to his left hand having been secured to his trousers to force the left-handedness out of him. Left-handedness was viewed as evil in those days.[4] My mother favoured romantic novels. I, in my turn, have tried

---

2 Operation Motorman was the biggest British military operation in peacetime. 22,000 regular British soldiers and 5,300 members of the RUC and UDR smashed their way into nationalist districts in Belfast and Derry. In Derry they killed four people and in Belfast they seized control of GAA stadiums, schools and other facilities for use as barracks.
3 Internment without trail was a weapon often deployed against nationalists. In 1971 it was used again and led to a massive intensification of the conflict.
4 Myths about left-handedness go back to antiquity and the left has long been associated with evil and the devil. The superstition of throwing spilt salt over the left shoulder originated in the belief that it was here that evil spirits lurked. In Protestant culture in Ireland Catholics were referred to as left-footers signifying that they 'kicked with the wrong foot' and were intrinsically evil.

to inculcate a love of reading in all my children and grandchildren. I succeeded and am proud that I did.

From hospital I went to granny Lizzie Jackson's house, although she more often went under her maiden name Hagan. There was no love in that house for the Reverend Ian Paisley, the firebrand unionist preacher and hate-monger. Nor was there much love for Eamonn De Valera, the then Taoiseach. Pope John XXIII, Angelo Giuseppe Roncalli, was venerated in Lizzie's house. I was to learn that opprobrium was heaped on De Valera, 'The Spanish Gypsy', for allowing Sean McCaughey, Officer Commanding the IRA Northern Command, to die on hunger strike on May 11th 1946. Raidió Éireann or 'Athlone Radio', always played in the background. There was an enveloping sense of Irishness, with traditional and rebel songs and the odd hymn being sung. My mother, father and Granny Lizzie were all fine singers. Singing was a common pastime. The custom of singing rebel and traditional songs was widespread, despite the fact that Lizzie's father, John Hagan, and four of her own sons, my father included, served time in the British Army, like scores of other economic conscripts.

Inside Lizzie's house she was boss – and she wasn't shy about using her tawse to settle disputes.[5] Outside 17 Jamaica Street, Basil Brooke's Ulster Unionist Party ran everything else with an iron fist.[6] Brooke and his party had won 37 seats against seven for nationalists in the year I was born.

My parents got a house of their own in Andersonstown in spring 1961. They loaded up their meagre possessions on a horse and cart belonging to John Mallaghan, the local coal merchant. I was left behind in Lizzie's 'until they got settled in'. I stayed until early 1962, when granny became ill. I didn't move far, just around the corner to my other granny, Lizzie McNally (née Gilligan) and her husband Rabbie's house. I remained there until I reached school age. Granny-rearing was quite common. I'm certain it did me no harm. My grandparents had a profound influence on me. I was, as a result, said to be very old-fashioned. I was very articulate in both standard English and the country dialect, which Rabbie favoured. I was also full of the storytelling and superstitions.

---

5 The tawse was a leather strap used for corporal punishment.
6 Basil Stanlake Brooke, Viscount Brookeborough was the third prime minister at Stormont and virulently anti-Catholic. He once remarked at an Orange Twelfth of July march in 1933 in Fermanagh that he 'wouldn't have a Roman Catholic about the place'.

Although my grandparents influenced me greatly, I was never in any doubt as to who my parents were. I was a pleasant and settled child, if rumours are true. But as far as my sisters and father were concerned, I was spoiled. My father formed the strong opinion that I was too soft and needed hardening up. According to Gerry if I didn't shape up, he would 'make a man of me'. Although I was soft-natured, I don't recall crying much at all. That is until I cried with abandon in the year of the 'Big Snow' in 1963. It was March, the snow lay at least two feet deep and my big, cuddly Granny Lizzie, who would bounce me on her knee while singing gently, was dead. I was heart-broken. I still clearly recall the noise of the shovels clearing snow from the road to allow her passage to Milltown Cemetery. The snow was piled as high as the window sills. She was the first person that I had lost in my life and it had barely started. I cried incessantly as I waited for my father to return. I was clearly annoying my poor aunt, who had been left to mind me. Her patience broke and she roared: 'Your da's not coming home; he's after falling into the grave with Lizzie because of all your crying.' I was terrified and stopped crying immediately. I never cried in front of anyone again, until May 5th 1981, the day of Bobby Sands' death. I'd learned a hard lesson, I'd learn it again and again. I would hide my feelings, bury my sensitive nature, and make sure that I made a man of myself – practice which would come back to haunt me.

Gaein tha heap a hoak / Poking the pile

A door never closed but another opened. I was bidding goodbye forever to Jamaica Street and saying hello to Northwick Drive. I settled with no problems in the McNally household, having already been in semi-permanent residence for almost a year with Rabbie and Lizzie. My uncle Joe and aunt Margaret would be gone that year, both having married – Joe to Kathleen Grogan from Sailortown and Margaret to Justin Zelewski from Earlswood Road and before that Poland. Only uncle Bobby, myself and the old couple remained.

With each passing week I grew more curious about the world. Granted my world was limited enough, but I was hungry to know everything. I would listen with full attention as Rabbie told tales and discussed all manner of things with me. I also constantly pestered him with questions, which he patiently and fully answered. These sessions mostly happened as he prepared plants and vegetables in his tiny backyard, which also housed our toilet. The seedlings would eventually end up in an allotment he rented from the then Belfast Corporation above in the Oldpark.

Rabbie was the son of James and Mary Elizabeth McNally. He was born in 1889, and his father James was born in 1850 at the tail end of An Gorta Mór.[7] History is closer than we imagine. Rabbie was born in Cranfield in the townland of Creggan, close to Randalstown in County Antrim. Cranfield housed Saint Olcan's Well. Olcan was buried there in blessed soil brought from Rome, according to local lore. Olcan was a fifth century member of the Royal House of Dál Riada. Of course he was baptised by Saint Patrick, an incredibly busy man, if he did the half of what he was said to have done. Superstitions associated with Olcan are still strong in Cranfield. It's said that the newborn Olcan was found at Drumbolcan in Rasharkin, but the people of Armoy dispute the fact, claiming him as their own. Whatever the truth, there is no doubt that he founded his monastery at Rasharkin. The ruins of a 13th century monastery associated with Olcan still stand at Cranfield, along with a holy tree. Both look out over the majestic expanse of Lough Neagh. In childhood I would often visit the spot with my father for a bit of fishing. My grandfather told me of a strong superstition which stated that the amber pebbles from Olcan's well were protection for pregnant women and from fire. He also told me how his own grandfather told how those fleeing An Gorta Mór swallowed the pebbles to protect them on their journey on the famine ships.

Rabbie married Lizzie Gilligan, a daughter of Christopher and Bridget Gilligan of Irvinestown, close to the shores of lower Lough Erne in County Fermanagh. Rabbie was more than six years Lizzie's senior. He had married in his mid 20s – just like myself. I married Chrissie Keenan, a daughter of Brian Keenan and Chrissie Campbell, in my mid-20s and was also more than six years her senior. Back in 1963, however, I had no notion of marriage. There were, however, changes afoot in the Big House at Ballymascath. Isn't it ironic that Stormont sits in a townland known in Irish as the 'Town of the Shadows'! Terence O'Neill was running the show. John Fitzgerald Kennedy, 35th President of America, the first Catholic to hold the office, was on a tour of Ireland. His portrait adorned my granny McNally's wall alongside Pope John XXIII, who had died less than three weeks before Kennedy touched down in Ireland. Roncalli's

---

7 The Great Hunger or Irish Holocaust of 1845-1852 which saw death and emigration reduce the population of Ireland by close on three million.

portrait would eventually be replaced by one of Pope Paul VI. The great demagogue, Ian Paisley, was inciting trouble as usual. He mocked the dead pope: 'This man of Rome and sin is in the fires of hell.' Earlier that year Cardinal John D'Alton, Catholic Primate of Ireland, had also passed on, as had my mother's favourite singer, Patsy Cline. The Beatles were playing in Dublin; the Cuban Missile Crisis was settled. Before year's end Kennedy would be dead. His nemesis Nikita Krushchev would be secure in his leadership of the USSR and firmly ensconced in the Kremlin, welcoming Fidel Castro to Moscow. The people of Yemen had risen against the British. Jomo Kenyatta had wrestled freedom from Britain in Kenya. The unravelling of the hated and murderous British Empire, which had blighted humanity, raped, pillaged, slaughtered and exploited millions across the globe for so long, was now gathering pace.

In the midst of the tumult I had made my first visit to the Crumlin Star Picture House. My father had brought me to see Ben Hur. I was spellbound by our own Stephen Boyd playing Roman villain, Messala, the scourge of hero, Judah Ben Hur, played by Charlton Heston. When the chariot race got under way I knew that I was witnessing an epic moment in cinematography. I can still see myself as we returned to granny's. I was a king, on top of the world, riding home on my father's shoulders. I wore my little blue anorak, a quarter bottle of whiskey hidden in the pocket for Rabbie, secreted in case Lizzie found it. I wore my brown balaclava, not the balaclavas people would wear in later years, but the itchy kind our grannies used to knit for us. The night was brittle and cold. It was a night when sounds carried forever. Not a breath of wind stirred. My hands were toasty warm from the paper roll of chips I held in my grip. I was in seventh heaven making my way down Brompton Park. Ardoyne Heights and its lights twinkled before us, like so many stars in a winter sky. Those were the days when neither I, nor any one else, could have envisaged what lay ahead of us.

Rabbie, it transpires, had some Irish. I regret to say I never heard him use it, other than the odd word. I didn't learn that he had Irish until after he died. He spoke to me only in his quaint, country dialect of English. I can still hear him speaking as we arrived at his allotment: 'Gie thon haep a hoak for hirchins. Am awa tae draa dung' – 'Give that pile a shake to see if there's any hedgehogs. I'm away to get manure.' It would come in useful when I wrote a column called 'Jist Bletherin' in the Irish language paper *Lá*. I was as good a hand at it as were those who were claiming to write and speak what they claimed to be 'Ulster Scots'.[8]

I was beginning to show an interest in newspapers. We had an outside toilet with squares of the *Irish News* impaled on a nail. 'Best place for it,' Rabbie would say, 'At least it'll be of some use.' Before I myself would use it I made valiant efforts to read, what for me, was an indecipherable jumble of letters. I couldn't wait to be able to read a whole *Irish News* – as they say, however, be careful what you wish for. I was also hugely interested in many of the rituals practised by Rabbie. He would, for example, take his mixture of tobacco, consisting of Warhorse Ready Rubbed and Condor Plug, and lay them out in the backyard on a double page of the 'Vatican Echo', as he called the *Irish News*. He would pare, slice and rub the Condor to get the required consistency, then blend both together. This task completed, he would sprinkle the mixture with poteen and place another sheet of newspaper over the top, allowing it to dry before packing it into empty marmalade jars. He would sometimes allow me to do the packing. 'Aisy noo, Barney,' he would say, using the nickname which he'd given me for reasons I never understood. I was mesmerised by the accoutrements: penknife, tobacco tins, pipe cleaners, little silver covers for his Peterson Pipes, Swan Vesta matches and a little pipe rack. I would sit watching Rabbie indulge in cleaning, filling and smoking his pipe. The smell of pipe smoke always brings me back. My father smoked a pipe and it was a treat when he took me to Leahy Kelly's Alladin's cave in Belfast. I know tobacco causes huge health problems, but it didn't appear to do Rabbie any harm. He smoked Players Navy Cut like a train, as well as his pipe. He drank poteen and whiskey with gusto. Yet he lived to a ripe old age of 86, unlike his teetotal, non-smoking wife who passed away at 79 years-of-age. Her passing robbed him of any spirit or any will to live. He died within two weeks of Lizzie's passing.

Rabbie never amassed any money. He lived from hand to mouth. But on his passing he left me two pennies of huge value. One, dated 1898, bears the image of the British Queen Victoria, saved from his first wage. The second bears the image of the British King George V, retained from his wage the week the Titanic left Belfast. He worked

---

8 A much disputed dialect, promoted by sections of unionism, mainly as a spoiler against Irish Gaelic. For many it is an object of fun and ridicule. The dialect is controversially recognised as a language under the European Charter for Regional and Lesser Used Languages. Aside from the political chicanery associated with it, it is a version of English used in some rural parts of Ulster from Donegal to County Down.

on the 'cursed ship', as he called it. Like the ship, he was to leave the shipyard himself some months later in the company of 2,000 other Catholics and trade unionists, driven from the place by loyalist mobs angered at talk of Home Rule.

As 1963 gave way to 1964 I was spending more time with my parents in Andersonstown, where I now had four sisters. I realised my time with Rabbie was drawing to a close. I wasn't happy. Alas, at summer's end, my start date for school approached. My race was run. I was heading for permanent residence in Navan Green, a street, at that stage, on the very edge of the countryside at the foot of the Belfast Hills. I was unsettled. At least this time no one had died. Rabbie and Lizzie would live on for another 10 years and I would visit them regularly.

Other changes were afoot, which gave us a foretaste of what was to come. Ian Paisley was at the centre of things again. He threatened, during the 1964 Westminster election campaign, that he would march on Divis Street in the Falls to remove an Irish Tricolour from the window of the Republican Party, a cover name for the outlawed Sinn Féin. Paisley's threats, and a telegram from Jim Kilfedder to Home Affairs Minister, Brian McConnell, had unsettled unionists. McConnell decided to send in the RUC to forcibly remove the flag, precipitating the worst riots since the 1920s. The spectre of loyalist violence and nationalist resistance was again abroad on the streets.[9]

In that election, unionists won 81.8 percent of the vote, nationalists 18.2 percent. Nationalists would never again fail to secure a seat at Westminster. In the election of 1966, Gerry Fitt from Republican Labour won West Belfast. Unionists had held the seat since the foundation of the statelet. They never held it again and by 2020 found themselves with only a single seat in Belfast. In that ground-breaking election John Finucane, son of murdered human rights lawyer, Pat Finucane, dealt unionism a huge blow by ousting Nigel Dodds, the deputy leader of the DUP. Even back in 1964 change was coming and unionism, as always, was finding it difficult to cope. The campaign for civil rights was about to go into full swing. Everything was changing and the unionist response would be what it always was: threat, bullying and violence.

---

9 Jim Kilfedder, 1928–1995. Kilfedder won the support of loyalist paramilitaries in the bid to be the unionist candidate for West Belfast in the 1964 Westminster election. He was the last unionist to ever hold the seat. He ended his career as the sole representative of the Ulster Popular Unionist Party.

Andersonstown

I was on the cusp of a new life. The old life wasn't coming back. If truth be told, it was a new lease of freedom, a time filled with new wonders, new explorations, new adventures and apparently no limits on freedom. There was any amount of space, fields, farms, rivers and hills, all on our doorstep. I would need a few more years before I could fully indulge the new-found freedom and wander far and wide with the big boys. It was another world compared to the narrow streets of Ardoyne, filled with dust and chimney smoke. I could wander out around the green in front of our house, as long as I didn't venture beyond the entrance to Johnny Smith's farm. Such freedom! What was even better was the street was full of children, many my age and others just a little older. Next door to us were the six McDermotts, the eldest, Terry, only five years my senior. On the other side were the seven Weirs, all but one of whom were girls. Beyond that were the six Quinn boys, all hurlers, then the six Donnellys and the McLarnons with three boys and a girl. Our row finished with the Cassins, an exception to the rule, with only a single child called Colin. The lack of Cassin children was more than made up for by the lush fruit bushes which grew in profusion in their garden. Around the small green on our side of the street, which only had 15 houses, there were 70 children. This number would increase to 83 by the time Eamonn, the last of the Jacksons, arrived.

The oldest boy in the street, Jim Butler, was a man to us, though he was only 15. Jim was one of seven children. The children I'm counting were only those in our square; there were two other arms of 32 houses, radiating out from the square, equally filled with children. Our street was semi-circular in shape and was free from traffic other than coalmen, binmen, bread and milk delivery men and the fish man on Fridays. There were the McDonalds and the Johnsons, with more than 20 children between them. Oh blessed life, I was one contented boy! The mid to late 1960s were a lovely time for us. The miracle of TV arrived in our lives. Small black and white sets broadcasting on UHF. We only had BBC 1, BBC 2 and ITV. We'd never seen the likes of it. TV was not on my radar until Blue Peter's John Noakes, Valerie Singleton and Peter Purves appeared. It ran twice a week on the 'squawk box', as my Da called it. When the shout for Blue Peter went up, sloitars,[10] balls and hurls were flung aside. What innocence! Throughout the 1960s I watched 'The Beverly Hillbillies', Johnny Morris' 'Animal Magic', 'Thunderbirds',

---

10 A small ball for the national sport of hurling.

'Bonanza', 'The Lone Ranger' and the boys' friend, 'Doctor Who'. The first colour TV in our street belonged to the Quinns. We saw it through their window, thanks to Barney and Kev. A crowd of us were gathered in the garden to see 'The Flintstones' in full colour. We made so much ruckus that Mr Quinn arrived undetected in our midst and administered a kick in the arse to anyone not quick enough to get offside.

I've mentioned my father's crusade to 'make a man of me'. Looking back it affected me, and remoulded me. It wasn't healthy, or to my benefit. I was soft-natured, open, and easily offended. I made a conscious effort, under withering criticism and ridicule from my father, to hide my nature. It was my practice to show a front: cynical, tough, headstrong, aloof and even arrogant. I clearly remember, and still feel deeply hurt, at the way in which he treated me when I made any complaint. He would put on a whining, childish voice and repeat my words and would then sing the song: 'I dream of Jeanie with the light brown hair'. It cut me to the marrow. I would fill up with anger and loathing and shame, tightly clenching my hands and teeth. I would never shed a tear. I wanted to run to mammy for comfort. Mammy, however, never interfered when Gerry was 'putting manners on the children'. After he'd had his fill, he would stop the singing. He'd 'taught me a lesson'. Over time, all he had to do to was to ask in a mock baby voice: 'What's wrong with poor Jeanie?'. I know now he was only, in his own way, trying to protect me and ensure I could stand on my own two feet, in a world which was cruel and hard. I would make a huge effort not to feel emotion, even though his merciless taunting wounded me like arrows. Contrary to my nature, I managed to become adept at hiding or even feeling emotions. I would take insult and hurt, closing them up in a mental compartment. In truth, I became more than adept at deploying this survival strategy.

Halcyon Days

My sense of my father's dissatisfaction with me, was constant. He'd lost his own father at the age of 10 and was one of 15 children. He found out in later years that his youngest brother Bert had been thrown out 'on the wrong side of the blanket'.[11] My Aunt Annie explained to him in his late 50s: "Mammy reared him as one of her own." Bert was the son of my father's eldest sister. When my father asked why he hadn't been told, Annie said: 'It was none of your business'. Women did what they had to in those days when men held all the cards.

---

11 A euphemism used in Belfast to denote illegitimacy.

I had been a little spoiled by my granny-rearing. But within the bosom of my own family, I was surrounded by girls: Pauline and Carol above me, Collette and Theresa below me. There was at most a year and a half gap between each of us. I had blond curly hair, which darkened to mousy brown as I grew older. I was also always a bit baby-faced and totally petted on by my mother. I tried my best to adopt the air of a tough little man. In all honesty, it was against my naturally soft-hearted and sentimental nature. My father's moulding wasn't good for me. It shaped me in ways which were less than healthy and brought me an unnecessary degree of suffering, which I didn't fully comprehend or deal with, until I myself was in my late 50s.

In 1964, or perhaps 1965, we were visiting relatives in Ardoyne. I was asked to bring a pot of soup up to my uncle Hughie. I was well warned not to spill a drop. I made my way very carefully up across the cinder pitches at the Bone Heights. I lost my balance and felt I was going to fall on my face. Steadying myself as best I could, and holding the pot above my head, I fell to my knees. It was excruciating as the cinders cut into me, but I never spilled a drop of the soup. I got back to my feet and could feel the blood running down my shins. I didn't care, the soup was safe. On arrival at Hughie's, his wife shouted out that I'd fallen and cut myself. Hughie asked if the soup was safe. I told him it was and he shouted out: 'You're a good wee soldier. Away on now and she'll clean you up.' The lesson wasn't lost on me.

Back in those halcyon days, everything had its season. The seasons dictated everything, from the food we ate to the things we did. There was the season for Bridget's Crosses, frog spawn season, newt season and the season for hunting nests and eggs. That was our spring. With the arrival of summer, it was the season for fishing for small trout and spricks, or going to Colin and McCance's Glens to harvest hawthorn and willow branches for bow-and-arrow making. We always wanted to be the Indians, despite the cowboys being the heroes on TV and in the comics. We had lots of other pastimes. There was the season for the 'Cooler', when hundreds of children would descend on the open air swimming pool in the Falls Park, where brass bands performed on the old bandstand. The 'Cooler', the brass bands, and so much else from our childhood, are long gone and forgotten. We were also, in those days, blessed by 'free' fruit, which grew in the gardens of the more affluent houses on the outskirts of Andersonstown. We knew early summer would bring damsons, plums and certain types of apples. The owners of these gardens also knew that we knew, as did their dogs. It was a cat and mouse game.

Reputations could be made or broken in this battle with owners and dogs. The conflict would rage all summer and would end with the appearance of the soft fruits in late summer and early autumn, when berries, wild strawberries and my own favourite, blueberries, would be available for free. We would wander fields and hills foraging and feasting on other free foods like sorrel, goosefoot and lamb's leaf. We would raid a few potatoes and sometimes boiled eggs and biscuits and would take to the Black Mountain, which looked down on us and the city. We would try to snag a few trout and spend the day playing, adventuring and getting sunburned. As evening fell, we'd light a small fire and roast the potatoes which, along with the herbs and anything else we'd foraged, would make a fine feast. Our boyhood feasts were meagre, but for us, they surpassed the fabled sultan's feast. We'd have more sport later, peeling the skin off our backs and arms as the sunburn settled down.

Johnny Smith had a farm next to Navan Green. Then there was Horner's Field, housing the canvas tents of the Travellers. In those days we called them gypsies, as they called themselves. I remember one memorable night in August 1969 spent with the McDonaghs and Purcells, who had helped evacuate the Catholic refugees fleeing the pogroms. One of the McDonagh elders sang 'I'll take you home again Kathleen', as we sat around the camp fire; it was magical. Beside Horner's was free land, later to become the first urban Gaeltacht.[12] We didn't know anyone from the Gaeltacht back then, but we all knew their big hound Mil, who ran wild through the fields just as we did. The fields stretched from Horner's to the outskirts of Lisburn and all the way to Colin Glen on the other side. These fields had little streams and small lakes. The biggest was the Half Moon Lake. There were other lakes at Colin and McCance's Glens, but they didn't have names. At the edge of our domain there was a lake at the old quarry which we called the 'Rumble Hole'.

My Da often told the tale of my mother asking who owned the big field behind us when she moved into the house. Our garden always had a good supply of fruit and vegetables. The neighbours would work in unison and grew food communally. In those days working families depended on this supplementary food. We were all poor,

---

12 An area where Irish was the language of the home.

despite not knowing it. There was no notion of fancy clothes or shoes back then. We wore plastic sandals in summer – red for the girls, brown for the boys. In winter it was waterboots. We had school shoes and, if we were lucky, football boots. Boys wore short trousers, girls a variety of skirts and dresses. Most of these were hand-me-downs from older siblings and cousins.

We spent a few summer weeks at Uncle John Hannin's farm in Tornaroy. We learned all about nature and foraging. John was immensely knowledgeable. Of course it meant work, and hard work. But it was fulfilling and enjoyable. We learned a lot of lore and all the superstitions, which were still observed by the country folk in Hannahstown. Even though these people only lived on the other side of the mountain from us, they were a different breed.

My favourite time was the 'saving of the hay'. A meitheal would gather at John's early in the morning.[13] Each man knew his task. There were boiled eggs and homemade wheaten bread, all devoured before sunrise. Children sat at the edge of the throng, listening intently to the adults' talk. Every adult had an opinion on the best plan of action. Weighty matters of the day were also aired. We sat quietly, greedily drinking from these fonts of wisdom. We weren't permitted to talk, except when given permission to ask a question. With the sun in the sky, John would announce: 'Time to strike the iron while she's hot'. We'd set off from the farmyard to the meadows. Children would be loaded onto the trailer, with the graips, forks and rakes.[14] We were pulled along behind the tractor. John, being a Catholic, had the bog-standard Massey Ferguson 135, unlike the more affluent Protestant farmers, with their John Deere 1010s.

Work would begin at the edge of the meadow. We worked inwards in a circular motion, as had happened with the cutting. There were periodic short breaks to allow small creatures to escape. Field mice, voles, meadow pippets and even the odd corncrake could be seen. Frogs were plentiful and we would squeal with delight as they flopped and fled. Putting the hay up into rucks was hard, back-breaking work.[15] Rucks had to be evenly spaced and neat. John would tongue-lash anyone for shabby work. After a long morning's toil we would break for wheaten

---

13 A work gang of neighbours.
14 In Hannahstown a graip was a long-handled, two-pronged pitchfork and a fork was a shorter four-tyned version. I have since heard that it is the opposite in other parts of the country.
15 The name used for a haystack. Derived from the Irish word cruach for stack.

bread, cheese, boiled eggs, biscuits and bottles of tea, carried to the meadow by Aunt Sheila and the other women. Then it was back for another long shift, which would last until nearly nightfall. When all the work was finished John would approach a piece of hay which had been left uncut. He would tie it in a knot and set fire to it, telling us he was 'burning the witch'. We didn't really understand its significance. It was clearly some ancient pagan ritual which came from the mists of time. We were happy contented kids, with not a worry in the world.

Dark clouds on the horizon

I wasn't aware then, but the days of innocence were almost gone. As the 1960s drew to a close, dark days arrived for us all. Between 1966 and 1969, the UVF and other loyalist terror gangs were again active, just as had been the case in the 1920s with RIC Inspector John Nixon's murder gangs. It was little surprise that Nixon had chosen the name of the Cromwell Clubs for his terror gangs, honouring one of the most hated figures in Irish history.[16] Gusty Spence was to lead the UVF gang on the Shankill Road. Spence would later recount being approached in 1965 by two unionist politicians, one of whom was at the time an Ulster Unionist MP. They invited him to get involved with plans to revive the UVF. Other gangs active at the time included Tara, led by Orangeman William McGrath. McGrath, a lifelong Paisleyite, would later be convicted of gross indecency, buggery and indecent assault of young boys in his care at the infamous Kincora Boys' Home for which he received a four year sentence and served two years. McGrath would be a prominent supporter of Spence, when the latter appeared in court on charges of murder.

Between April and June 1966, Spence's gang murdered two Catholics, John Scullion (28) and Peter Ward (18), and also shot another three. Matilda 'Tilly' Gould, a Protestant in her 70s, had been the Spence gang's first victim. She died in excruciating pain several weeks after the gang threw a petrol bomb through her living room window. They had mistaken her Upper Charleville Street home for that of a Catholic. Two weeks after the murder of Tilly Gould the UVF issued a statement to the media saying:

> From this day, we declare war against the Irish Republican Army and its splinter groups. Known IRA men will be executed mercilessly

---

16 Oliver Cromwell 1599-1658, had during the Cromwellian settlement of Ireland from 1649 until 1653 launched an unparalleled reign of terror, murder, land clearance and enslavement. He remains a hero for unionists and loyalists to this day.

and without hesitation. Less extreme measures will be taken against anyone sheltering or helping them, but if they persist in giving them aid, then more extreme methods will be adopted.

Spence would later explain their approach: 'At the time, the attitude was that if you couldn't get an IRA man you should shoot a Taig; he's your last resort.'[17] The UVF also bombed three Catholic primary schools and two Catholic businesses. After Spence and his gang were imprisoned, the UVF campaign abated until January 1969 when bombs were placed at water and electricity installations on both sides of the border. This was an attempt to force unionist premier Terence O'Neill from office, following his indication that he was considering reforms in response to the growing civil rights' campaign. As the year progressed loyalist violence increased. After the RUC held Derry's Catholics under siege between August 12th and August 15th 1969, things spiralled rapidly downward.[18] Backed by heavily armed RUC men, loyalists began driving Catholics from their homes in Belfast. It was open season on Catholics. Eight were murdered, hundreds injured and thousands made refugees. Catholic businesses and homes were burned wholesale. The first victim of the Orange pogrom was nine-year-old Patrick Rooney, cut down by RUC machine-gun fire which raked the home of his parents in Divis Flats. Young Rooney joined other Catholic victims, murdered by the RUC, including Francis McCloskey, Samuel Devenny, John Gallagher, Hugh McCabe, Samuel McLarnon and Michael Lynch.

From August to December 1969, the UVF and the Orange Volunteers carried out five bombing attacks in the south of Ireland. One claimed the life of one of their own, Thomas McDowell. The father of 10 died planting a bomb at Ballyshannon on October 19th 1969. Convicted loyalist killer Billy Hutchinson in his 2020 memoir *My Life in Loyalism*, recounted an encounter with Ian Paisley, who refused to share a lift with him in Stormont, calling him a UVF murderer. Hutchinson replied: 'It didn't worry you too much when you were sending Tom McDowell to his death.'

On Saturday October 12th 1969 the UVF murdered the first RUC man killed during the conflict, gunning down 29 year-old father of one

---

17 A pejorative term used by unionists and loyalists to describe Catholics.
18 Known as the Battle of the Bogside, the worst trouble of the early conflict saw Derry Catholics besieged by hundreds of RUC men and unionists. The city's Catholics fought the RUC to a standstill between August 12th and August 15th. On August 15th with the RUC on the verge of collapse, the British government sent in British troops to stave off the collapse inaugurating a 30 year-long conflict.

Victor Arbuckle on the Shankill Road. On the same night, during vicious rioting, the British Army killed Protestants George Dickie, shot at the corner of Downing Street, and Herbert Hawe, shot at Hopeton Street.

Meanwhile I was beginning my last year at primary school in the old stand at Casement Park GAA grounds. The Urban Gaeltacht pioneers were beginning to occupy the self-built houses at Shaws Road, inaugurating a cultural revolution whose positive benefits are still unfolding. I had also joined the ranks of the Republican Movement. I would remain loyal to the Movement until my resignation in 1997. I was to serve two terms of imprisonment during this period. I am still immensely proud of the role I played, although I regret the conflict happened. My first clear memory of republicanism was the 50th anniversary of the 1916 Rising in 1966. My father brought me to the celebrations at Casement and McRory Park. I saw the faces of the executed signatories of the 1916 Proclamation displayed on banners strung between Slemish Way and the gates of Casement Park. I knew I wanted to emulate those men, to stand my ground for Ireland and her downtrodden people, should I ever be worthy and brave enough to follow their example.

Leaving Primary School and Days of Innocence.

With my final year in Holy Child Primary fast approaching, we found ourselves moved to classrooms below the stand at Casement Park. Another Catholic baby boom was to blame. Holy Child had no room for us. Mr O'Neill was our teacher; he mesmerised me with his ability to insert a whole Jaffa Cake in his mouth. He always kept a ready supply of the biscuits in his desk. I always enjoyed primary school. We had Mrs Crilly in primaries one and two and Mr McKeith, who was very cruel to us, in primary three. In our communion year we had Mr Grace, a wonderfully kind and nurturing teacher. In primary five we had Mr Lacey. Finally in primaries six and seven we had Mr O'Neill, a kind, knowledgeable and interesting man. He had a great command of Irish history. We had him for a year at Holy Child and another at Casement Park, where the Falls Road trolley bus terminus was located. I loved Casement. We had lots of space. When the weather turned bad the faulty heating system was of little use and we were obliged to run around the pitch to get a bit of heat into our bones. There were four classrooms, accessed by a set of concrete stairs. Toilets were in the middle, two classrooms at either side. We occupied the classroom at the far left, as you looked from the front of the stand. It was a reasonably-sized room, adorned with a huge crucifix which faced a portrait of George Gavan Duffy, on the back wall.[19] We didn't have natural light, but there was a storeroom attached to the classroom with a small casement window. When we were placed in the storeroom for misbehaviour I loved to climb on the old desks. I'd gaze out the window looking at the lorries whizzing past on the M1 motorway, wondering and imagining their final destinations.

Many years later, in 2004, I got the opportunity to visit the storeroom, during an Antrim and Cork hurling game. After the game I spoke with the groundsman who brought me to the old storeroom I hadn't seen in 35 years. I was astounded at how small it was. As a child I believed it to be a fairly large. The room hadn't changed much and there on the wall, written in crayon, was 'Jake and Bow 1969'. Clearly myself and my neighbour Bow Weir, were in there at some point in 1969 for misbehaviour and had left our mark.

Outside the cocoon of our classroom, behaviour was also deteriorating. Storm clouds were amassing. It wouldn't be long until the tempest broke. I remember clearly an incident in 1968 which awakened me to impending danger, allowing me to grasp that there was a group of people who didn't like Catholics and who could be a threat. A group of us had tagged along with the bigger boys on an adventure to Lady Dixon Park. It was an area seldom visited by young Catholics. Jim Armour, Kev Quinn and Vinty Heatherington, were leading us. Vinty was to be killed in 1976, accused by the IRA of being a British agent. The adventure to the park was a big one for the likes of me. It sat only a few miles from us on Malone Road, but may as well have been on the other side of the planet. I'd never ventured so far from home. We approached the field where the Orangemen held their 12th of July parade, although it is now a GAA training ground. An old tan-coloured Austin Maxi was parked at Ardmore Park; a man leaned against its bonnet. He wore bottle-green trousers with a gun at his waist. His white Aran jumper grabbed my attention. He shouted and began approaching us. A stream of angry curses, punctuated by the instruction that we should take ourselves back to where we came from, heralded his approach. I wasn't sure what was happening, but

---

19 George Gavan Duffy 1882–1951. Gavan Duffy, a signatory to the Anglo-Irish Treaty of 1921, was one of the Sinn Féin MPs elected in the historic 1918 election. Duffy had represented Roger Casement during his trial and conviction in London. He was one of the representatives of Ireland at the Paris Peace Conference and had a long and distinguished career in the law and then in politics.

sensed fear from the bigger boys who said he was a B-Special.[20] Clearly we needed to leave.

Back at home I spluttered: 'Mammy, mammy, there was an old man. He had a gun. He said bad talk. He called us fenians.[21] We were down Finaghy. We had to run. Vinty and the big boys were afraid.' 'Slow down,' my mother told me. I drew breath: 'Don't go down there again!' That was it. No explanation. I learned lots later about the Specials from my friends and my granny, who told me how they had crucified Malachy Halfpenny. She described how, with scores of women, she knelt outside Holy Cross Chapel praying the rosary while Halfpenny's screams filled the air. The bigger boys told me the Specials were policemen, but much worse than the ordinary RUC men. The RUC were always seen as the enemy. I remember my grandmother sprinkling holy water if the RUC came near the house. The Specials and the RUC were on the side of the Orangemen and the British. We avoided them at all costs.

Another incident occurred that same year, reinforcing my understanding of another tribe who didn't like us or our Irishness. They could be a threat to us and had the upper hand, which would be used with great violence, if we rocked the boat. My mother was taking my sisters Pauline and Carol and myself to visit the home of a long-time friend in a loyalist estate. She was a Protestant with who had worked in Greaves' Mill since they were young teenagers. I remember it being near Easter time; the bands were beginning their practice. When we reached her friend's house, who we all knew well, she opened her door, held it with her foot and said before slamming it in our faces: 'You're not welcome here anymore.' I sensed mammy's fear. I still thought my parents omnipotent at the time. The fear infected me. 'Come on, come on. Don't be asking questions. Home now,' said mammy, hustling us away. I knew life had changed. I wasn't sure how. I had the vague, but unmistakeable feeling, things would never be the same again.

When we reached my grandfather's house he brought mammy into the kitchen. I could hear him say, 'I told you they'd never be your true friends. I told you they would turn on you.' I had a similar experience with a boy I knew, James Watt, nicknamed 'Tonto'. He was six years my senior. The Watts were Protestant. Tonto's father was the groundsman at the Oldpark playing fields beside my uncle Hughie's house.

---

20 The B Specials were a particularly sectarian and feared element of the RUC.
21 A pejorative term used by Protestants to describe Catholics.

I wasn't to see 'Tonto' again until 1977 in Crumlin Road Gaol. He was facing charges of murdering nine Catholics. The youngest of his victims was 10 year-old Kevin McMenamin, killed in Beechmount on Easter Sunday 1977. 'Tonto' was one of the UVF's bombmakers. He was also part of the UVF gang which murdered Gerard Grogan, a brother of my aunt Kathleen. Members of the Shankill Butchers gang accompanied him on that killing mission.[22] Gerard was 18 years-old and in his first job. The gang entered Casey's Bottling Plant in Millfield. It was October 2nd 1975. Lenny Murphy, a leader of the Shankill Butchers, led the gang. They found four Catholics: Gerard Grogan (18), sisters Frances Donnelly (35), and Marie McGrattan (47), and Thomas Osborne (18). Murphy knelt the two young men down and shot them through the back of the head. William Green did likewise with the sisters. The victims were among 12 Catholics murdered by the UVF that night, 45 others were injured. I've since heard that Tonto became a born-again Christian in prison and a lay preacher on his release in 1989.

---

22 A notorious gang of UVF men who terrorised Catholics in the 1970s, grotesquely mutilating their victims. They abducted, tortured and slashed their victims with cleavers and knives, often cutting the throats right back to the spine. Between 1975 and 1982 the gang murdered 23 Catholics and also killed six Protestants mistaken for Catholics.

Chapter 2

In the eye of the storm and the midst of conflict

'A story is always good until the next one comes along' (Seanfhocail Uladh 410 b Ulaidh/Roibeárd MacÁdhaimh)

By the decade's end things were moving at pace. The television was full of images from the United States where African-Americans demanded civil rights, whilst state forces tore into peaceful demonstrators with savage violence. The marchers sang 'We Shall Overcome' as they were batoned and attacked with tear-gas. It was soon happening in the north east of Ireland. Demonstrators sang the same song and faced the same violence. There was fearful talk about the B Specials and RUC. People thought they were going to invade our areas at any time. Talk of things being about to explode was becoming common-place. I was active in the youth wing of the Republican Movement by this stage and attending lectures on Irish history, which was adding to my understanding of Ireland's 'British' problem. I was also learning new skills which would be of use to me as time and events progressed. The North was descending into chaos. I never revealed my involvement to my family, although three of my sisters and a brother would also join the Republican Movement. Three of us would see imprisonment and would serve 23 years in total. My mother visited prisons continually from 1975 until 1995. The situation was the same for many other families. Between blood relatives and in-laws my own and my wife's family served 84 years in prison.

The decisions I, and other young people, were making at that period, need to be viewed in context. I knew by 1968 that my community faced challenges and threats. I knew where I wanted to stand. I was only 10 years-old, but I knew what path I wanted to follow.

Eventually I found myself in the Republican Movement. I was so proud. 'Infiltrate, educate and agitate' was the slogan of the time. Looking back it is easy to claim that we didn't properly understand these things. That's not how it seemed to me. When the movement split into Official and Provisional wings I followed my neighbour Terry McDermott siding with the Provisionals. It seemed they were the grouping most likely to take action against the British, who now militarily occupied the Six Counties. Terry was the first person I knew to die on armed service for the IRA. He lost his life at 19 years-of-age, when a bomb he was planting exploded prematurely on October 2nd 1971. He was killed by the same type of device which killed the first British Army bomb-disposal expert, Captain David Stewardson (29) at Castlerobin, one month before Terry's death. Early IRA bombing technology was a remnant of the 1950s campaign. It was often unreliable. In total 120 IRA Volunteers lost their lives as a result of accidental explosions. I was shocked and deeply saddened by Terry's death. I was honoured when I and three of my school friends were allowed to be in his honour guard.

A few months before Terry died, the first paratrooper to die in the conflict, was killed in Andersonstown. Richard Barton (24), from Barnstaple, died less than 100 yards from my home. I witnessed his demise. During the internment swoops of August 1971 the regiment murdered 11 people, including a Catholic priest, in Ballymurphy and shot dead Desmond Healy (14) and Francis McGuinness (17) in Andersonstown. Later, the same soldiers would murder 14 innocent civilians in Derry. We tasted the brutality of the paratroopers when they smashed their way into Terry's funeral. They attacked us with batons and CS gas. We reformed and marched on. When the cortège reached the apparent safety of St Agnes' Church they fired CS gas and rubber bullets through the windows. It was clear that the premier of the Orange state, James Chichester-Clarke, had indeed been true to the words he had uttered after the death of Robert Curtis (20), the first British soldier to be killed by the IRA. Clarke had stated on February 6th 1971: 'We are at war with the IRA Provisionals.' War had arrived and we were in its midst. A total of 171 people were to lose their lives in the conflict during 1971. The following year, the bloodiest of the war, was to see 476 people die.

Our lives were turned upside down. We witnessed attacks on civil rights marchers at Duke Street in 1968, at Burntollet Bridge in January 1969 and endured the horrors of the Orange pogroms of 1969 with the burnings, killings and the enforced exile of thousands of Catholics. Internment, and the killings which accompanied it, were seared into our minds as was the loyalist murder of 15 innocents in McGurk's Bar in Belfast. Horror upon horror was visited on our community and eventually, by 1971, the IRA was taking the war to the British. The IRA in total killed 763 front-line British soldiers during the conflict and would injure over 6,000 other soldiers. By 1972 I had turned 14 and I was certain that the role I needed to play was in the Republican Movement. My parents were supportive of the republican cause but I was to have a sobering lesson from my father about the horrors of war. My father had been a Sergeant Major in the British Army. I was ashamed of this part of his past, but very proud when he agreed to give military training to the IRA. He knew nothing, as far as I was concerned. We knew it all. We were the generation who would finish off the Orange state.

My lesson came on July 21st 1972. A number of us were on the Glen Road observing British forces' movements. Others were on all approach roads to West Belfast. The barricades, put in place following 1969, and strengthened following internment, were still in place. We could see IRA Volunteers heading city-wards. Around 2.30 p.m. we heard an explosion. Smoke rose over the city. For the next 90 minutes explosions rocked Belfast. Columns of smoke were visible. The noise of the detonations was unmistakeable. The IRA had driven 23 bombs into Belfast. Warnings were given. The Samaritans confirmed that, for the explosions which claimed lives, they had given between 22 minutes and one hour's warning to the RUC. The British said their forces were overwhelmed. Seán Mac Stíofáin, IRA Chief-of-Staff, said: 'One policemen with a megaphone could have cleared every street.' Regardless, nine people were killed, including two British soldiers and an RUC man. In total 130 civilians, including 77 women and children, were injured.

That evening, my father was furious. He was a bus man and had been near the scene of the Oxford Street bombing. He assisted with the initial clean-up. Four civilians and two British soldiers died at Oxford Street. They were so badly mutilated the corpses had to be shovelled into plastic bags. My father said he was disgusted and ashamed of what had happened. I began defending the IRA saying warnings were given. 'The world isn't black and white,' said my father, 'but black can never be made white. What happened today was wrong and anyone associated with it or defending it shares the full guilt.'

In August 1973, myself and three friends were caught up in an accidental explosion. I experienced some of the confusion and fear, which any victim feels. We were in a field beside my home when a device exploded. My school uniform was blown off me and left in shreds. My body was scorched, thankfully not badly. My first concern was that I would be in trouble. Uniforms were expensive and money scarce. As that thought was going through my mind I was also aware that the air around us was slowly expanding and contracting, seemingly all at once. I felt I was witnessing this from afar but also from the epicentre. A huge roar ripped through my ears seconds afterwards. Dirt, dust, smoke and earth were all around us. In the middle of this maelstrom, flames were swirling and I could feel intense heat. I saw my friend Peter Johnson tumbling through the air and disappearing over a nearby hedge. I experienced a hammer blow to my chest and sensed a fiercely hot blast of air which sent me hurtling backwards. The remnants of my uniform were on fire and my mouth, ears and eyes were filled with earth.

I must have momentarily passed out, as I remember being shaken into consciousness by a neighbour from Bingnian Drive who seemed to me to be pulling my jumper off in slow-motion. He carried me to Eddie McArdle's car, which was parked in Navan Green. I was placed in the back on top of manure sacks. Eddie was a keen gardener. Peter Johnson was placed in beside me and we drove to the Royal Hospital. My nose was filled with the smell of manure and the acrid smell of the explosion. To this day when I smell manure I recall that day. I can still feel and experience the events of that day as if it were yesterday. The world stood still, but was, at the same time, moving in hyper-drive. I can see the cloud of smoke and flames expanding and contracting. I can hear Peter's screams and the deafening roar of the explosion. Back then I did what we all did. We were in the midst of the storm. Fear was our only enemy. I minimised the event, consigned it to its box, dried my eyes and got on with it. As we often heard, 'If you can't stand the heat, get out of the kitchen.'

Dry your eyes and get on with it

I would need to dry my eyes again and again. Conflict raged all around us. The British Army had taken possession of Saint Genevieve's school, which adjoined our school at La Salle. Break and lunchtime witnessed riots at the gates and fences of the school and at the corrugated iron outposts, which were manned by the British. The IRA also targeted and destroyed the school kitchen, which had been appropriated by the Crown forces, injuring a number of soldiers. On one occasion a number of my friends managed to wrest a General Purpose Machine Gun from the hands of one of the sentries manning an outpost adjacent to our school yard. The gun, a hefty belt-fed weapon, was delivered to IRA men in a waiting car to loud cheers from all the students.

I recently discussed these times with Fr Patrick McGlynn, a friend from my time at Queen's University. He marvelled that schools were even able to function, given the number which had been occupied or which had huge British Army barracks erected next to them. They were an early example of the British use of human shields. I suggested he consider recording the challenges faced by educators under British occupation. It is a subject which has never been properly addressed. Those who ensured the education of children deserve proper recognition. By late November 1972 the British ended their occupation of our school and retired to a huge barracks named Silver City, yards from our school gates. West Belfast was a veritable armed camp. Casement Park was occupied, McRory Park was occupied, as was the Woodbourne Hotel, the Whiterock Industrial Estate and a number of the local mills. Outposts were also erected in private dwellings in Lenadoon and on the tops of high rise flats at Divis and Broadway. There was Fort Jericho, Fort Monagh, Fort Pegasus, Silver City and Black Mountain Fort. All huge monstrosties. That was before you counted the RUC barracks, which had been made all but impregnable. These sat at Andersonstown, Hastings Street, Springfield Road and Grosvenor Road.

Death and violence were common place. Séamus Simpson (21), a brother of my childhood friend Seany, was shot dead by the British Army on August 11th 1971. On November 1st I was at Avoca Park when an IRA Volunteer shot dead two plain-clothes RUC men. She had lain in wait for them at a fashion boutique. They were Stanley Corry (28) and William Russell (31). More than 200 members of the Crown Forces died between 1971 and 1972 out of a total of 21,000 who swamped our streets and destroyed our homes. Before the IRA killed the first British soldier on November 9th 1971, the British forces had declared open season on nationalists, gunning down and injuring scores of innocents and killing 41 civilians in the process. Some deaths stand out more than others in my memory. I recall clearly the death of Major David Storrey (36) and his colleague, Brian Hope (20), blown up in a field behind Owenvarragh on August 11th 1972. Then there was Alan Tingey (25), a British soldier killed on patrol at Kenard Avenue on August 23rd. As my mother would say and as I appreciate more now: 'They were all somebody's son or daughter.'

We were getting accustomed to walking behind the funeral cortèges of friends and neighbours murdered by the state forces or by their proxies in the loyalist gangs. During this period the British Army killed 106 civilians. Loyalist proxies killed a further 93 and the RUC, relegated to a secondary role with the arrival of British troops, had murdered 5 people. By March 1972 Stormont – 'the Protestant parliament for the Protestant people' – had fallen. We imagined that the end was in sight. We were euphoric. How wrong we were. I felt at the end of that bloody year that I faced two possibilities, death or imprisonment. That is the dark and unforgiving place into which unionists and the British had driven us with their violent and bloody response to peaceful demands. I would be in prison within three years.

As far as the Free State government was concerned, we initially hoped they would come to our defence. IRA Chief-of-Staff, Cathal Goulding, issued a statement following the deployment of British troops saying: 'We have sent a number of fully equipped units to the north of Ireland … this organisation calls on the Dublin government to use the Irish Army in the north and to call an emergency meeting of the General Assembly of the United Nations.'

Taoiseach Jack Lynch had said days earlier on August 13th:

> It is clear now that the present situation cannot be allowed to continue. It is evident also that the Stormont government is no longer in control of the situation. Indeed, the present situation is the inevitable outcome of the policies pursued for decades by successive Stormont governments. It is clear also that the Irish government can no longer stand by and see innocent people injured and perhaps worse. It is obvious that the RUC is no longer accepted as an impartial police force. Neither would the deployment of British Army be acceptable nor would they be likely to restore peaceful conditions, certainly not in the long term.

We were hopeful. Instead Irish Army camps were opened to receive the flood of refugees pouring into the Free State. We continued to hope, but again, how wrong we were. Goulding received his reply from Jack Lynch in a statement delivered in Tralee, County Kerry, on September 20th 1969. Lynch made clear that he would meekly follow the lead of the British government in addressing the Northern crisis, a craven position followed by those who succeeded him. We were on the long finger. To underscore that position and ensure it never changed, loyalists, with the active assistance of the British forces, would periodically bomb targets in the South. The first UVF bombing was at RTÉ's headquarters on August 5th 1969. In this attack and the subsequent 25 loyalist bombings in the South, 36 people died and 400 were injured. RTÉ chose to focus solely on 'IRA violence' as the cause of the conflict.

In the North the UVF, Red Hand Commando, UDA and smaller loyalist gangs would claim the lives of 1,027 innocent Catholics, besides the thousands they wounded. All of this with the active assistance, or at the very least acquiescence, of the British state. Sir John Stevens told a parliamentary committee in 2011 that of 210 people he arrested during his 14-year investigation of loyalists and state collusion, 207 were in the direct employment of the RUC, MI5 or the British army.[23] He also stated state collusion was a factor in many of the killings carried out by loyalists. These death squads were in effect, wholly-owned subsidiaries of the British Security Services, directed to achieving British political policy objectives. You would have struggled to know any of this had you been depending on a censored RTÉ or on Dublin politicians for your information.

I was to get a personal taste of British brutality in the early morning of February 5th 1974. I was on my way home when I was placed spread-eagled against a wall at Slievegallion Drive by members of the Royal Regiment of Fusiliers. Without warning they began to batter me mercilessly with fists, boots and rifle butts. I was shocked but I leapt from the wall and began defending myself. I was beaten to the ground and pounded as they screeched that I was murdering scum. Blows and British obscenities rained down on me. Luckily some local women emerged from their homes and ran towards us shouting. The Brits ran off. I subsequently found out that many other young nationalists had suffered the same fate and worse that morning. It was in revenge for an IRA bombing of a British Army bus on the M62 in Manchester on February 4th 1974. Twelve had perished in the attack, nine soldiers

---

[23] Parliamentlive.tv Draft Detention of Terrorist Suspects (Temporary Extension) Bills Committee, Tuesday 3 May 2011, at 16:46:24. Sir John Stevens, later Baron Stevens of Kirkwhelpington, a cross bench peer in the British House of Lords, was a former head of the Metropolitan Police. His final report, issued on April 17th 2003, concluded there was collusion in the murders of solicitor Patrick Finucane and student Brian Adam Lambert. .

and three of their relatives. Among the four dead Royal Fusiliers was Clifford Haughton, whose wife Linda and two sons, Lee (5) and Robert (2), had died alongside him. An innocent English woman, Judith Ward, was wrongly convicted of the bombing and served 18 years in prison before her conviction was overturned. The IRA was in the midst of a concerted bombing campaign in England. Before the year was out, the Guilford Four, Maguire Seven and Birmingham Six would all be framed by the British state and wrongfully imprisoned for horrendous periods of time before eventually being vindicated following huge international campaigns. The youngest innocent victim of this police and judicial stitch up was Patrick Maguire (14), the eldest was Giuseppe Conlon (52), who had only gone to England to visit his imprisoned son Gerry. Giuseppe died in prison in 1980.

The leading British judge, Baron Alfred Denning, declared in 1979 in relation to the possible release of these innocents: 'It will mean that the police are guilty of perjury, that they are guilty of violence and threats, that the confessions were invented and improperly admitted in evidence and the convictions were erroneous… This is such an appalling vista that every sensible person in the land would say that it cannot be right that these actions should go any further.' Denning also said: 'We shouldn't have all these campaigns to get the Birmingham Six released if they'd been hanged. They'd have been forgotten and the whole community would have been satisfied.'

By the end of 1974 I was caught up in another explosion. A friend and I were walking along Finaghy Road North beside Brenda Park when a car sped towards us from the Andersonstown Road. We were immediately on alert as drive-by shootings and bombings by loyalists were common place. The car slowed momentarily and a bomb was tossed towards us. We dived for cover behind a garden wall and were unscathed in the explosion, which blew out windows and caused damage to a number of homes. Many others would not be as fortunate that year. Some incidents stand out for me: the Dublin and Monaghan bombings, which claimed 33 lives and injured 300; the death of 21 year old Mayo man, Michael Gaughan, who died on hunger strike on June 3rd; and the death of Volunteer Gerry Fennell (28), who was gunned down by the British Army on the Stewartstown Road on August 8th. I was privileged to serve in his guard of honour. The Catholic Church adopted a new policy at Gerry's funeral, which would dishonour the sacrifice of dead Volunteers. The priest prevented the Tricolour-draped coffin from entering the church. People were rightly furious given that the same Catholic Church, to its eternal shame, was more than happy to allow coffins draped in the 'Butcher's Apron' (the Union Flag of Britain) to enter churches.

For my sister Pauline and me, the following year, 1975, didn't have a great start. It wouldn't have a great ending either. In January we found ourselves in the Contagious Diseases Hospital at Purdysburn. We had both eaten from a food outlet and contracted hepatitis. My main memory is of the boredom of forced confinement, the foul taste in my mouth and throat, as well as the awful running to the toilet. It was timely practice as it turned out, since both of us would find ourselves incarcerated in prison by the end of the year. Pauline was captured following a siege in a house at Finaghy Road South, along with Gerard 'Raddo' Brady and Harry Maynes, as they prepared to ambush a senior RUC man. The scene was placed under siege by undercover British Army and RUC units and a five hour stand-off ensued. The arrival of a Catholic priest ensured safe passage from the scene, although it didn't prevent them enduring a severe beating. The driver on their mission had parked around the corner and was able to make good his escape. They all received five year terms of imprisonment. Pauline was 18 years-of-age at the time. She later married 'Raddo' Brady and they raised their two sons and five grandchildren as Irish speakers. Pauline became a teacher, a job she loved and which she reluctantly had to leave due to cancer. She remained a staunch and proud Irish republican until her death at the age of 64 in January 2020. She was always one of my heroes.

Another famous siege grabbed headlines shortly afterwards at Balcome Street in London between December 6th and 12th. I watched this unfold in Crumlin Road Gaol where I was now on remand. I would later get to know Hughie Doherty, the IRA commander at Balcome Street, after his return to a prison in Ireland. He is a wonderful and talented artist and one of the most mild-mannered and gentle human beings you could hope to meet.

Back in 1975 this was all still ahead of me. My school-days, the days of my youth and the days of whatever innocence I retained, were gone from the first day I entered Crumlin Road Gaol. What a first day that was. I had been water-boarded and beaten during interrogation by the RUC.[24] At the subsequent court appearance I was charged with 11 counts of conspiracy to cause explosions. The charges were based on

---

24 A form of torture where water is cascading on a hooded prisoner to induce feelings of drowning.

documents detailing plans of British barracks and other installations. I had remained silent in the barracks and had refused to recognise the right of a British court to try me on any charge. I was only guilty of defending my country against a foreign occupier, a view that I hold to this day. Water-boarding was in the news during the illegal American and British occupation of Afghanistan and Iraq. Back in the 1970s I'd never heard the term, although many had been subjected to it. Years later I saw one of my torturers on a television documentary. He was being interviewed in Europe, where he had retired on his huge RUC pension. 'Look at that,' I said to my wife. 'That's one of those who water-boarded me.' She asked what had happened and I explained to her that I was brought to a room with a bath in it and forced to strip to my underpants. I was then forced under the water. It was freezing and took my breath away. When I surfaced I was dragged to a plastic chair and held down by two men. A third man from behind me placed a towel soaked in water over my face. I was terrified and thought I was drowning. It all happened very fast. One minute I was sucking air into my lungs with relief following the submersion. The next moment I was inhaling water and panicking with the towel over my face. Despite the firm grip, which secured me to the chair, the panic gave me a strength which surprised even me. I managed to wriggle free and dislodge the towel. Suddenly my feet were gripped and I was dragged to a window and held dangling above the ground by my ankles. In all, I suffered three bouts of water-boarding. I eventually lay spent on the floor breathing deeply and rejoicing that I hadn't spoken. During all my interrogations, then and since, I adopted a strategy of giving all my attention to entering my mother's home. I would walk through the front door, noting every detail. Every time my interrogators would break my train of thought I would return to the front door and begin my journey again. Rosie's front door always stood between me and any threat from outside.

I was transported from court to Crumlin Road Gaol in the back of a van by myself. Sounds of the street came in through gaps in the van, which was windowless. The mundane sounds filled my heart with an indescribable pathos. I was a staunch, undefeated republican but the ordinary sounds of the street filled me with a loneliness and anguish which almost broke my heart. If loneliness unsettled me, my arrival in Crumlin Road Gaol taught me that there were worse things than loneliness. I spent my first night in 'B' Wing, which also housed the punishment block. I had never experienced such a din in all my life.

Prisoners roared and shouted throughout the night. Loyalists were housed in 'C' Wing across the yard. They hurled sectarian abuse at us that was deeply offensive and gave warning of danger. Nightfall brought an even more cacophonous noise. I was encased in an old Victorian cell, a high window stood above the beds. It had small panes of glass, most of which were broken. Outside of that were the prison bars. Inside the cell it was narrow and claustrophobic. Two bunk beds and a small wooden cabinet were the sole furnishings. A chamber pot and a bible completed the cell's contents. A small circular hole with an outside cover adorned the door.

The Crum, as it was called, was built during the famine years in 1845 by Charles Lanyon. I knew that so many republicans had passed through before me and I drew strength from the thought. I thought of Tom Williams (19), hanged on September 2nd, 1942. It was an imposing prison, which I knew well as I had often observed it from my Aunt Marie's house in Cliftonpark Avenue. It was constructed from black basalt. I had been intrigued as a child as I had watched prisoners walking around the prison yard in circles. I understood that much better after I served my time there. Prisoners have only one hour's exercise per day and walking systematically around the yard is the best way to maximise the benefit. In my cell on that first night, I had 10 Players No. 6 cigarettes. Unfortunately I had neither matches nor a lighter. Around 9 p.m. I spotted a screw[25] through the hole in the door. I let out a whistle and asked him if he had a light. 'Who do you think you're whistling at, you vermin?' he roared: 'I'm looking a light,' I replied. 'You'll learn manners when the Day Guard arrive,' he said. 'Now get to bed, you piece of IRA shit.'

I got neither a lighter nor very much sleep that first night. The cell had no light but was well illuminated by the external security lights. I noticed a Gideons' Bible on the cabinet. The only other thing I could see was the piss pot. I lifted the bible and began to read it. I had no notion of the bible, except for the extracts which were read at Mass. I started reading it from the beginning and resolved that I would read it from cover to cover. I succeeded in that aim and had read it five times before my final release. As literature it was a reasonable collection of disparate works, but as to its veracity I formed the opinion that even a hungry crocodile wouldn't swallow the half of it. My favourite piece was Ezekiel chapter 23, verses 1-21.

---

25 The name given to prison wardens.

Sleep eventually came, but it was rudely interrupted by a gang of screws who burst into my cell around 8 a.m. They were highly excitable and roared that I was to accompany them to see the governor. They frog-marched me to an office in the central circle, from which the various wings of the prison radiated outward. Behind a plush desk with a green leather top sat a be-suited man. Blue-shirted screws to either side of me were poking and prodding me in the arms, telling me to stand to attention and call the governor 'sir'. A white-shirted screw, who introduced himself by name, told me that he was the Principal Officer. He stood in front of me and began shoving his finger into my chest. My patience eventually gave way. They descended on me like a pack of wild dogs. One blow wasn't waiting on the other. They beat and hustled me back down 'B' Wing. I had very long hair in those days and one of the screws used this to drag me along. The whole episode was a bit of a blur. They dragged me towards the punishment cells, behind a long wooden and wire screen fence. Halfway down the fence I noticed two doors opening at once, a door in the fence and a cell door facing it. A screw came through the fence door and managed to land a well-placed boot to my lower abdomen which completely winded me. I was dumped into the cell and the door was locked. I lay there feeling sorry for myself. Suddenly the door opened again and a gang of screws, some with batons drawn, were standing there ordering me to throw out my boots. I did so. They ordered me to remove my jumper. I had half completed this task when they rushed at me with a vengeance. Boots, fists and batons rained down on me. They repeated to me in rhythm with the blows: 'Never lift your hand to an officer again.' All I could think of was an old neighbour of ours who used to swing her kids round by the hand beating their arse and intoning their offence in perfect rhythm. The mind is a strange thing.

The screws left and I licked my wounds. My first full day in prison was complete. It was a steep learning curve. I missed my committal visit with my family due to being on punishment. I didn't get a visit for the first month, as I'd lost visiting, parcel and association privileges. In a way I was glad as I didn't want my family distressed at the sight of me. My mother came on her first visit and my father accompanied her. My father said he was proud of me, but that he wouldn't be coming back on visits as it was too upsetting for him to see me in prison. Now with children of my own, I can understand what he meant, but in all honesty, I don't think I would refuse to visit my children.

Early days of imprisonment

So much happened in prison that it is deserving of a book in its own right. The scope of this book however is broader so I will only recount some of what transpired. There are excellent books covering the recent prison experience and I would single out four must-reads: *Ten Men Dead* by David Beresford, *6000 Days* by Jim 'Jaz' McCann, *Time Shadows* by Laurence McKeown and *Nor Meekly Serve my Time* by Brian Campbell, Laurence McKeown and Feilim O'Hagan.

The first thing I was to discover in prison is that it contained more innocent men than would be found in your average monastery. I also learned that when prisoners were discussing their own cases, one was well advised to keep the salt handy; a pinch or two was sometimes required. I heard things in the Crum which stretched credulity further than even the most bizarre religious mumbo jumbo. I was a few weeks in 'A' Wing, which housed republican prisoners, before I was allowed association due to my loss of privileges. 'C' Wing was the preserve of the loyalists. Under the regime we were permitted to wear our own clothes, having political status thanks to a hunger strike in 1972. The only authority we recognised was the IRA, headed by the Officer Commanding. Ours was a man from Andersonstown. He was a very decent man and a good Gaeilgeoir.[26] When not restricted by punishment we were entitled to free association with fellow prisoners from 10 a.m. to midday in the yard and the canteen area. Again we had yard and canteen access from 2 p.m. until 5 p.m. in the afternoon. Association from 6 p.m. until 9 p.m. was solely in the canteen. Confined to my cell, I was nonetheless able to speak with fellow prisoners through the cell door and I gained a lot of useful information. We also had to go to the remand courts once a week and I got to know the 'Friday Crew' well in this way. I was initially in cell 22 on the garden side on the ground floor in 'A' Wing. Two other floors were above me, accessed by an old wrought iron Victorian stairway. The first book I read in the Crum, aside from the bible, was *Catch 22* by Joseph Heller.

On Fridays the screws would move a group of us from our cells and hand us over into the custody of the RUC, who would handcuff us and transport us by van to Townhall Street Court. I always travelled in the van with Brendan 'Bik' McFarlane, Peter 'Skeet' Hamilton, Robert 'Cheeser' Crawford, Norman 'Basil' Hardy, John 'Nodger' Todd and Micky Donnelly, all from Ardoyne. I was among friends. On my

---

26 An Irish Language speaker.

first trip the questioning was all about myself and the beating I'd got from the screws. My eyes, face and upper body were still marked and bruised. The lads were all angry and said that I should point out any of the screws involved if they ever came on to 'A' Wing. I looked forward to spotting any of my attackers, but as always it is best to be careful what you wish for.

Several weeks later I spotted one of the main perpetrators on duty at the gates between the canteen and the wash-rooms. I pointed him out to Bik McFarlane and big Pat Thompson from South Armagh. Three of us were permitted into the toilet and wash block at the same time. Out we went. Bik shoved the screw into the wash-rooms. Big Pat motioned me in and blocked the exit. I was sure the screw would pay for his brutality. 'Are you one of the brave men who beat this young lad?', asked Bik. The screw admitted that he was. 'We'll see how hard and brave you are now that you're on your own. Give the lad a fair fight.' My stomach somersaulted. This was not what I'd envisaged. The screw squared up to me and not wanting to appear cowardly or foolish I made a go for him. Without the help of the other screws he managed to again give me a sound beating. The two lads quickly broke it up, honour was apparently satisfied. I had learned a lesson: if you can stand on your own two feet it's always best to do so, but one always needed to be careful which fights one picks and on which terms they will be fought.

My first Christmas in prison is worth noting, I was to spend eight altogether in prison. At Christmas 1975 I was still in cell 22 on 'A' Wing, which I shared with Séamy Lawlor. My first surprise was learning that republican prisoners refused to eat dinner on Christmas Day and St Steven's Day, choosing instead to stage a symbolic fast. Two full days with no food! Worse still we were inflicting this on ourselves. I questioned the policy. 'That's how it has always been,' I was informed. 'Why?', I asked. 'It has been that way for years,' he said. 'Why?' 'I'm not sure, but it's best not to start nor break a tradition,' I was told. 'As far as I'm concerned it's a nonsense,' I said. 'It demonstrates that we have discipline and self-sacrifice,' came the reply. 'It shows that we're mad,' I said. The tradition wasn't broken that year though it would be later. Merry Christmas.

Aside from the lack of food, there was another thing that made this a less than merry Christmas for me. Around midnight, I heard the voices of a group of young women. I reckon they must have been at Landscape Terrace or Cliftonpark Avenue. They were most likely going to or coming from a party. It was a windy and slightly rainy night, but their voices carried clearly over the prison walls. They were singing Queen's 'Bohemian Rhapsody', which was No 1 in the charts. 'Is this the real life? Is this just fantasy? Caught in a landslide, no escape from reality,' they sang. I had no escape from my reality.

The sound of female voices made my suffering all the more acute. Escape was a constant preoccupation and duty for all republican prisoners. When Martin McGuinness came into the Crum, his first question was: 'Is it possible to escape from here?' Now why didn't we think of that? I would get to know Martin very well in later years. Back then he was one of the more widely recognised members of the Movement. He never did escape and served only a short time on remand before charges of IRA membership were withdrawn. I myself was involved in two serious escape attempts and more farces than I care to recall. In the first case the 'Friday Crew' had, over a number of weeks, managed to move aside a concrete block, which covered an old skylight. We first had to remove and then replace a metal cover. On the day of the planned escape we were placed in another cell. Our misfortune was the good fortune for five IRSP prisoners who escaped from our former cell.[27]

The second attempt involved the smuggling in of explosives. IRA Volunteers were to tunnel into the space between the two external security walls. A gate on the inside wall would be blown open allowing access to the tunnel and freedom. The plan was compromised by an informer and the explosives were captured during a British Army search of the prison. The informer was spirited away during the search. In the third attempt I was to emulate the 'Crumlin Kangaroos', Martin Meehan, Dutch Doherty and Hugh McCann, who disappeared over the perimeter wall in December 1971. John Dornan from Belfast and Martin Donnelly from Tyrone loaded me into a big laundry bag which was then placed beside the yard gate leading to the hospital wing. From there I was to make my way to a rope ladder and over the perimeter wall. Volunteers would be awaiting my arrival at the other side. I was to remain in the yard, secreted in the bag, until everyone had gone back to their cells, allow five minutes and then emerge from the bag and

---

27 Irish Republican Socialist Party, one of the many off-shoots of the Official IRA. The group was formed in Lucan, County Dublin on December 8th 1974 by former members of the Official IRA and Official Sinn Féin. Its first chairperson was Seamus Costello, who would be murdered by his former comrades in the Official IRA on October 5th 1977.

shoulder open the gate, which would be unlocked. I waited what seemed like an eternity. The yard was totally silent. I leapt out and crashed into the gate. It didn't budge. Suddenly an unbelievable noise erupted in the yard. I stood there feeling very foolish and very sheepish. I was the butt of a cruel joke by all the prisoners who were now laughing uncontrollably at my discomfort. I was a bit more careful about what I believed after that.

Musical instruments were allowed in the Crum and I was enchanted by Bik McFarlane's rendition of Rod Stewart's 'Mandolin Wind'. There were some very talented musicians and no shortage of excellent singers. I loved the music sessions and was able to add to my already extensive repertoire of songs. 'Mandolin Wind' always takes me back to the Crum. By early 1976 we had embarked on a protest against the removal of P.O.W. status, which had been announced on November 4th 1975 by British secretary of state, Merlyn Rees. He had announced that political status would be denied to anyone convicted after March 1st 1976. We decided that we would go to court dressed only in our underwear. We were the first to appear in court on January 2nd 1976. We were pulled from our cells and beaten and battered down the wing. There was a screw on duty at the gates of 'A' Wing. As we were beaten towards him he removed his hat and threw it up the wing declaring that he wouldn't take part in brutalising prisoners. He left and was never seen again. While he was unwilling to brutalise prisoners, there weren't many other screws who felt the same. I respected the stand taken by this screw but also understood the stance of the others. After all, we were attacking their state and their neighbours. It was a rough but short enough bad patch. Much worse would come as prisoners began to arrive in the H-Blocks.

There was always a great comradeship among the prisoners and lots of messing and playing of tricks. One will serve to illustrate the type of antics prisoners engaged in. Frank 'Bap' McGreevy, one of the biggest messers, had pulled some prank and we retaliated sewing onions and cabbages into his pillow. His head had been turned with the smell, before he worked out what it was. He had his revenge when he caught a seagull in the yard and deposited it in our clothes' locker. The bird shat all over our clothes and we had to spend the night in the cell with the deranged gull, as it was too big to push out the small window panes. Bap, who hailed from the Lower Falls, was a great fella, a dedicated republican and one of the funniest people you could meet. He was unfortunately to lose his life to criminals who entered his home in March 2008 and murdered him in his bed. He was 51 years-old.

Our day in court

We all would have our day in court. IRA Standing Orders decreed that no republican should recognise the jurisdiction of any British court in Ireland.[28] The courts we appeared before were Special Courts. They came into existence after a report by Baron Kenneth Diplock in 1973.[29] The court consisted of a single judge and no jury. Diplock courts were in fact fashioned by the doctrine of Brigadier General Frank Kitson of the British Army as expounded in his book *Low Intensity Operations: Subversion, Insurgency and Peacekeeping*.[30] He stated succinctly that the courts should be an instrument of support for British Army policy. Kitson honed his skills during the British terror in Kenya and Malaya. Kitson wrote: '… the law should be used as just another weapon in the government's arsenal, and in this case it becomes just a propaganda cover for the disposal of unwanted members of the public.'

My own disposal as an 'unwanted member of the public' began with me walking, like hundreds before me, across the tunnel connecting Crumlin Road Prison with the High Court. It was from this same tunnel in 1980 that eight republican prisoners would escape. Seven of the escapees were from Belfast and the eighth was Michael 'Pete' Ryan from Ardboe, County Tyrone. Pete would be executed along with two other IRA Volunteers, Larry McNally and Tony Doris, in an SAS ambush in Coagh, County Tyrone on June 3rd 1991. I first met Pete in 1986 at a party in Monica Brolly's house in Dublin following the Sinn Féin Ard Fheis decision to end the ban on taking seats in Leinster House. This decision saw Ruairí Ó Bradaigh and others form Republican Sinn Féin. Myself and Chrissie, Marie Ferris and a few other friends from Kerry were there. Nessan Quinlivan, who would escape from Brixton Prison

---

28 The IRA orders in use at the time came from the 1956 version of the IRA 'Green Book'. This would be updated in 1977.
29 William John Kenneth Diplock, 1907–85. Diplock was a life-long member of the British judiciary. At the time of his death he was the longest serving member of that establishment and a sitting Law Lord.
30 Born 1926 and now a retired General, Frank Edward Kitson was the man most responsible for British counter-Insurgency theory and practice in the North of Ireland. In 2015 Mary Heenan, whose husband Paddy was murdered by a loyalist gang in 1973, served papers on Kitson and the Ministry of Defence for 'negligence and misfeasance' due to 'the use of loyalist gangs to contain the nationalist-republican threat through terror, manipulation of the rule of law, intimidation, infiltration and subversion.'

in 1991, was among them. Also at the party that night were Paddy Kelly, Jim Lynagh and Pádraig McKearney, all three of whom would be killed seven months later at Loughgall in County Armagh. They were among eight IRA Volunteers and a civilian who were cut down in a ruthless killing zone established by undercover Crown Forces on 8th May 1987. We had a wonderful night; the singing and the craic were first class. I was 28 years-of-age at the time and it is sad to think that so many of the young people there that night would die as a result of the conflict.

My appearance in court was before Robert Babbington, a former UUP MP and member of the Orange Order. Babbington was educated at Saint Columba's College and Trinity College, Dublin. He was acting under the Special Powers Act and sitting alone as was permitted under Diplock Court rules. I refused to recognise the court and took no part in the two day trial, other than to offer token resistance when I was dragged to my feet for 'His Honour'. At the end of the first day Babbington, sitting in his scarlet robes and clown's wig, told me that I was young and was probably under the influence of older and more sinister figures. He told me he was sending me back to prison to think about my attitude to the court overnight. I returned the following day and again refused to recognise the jurisdiction of the court. Babbington, in his best theatrical voice, told me that it was with a heavy heart that he was finding me guilty on the 11 charges and giving me consecutive terms of three years for each one. He acquitted me of IRA membership, which he said couldn't be proven without an admission. I was also to be acquitted of IRA membership in my second trail. I can therefore safely say that I have the word of two High Court judges that I wasn't in the IRA.

I had now had my two days in court and was content to be heading to Long Kesh; at least this time I would reach the place. I'd made an earlier attempt in 1974 with hundreds of others and was to get a beating for my efforts. It was a Political Hostages Release Committee march. We reached the bottom of the Suffolk Road where scores of RUC men blocked our progress. We waded across the river in Colin Glen and crossed fields until we reached the Stewartstown Road but were faced again with a phalanx of riot-clad RUC men. They boxed us in, and with support from their colleagues at Suffolk Road, they battered us back to Colin Glen. We never reached the Kesh but quite a few reached the Royal Victoria Hospital. My sister Carol was among them, having taken a hefty blow to the head from an RUC baton.

I was whisked to the Kesh by an RUC escort who dumped me at reception where I was quickly processed and dispatched with little fuss to Cage 11. I noticed that the cage had a sign describing it as 'Austin Currie Cage' after the SDLP politician.[31] It was the custom of republican prisoners to name cages after members of the SDLP.

The University of Long Kesh

The first person I met on my arrival in Cage 11 was Davy Wilson. Davy was on duty at the gate when I arrived. It was the custom in the cages that a prisoner was always on duty at the gate to act as a go-between for the IRA structure and the screws who guarded the outside of the cage. Screws only entered the cage to lock the huts at night. When they came to carry out searches they were accompanied by armed British soldiers. We were under the sole command of the IRA within the cage. Each cage had the same layout. There were 19 cages, each with a complement of around 120 prisoners. Cages one to eight housed internees. Cages 9 to 15 housed prisoners under the command of the Provisional IRA. Cage 16 housed the remnants of the Official IRA and cages 17, 18 and 19 housed loyalists. Each was surrounded by high steel mesh security fencing topped with coils of razor wire. In the front corner there was a watch hut staffed by the screws. Screws occupied internal security towers between cages. The perimeter was guarded by armed British soldiers who also had a full barracks within the Long Kesh complex. Inside each cage were four corrugated iron Nissen huts, behind these were two wooden structures, one housing a study room, the other housing shower, toilet and washing facilities. The polytunnel-shaped Nissen huts were stifling in summer and freezing in winter. Each hut contained tea-making facilities, a sink and a toilet and were divided along each side with seven foot high wooden partitions. These were separated from each other to give semi-private sleeping cubicles but had open doorways. Prisoners on the top bunk beds could see each other over the wooden partitions. The cubicles contained a single set of bunks and were decorated with personal photos, wall art and momentos. In republican cages there was a total ban on any pornographic material. Although some prisoners did smuggle magazines in, they could be subject to IRA discipline if found in possession of pornography.

---

31 Joseph Austin Currie, the last remaining founder member of the SDLP. His political career in the North ended in defeat and by 1989 he had retired to the South where he eventually succeeded in having himself elected for Fine Gael in the Dublin West Constituency in 1989. He was to lose that seat in 2002 and immediately resigned from politics.

We had a regular visitor to the cages, a Capuchin monk called Father Joachim. Joachim always carried an umbrella regardless of the weather. I recall one day when he came upon a prisoner, who shall remain nameless, looking at pornography. Joachim let a roar out of him and the prisoner took to his heels with Joachim in pursuit, his umbrella raised like the Sword of Michael the Archangel. The Catholic Church still had a smidgin of authority in those days and we prisoners had a respect for the Capuchins in light of their role in ministering to and bearing witness to the last wishes of the executed leaders of 1916.

Personally I have no religion and view all organised religions with the deepest suspicion. I feel they are a sham and a money-making scheme and have brought much misery and suffering. I hasten to add that my view is in no way a judgment on their adherents. I was then and remain now an agnostic, but I have always had an interest in theology, philosophy and the history of religion. Another frequent religious visitor to the cages was Father Dennis Faul from Dungannon.

I settled well in Cage 11. During my first stint of duty on the gate there was a particularly bigoted and distasteful screw manning the outside gate. He was to be shown a lesson and I was therefore told to get four of the purses made as handicrafts and to send him to four cages in turn with a single purse. I sent him first to Cage 12 and immediately on his return sent him to another cage, and another and then another. He was none too happy but couldn't do a thing about it. I didn't take any of this stuff personally but the screw did, as I was to learn to my cost a few years later.

A Volunteer from Belfast, who I was to get to know well in later years, was the IRA OC in Cage 11. The leaders in Cage 11 had the reputation of being radicals. It was here in Cage 11 that I met many people with whom I would work and serve prison time in the years ahead. People like Danny Devenny, Gerry Rooney, Bobby Sands, Cyril McCartan, Brendan Curran, Tommy Carroll, Terry 'Cleaky' Clarke, John 'Duece' McMullan, Patrick 'Mooch' Blair, Brendan Hughes, Eddie Brophy, Gerry Adams, Joe Rafters, Joe Barnes, Dónal Billings, Séanna Breathnach, Sean Coleman, Paddy 'The Pinker' Donnelly, Christy 'An Francach' Keenan, Tom Boy Louden and Jim McCann, one of the founders of our local Irish medium school, Bunscoil an tSléibhe Dhuibh, and author of *And The Gates Flew Open*. I met many others, among them Denis Donaldson, who was a long-term British agent and who was shot dead in Donegal on 4th April 2006, following his outing as a spy, and Chris Black, who would become the first British supergrass in the 1980s.[32] I also met many lads from my home area in Andersonstown, people like Paddy Molloy, Stu Rooney, Billy Donnelly, Andy Gibson and Danny Lennon.

Danny Lennon was released on 30th April 1976 and returned immediately to active service with the IRA. He understood the dangers, but on August 10th he engaged a British Army patrol in a fire-fight in his native Andersonstown. A second British mobile patrol intercepted and chased the getaway vehicle. The escaping Volunteers turned onto Finaghy Road North and the British recklessly and with no regard for pedestrians or other vehicles opened fire murdering Danny and injuring John Chillingworth. It was a clear case of reckless and negligent discharge of firearms by British soldiers in a built up area. With Danny Lennon dead the car tragically mounted the footpath and struck Anne Maguire, who was out walking with three of her young children. Two of the children, Joanne (8) and six-week-old Andrew, were killed outright. Anne was badly injured and her son John (2) died the following day. The tragedy didn't end there as Anne would take her own life in January 1980. No British soldier was ever indicted for their actions that day. A month after Danny's death, another Volunteer and ex-prisoner was shot dead by a British soldier in Derry. James Gallagher (20) was shot dead as he travelled past a British Army base on a bus. Again no one was indicted for the murder.

The IRA had officially been on ceasefire since February 10th 1975. It had been a shaky ceasefire and an increasingly unpopular one within sections of the Movement. On September 22nd 1975, some seven months into the ceasefire, the IRA launched 15 bomb attacks within the space of a few hours, citing British violations of the truce and warning that it would continue to take retaliatory action for such violations. The ceasefire was ended with effect from January 1976. The leadership of the Movement, which had been involved in negotiations with the British, had declared 1975 as 'The Year of Freedom'. It was clear that many believed this to be the case. Bobby Sands had inscribed his copy of *Buntús Cainte*:[33] 'Roibeárd Ó Seachnasaigh Cas 11 Ceis Fhada, Bliain '75, Bliain Saoirse.'[34] A debate, mostly carried out surreptitiously, was ongoing among many prisoners.

---

32 An accomplice witness who was given immunity and paid to offer evidence against those he or she accused of involvement in anti-British activity.
33 A first level Irish Learners' book.
34 'Robert Sands Cage 11 Long Kesh, Year '75, Year of Freedom.'

This was against Army Orders which prohibited any activity which could 'undermine confidence in the Army leadership'. There was a general atmosphere of conspiracy. It was clear that the 'Old Guard' and conservative thinkers were on one side and the 'Young Turks' and radicals on the other. There was also fierce opposition from the radicals to any IRA involvement in sectarian murders, which some units of the IRA engaged in as retaliation for the murder campaign by loyalist gun gangs. Sectarian attacks by the IRA between 1972 and 1977 cost 92 innocent Protestants their lives. I personally thought, as did many many others, that these were wholly misguided and reprehensible actions. It suited the British claim of being 'honest brokers' trying to keep apart warring tribes. After that period a further 39 innocent Protestants would be killed by the IRA mostly in bombing or shooting attacks gone wrong like those at La Mon House in 1978 which killed 12 people and Enniskillen war memorial in 1987 which killed 11.

Another debate began around the building work which was clearly visible at the bottom end of the Long Kesh Camp. I remember Bobby Sands and indeed others whose view was changing about 'The Year of Freedom', and who were certain that what was being built in Long Kesh was a more permanent prison for republicans. It was in fact the construction of the H-Blocks. Many of us would end up there. According to the view of those prominent in the 'Young Turks', Britain was engaged in its own version of the 'Vietnamisation and Pacification Policy', which had been pursued by the Americans in the final stages of their slaughter in South East Asia. They dubbed this policy 'Normalisation, Ulsterisation and Criminalisation'. They were right as this became official British policy during 1976.

The prison leadership was largely conservative. Two incidents served to illustrate this for me. In one we had sent out a death notice to *Republican News* for Volunteer Danny Lennon, which ended with the word 'venceremos'.[35] It was blocked by the camp staff. The other incident involved a request I made for books through the IRA Education Officer, a man from Lurgan. I requested: *For the Liberation of Brazil*, a Marxist treatise on guerilla warfare by Carlos Marighella, *Das Kapital*, Volumes One and Two by Karl Marx and *Grundrisse* by the same author. He questioned me to find out who had asked me to read these books. He also informed me that it was against policy to promote or

---

35 'Venceremos', Spanish for 'we shall overcome', a slogan employed by several left wing newspapers during the Spanish Civil War.

propagate communist ideology or literature. He asked me why I wanted these books. 'To read them,' I said, 'Will you be promoting them?' he asked. I replied that I didn't know as I hadn't yet read them.

A growing number of prisoners were becoming convinced by the arguments of the 'Young Turks'. On their release many of these prisoners began building alliances to force a change in Army policy, which would eventually lead to the 'Long War Strategy' and a new IRA leadership. As a result of the growing demise of the 'Old Guard' thinking, the IRA handbook 'The Green Book', was overhauled. Things were beginning to change and the changes would accelerate. Eventually a new Northern leadership began to dominate the Army at national level. The process of change would enter semi-public view by the time of the 1982 Ard Fheis. The Éire Nua policy was removed as party policy signalling the beginning of the end for its major proponents, Ruairí Ó Brádaigh and Dáithí Ó Conaill. Their leadership was effectively ended with the election of northerner Gerry Adams as Sinn Féin president in November 1983.

Despite the changes, and the publicly espoused position of the leadership, I held the view in 1975, and still believe, that the Provisionals were never more than a broad alliance who agreed on broad strategy and on the main unifying objective of a united Ireland. The alliance was a broad church: radicals, communists, socialists, internationalists, militarists, Catholic nationalists and a few reactionaries. There were people who could talk the talk of socialist revolution, when it was expedient, but who were in reality nothing more than nationalists. I'm not in any way suggesting that these people were anything but committed to the struggle. They were wholly committed but they never really, in my opinion, sought genuine revolution. In my view the Movement never managed to promulgate a core ideology. Many in the leadership, in my opinion, paid only lip-service to the political education of Volunteers. They were more disposed towards narrow vanguardism, and neglected to bring larger numbers of the working class towards revolutionary politics. Rather than being Leninist in thought and practice they veered dangerously close to Stalinism.

Despite a progressive education policy in Cage 11, there was in my view, a weakness in that the republican objective of gaelicising the Movement and the country was never taken seriously. There were many great gaeilgeoirí, but the revival of Irish was always viewed as being of secondary importance. There was another weakness in my view and that was that any dissent from accepted policy was viewed through a conformist and Stalinist lens. Dissent was quashed and along with it healthy debate. The central leadership was always right and everyone had a bounden duty to adhere strictly to the party line. Despite past deeds and loyalty, anyone who deviated from the leadership line was swiftly sidelined.

I had always inclined towards socialism and internationalism and the need for revolution ever since I had read *The Ragged-Trousered Philanthropists* by John Noonan (Robert Tressell) and *The Thoughts of Mao Tse Tung* which my father had given my as a youth. I also received an exceptional political education in the cages and subsequently in the H-Blocks of Long Kesh. This strengthened my beliefs and inculcated in me an unshakeable belief that there was a better way to organise political, social and economic human affairs than either imperialistic capitalism or invidious neo-liberalism. Back in the 1970s I was absolutely certain that I would remain steadfast in my loyalty to the Republican Movement and the struggle.

Another important feature of Cage 11 was that the Irish irregular verbs, the learner's biggest challenge, were written in large letters on the outside of the cubicle walls. Many intrinsically valued the language as a shared and liberating heritage for everyone on the island and didn't view it as simply a support mechanism for the Movement. I attended my first basic classes in Cage 11 but at the end of March 1976 I got a transfer to Cage 10 to be beside my sister's co-accused, 'Raddo' Brady, and because Cage 10 had, in my opinion, the best Gaeltacht hut in the camp.

My first long-term teacher was Anton Ó Catháin, an Madra Rua (the Red Fox). He was an excellent teacher and much older than the rest of us. Anton had been seriously injured in a premature explosion at New Forge Lane on September 4th 1970 in which IRA Volunteer Michael Kane (35) lost his life. The Madra Rua had been active in the IRA campaign of the 1950s. He was a great seanchaí[36] and I learned a lot more than Irish from him. Anton resigned from the Movement in 1986 in protest at Sinn Féin's decision to take seats in Leinster House. Although our political views diverged, I remained friendly with him until his death.

On April 5th, shortly after my arrival in Cage 10 an incident occurred which I found puzzling. Myself, 'Raddo' Brady and a few others were

---

36 A traditional Gaelic storyteller-historian.

sitting in Raddo's cubicle talking. The radio news announced that there had been a bomb explosion at the Conway Hotel and a subsequent shooting in which one man had died. A wrangler jacket, which was hanging on a nail on the wall, fell to the floor. 'Raddo' blessed himself. 'I know who's dead,' he said. We never commented. Later that day we learned that Volunteer Sean McDermott (20) had been shot dead by an off-duty RUC man and that Mairéad Farrell had been arrested. 'Raddo' showed me the wrangler jacket which he had been wearing on the day of his arrest. It had SMcD written on the inside of the collar. Sean had been the driver of the car which 'Raddo', Pauline and Harry Maynes had travelled in on the day of their capture. The death of any Volunteer weighed heavily on us, especially if they were ex-prisoners or were known to us personally. During my first term of imprisonment Volunteers whom I had known – Paul Fox, Laura Crawford, James McGrillen, Sean Bailey, Francis 'Fra' Rice, James Gallagher, Danny Lennon, Paul Marlowe and Joey Surgenor – would all die in the conflict.

The following republicans whom I had known were also shot dead: Paul Best, Máire Drumm, Comgall Casey and Sean McNamee. The IRA also killed four they accused of being British agents, Séamus O'Brien, Brian Palmer, Myles McGrogan and Vinty Heatherington. I knew them all, but knew Vinty particularly well. Two other civilians I knew also died; Daniel McGrogan, was killed by Séamus O'Brien's agent provocateurs in a bombing at the Whitefort Inn, and Gerard Grogan, was shot dead by the UVF. Volunteer Frank Stagg also died on hunger strike in Wakefield Prison on February 12th. His death deeply affected us all.

Most of us in the cages were teenagers. Some were in their early 20s and a very few were much older. We distracted and entertained ourselves playing practical jokes on each other and generally messing around. We kept busy, chasing seagulls, planning escapes, attending political and military lectures, holding discussions, reading books, learning Irish, listening to music and any of a hundred other pastimes. No one was permitted to be idle. Outside teachers had been banned from Long Kesh since the burning of the prison during the riot of November 1974. We had to take care of our own education. There was no shortage of prisoners with a range of knowledge in a whole array of subjects, so we had a wide choice of studies available. I was responsible for teaching remedial English and Math to those prisoners who had been failed by the education system. I had one student who refused to attend class and who would hide just before class commenced. He was always, unsurprisingly, found and brought to class. He got there in the end and I was delighted when he managed to read his first book. We had television, radio, books, record players, snooker and table tennis tables and we were allowed to go to the prison football pitches once a week, to play football or soccer, although hurling was banned. Many of the lads also played soccer in the yard of the cage. Lots of prisoners joined the Britannia Music Club. You got your first order free and in this way we built up a considerable and very eclectic collection of records. We also had to make handicrafts which were sent to the Prisoners' Dependents' Fund and the Green Cross Republican Charity. Some handicrafts we made for relatives and friends. I was no great hand at making things, though I did make a nice wooden Celtic Cross and wooden harp for my mother.

I didn't back then nor do I now have any great interest in garrison games. Some of the lads were fanatical about soccer. It was possible to bolt the doors of the huts and turn off the power from outside. Some of us would do just that for the craic and the ruckus from the soccer fans was pure entertainment. Besides all the craic, the IRA permitted prisoners to make poteen twice a year, firstly at Easter and then at Christmas. Outside of the brutality during searches by the British Army and the odd fracas with screws on the visits – and of course the absence of freedom and females – we really didn't have much to complain about. The absence of women gave us more opportunity for messing. Many a prisoner found themselves writing love letters to Gerard in the next cubicle in the belief that they were writing to Geraldine in the Bogside. In the case of one prisoner, who wasn't the most handsome of men, the messing went as far as organising a visit for him with the fictitious girlfriend. As he made his way from his cage for the 'visit' the other prisoners were all on the roofs of the huts singing Elvis' 'Heartbreak Hotel'.

In relation to Irish language, the Gaeltacht huts were making great progress. Fluency was also aided by the arrival on the airwaves of Raidió Na Gaeltachta in 1975. We had an abundance of Irish language books and access to the Irish content of a range of daily papers and magazines. Speaking Irish on visits was strictly forbidden by the screws. We knew of the Gaelic Revolution which had taken place with the founding of the Gaeltacht on the Shaws Road in Belfast. In 1975 Bobby Sands wrote an article saying that the founding of this urban Gaeltacht 'is the most revolutionary thing that had happened in the struggle to date and republicans across the country should emulate their example'. I followed the philosophy of Máirtín Uí Chadhain, socialist, republican and Irish language activist who summed up his position in his famous dictum: 'The reconquest of Irish is the reconquest of Ireland and the reconquest of Ireland is the reconquest of Irish.'

All things pass given time and so, on Holy Thursday 7th April 1977 my release date arrived. I was presented with a leather wallet inscribed '4ú Cathlán Óglaigh na hÉireann' (4th Battalion IRA) along with a Bartholomew Edinburgh World Atlas, signed by all 41 prisoners with whom I had shared a hut. There were three IRA battalions in Belfast; 1st Battalion based in Andersontown, 2nd Battalion based in Ballymurphy and the Falls and the 3rd Battalion based in North Belfast. Long Kesh was styled the 4th Battalion. Among those signing were Hugh Hehir from County Clare who was killed by the Free State Special Branch on 6th May 1988. Three other names stand out as they were written in much larger letters than the others: Owen Gerard Brady ('Raddo'), who added 'I love Pauline' after his name and who would marry Pauline in 1980; Bobby Storey who added 'Riverdale' after his name. Bobby was from Riverdale, the area of operations for 'E' Company, First Battalion of the IRA. The third name was that of Brian 'Homer' Holmes, another man from my home district. I still have the book and a lot has changed politically since that edition was compiled. A number of others who signed the book should be mentioned. One is Brendan 'Ruby' Davison, who was shot by the UVF on July 15th 1988 and the other is John McVeigh from Lurgan, who was totally innocent and wrongfully convicted to life imprisonment. John's 15 years in prison were made even more difficult by the fact that he suffered psychological and other problems as a result of a road accident in which he was involved during the early 1970s. John wasn't an isolated case; there were others also who were wrongfully imprisoned for many years. I wonder if the RUC men who consigned him to prison ever thought of his plight as they sat enjoying fat pensions for their foul deeds. John died in February 2014. May he rest in peace.

A Taste of Freedom

As April 7th arrived I experienced the same feelings that many ex-prisoners recounted to me about their own release. I was elated but also sad. I was afraid to speak as emotion was choking me. I thought of the people who had died and also those I was leaving behind. I longed for freedom and was ecstatic at the thought of seeing my family. I was also eager to resume my role in the struggle. In my first days home I found myself a little nervous of the much increased traffic. I was amazed and a bit shocked to see the clothes worn by the punk rockers and astounded by video machines and the other technological marvels which had arrived. I found myself angry with people showing so much interest in celebrities, soap operas and British gutter newspapers. Didn't these people realise that there was an ongoing war and that people were dying? I know now these were crazy thoughts, but it is how I felt at the time and I felt very strongly about it.

A homecoming party had been organised for me at my mother's house. The welcome I received from family, friends and neighbours was overwhelming. It was a great celebration. My brothers were much younger than me and so it was a chance to get to know them better. My sister Pauline was still in Armagh Gaol and she was in all our thoughts. The following day I contacted an old friend telling him I was eager to resume an active role in the Movement. He advised that I should take at least a few weeks to relax. I was reluctant to do so. The war was still raging. On the day after my release two RUC men were killed in an IRA operation at Gortagily near Moneymore in County Derry. They were both young men, John McCracken (22) and Kenneth Sheehan (19). On the Saturday death was much closer to home when the body of Myles McGrogan (22) was found at Colin Glen on the Glen Road. He had been executed by the IRA, accused of being part of a gang of British agents involved in undercover activity. The leader of this counter-gang, Séamus O'Brien (25), had been executed on January 17th 1976 followed by two other gang members, Brian Palmer (39), executed on July 1st, and Vincent Heatherington (21), executed five days later. Vinty had been a childhood friend.

Events meant that any decision about taking a few weeks off was taken out of my hands. On Easter Sunday morning I met Bobby Storey, Patsy O'Carroll and Seany Simpson. We made our way to Beechmount for the Republican Easter Parade. As the parade was drawing to a close we heard the huge rumble of an explosion. We made our way out of Milltown Cemetery and gathered at McEnaney's Bar, across from Andersontown Barracks. A short time later the Easter parade of the Official IRA reached the cemetery gates. To our shock a member of the parade drew a Magnum .357 handgun and began firing in our direction. All the bystanders screamed and ducked for cover, as we did ourselves.

We had no idea what was happening. Two of us decided to head to a house in Ardmonagh Parade in Turf Lodge. We were in the house only a short time when another friend arrived with the news that the explosion had occurred just as the Official IRA parade was getting underway. A 10 year-old boy, Kevin McMenamin, had been killed. There had been other shooting incidents involving members of the Official IRA attacking known Provisionals. The Provisionals, in retaliation, shot dead John Shortt (49). Shortt turned out to be young McMenamim's uncle. Other shootings occurred across the city. It was eventually established that the bomb attack had been the work of the UVF. The bomb had been constructed by James 'Tonto' Watt and was planted by members of the Shankill Butchers' gang, including John Murphy, a brother of the Butchers' leader Lenny Murphy.

A few of us left the house at Ardmonagh some time later and made our way to a nearby flat in Norglen Parade. As we walked along the balcony of the flats we heard a burst of gunfire. We took to our heels, heads bent to minimise the danger. I turned my head and saw a known member of the Official IRA just as he loosened-off another burst of automatic fire from an AK47 assault rifle. It was a weapon none of us had seen outside of a book. We were extremely lucky that the gunman, who I still see from time to time, wasn't as efficient a marksman as the weapon he carried. He was following us with bursts of gunfire instead of aiming ahead of us and traversing the fire back towards us. We certainly lived in dangerous times. I was to find myself back in prison before this episode of sheer madness would finally end. I was utterly disgusted that inter-republican rivalry was ever allowed to get to such an awful position. The madness of the Easter outburst had been quickly resolved but it was to flare up again in July. A number of Provisonals on the New Lodge Road had physically attacked a group of Officials and the return to shooting quickly followed. It was to end on July 27th and culminated as badly as it had begun. The Provisionals shot dead Trevor McNulty (29). The Officials for their part killed Daniel Cowan (30), Tomas Tolan (31) and James Foots (29). Another 18 people were wounded. I remember my father-in-law saying years later that Irish history was littered with tragedy, which British colonialism had brought down on us. In his view, however, there were only two disasters, the Civil War and republican feuding. I completely agree.

During the months of April and May 1977 the pace of life was hectic. I was constantly busy and had little time for normal things.

One photograph was taken of me during that period and it thankfully survived. In the photo are Seany Simpson, Martin Lavery, Mart Holland and myself. It was taken in the Green Briar club. Martin would end up with me on the Blanket protest and Seany would also face future terms of imprisonment. Mart was spared the experience. Another personal tragedy was to strike myself and my friends before my return to prison. I was with a number of comrades, among them Brendan O'Callaghan. It was Saturday April 23rd. We had split up and Brendy made his way to the Hunting Lodge Inn. He was in the car park when a British soldier, concealed in a hidden observation post, opened fire without warning, killing Brendy instantly. I had first met Brendy when we were together in the Crum. He was the IRA Officer Commanding Lenadoon and his loss was a big blow to all of us. It was especially so for his wife Amelia and their two young children. Brendy always had an easy charm and an infectious smile. He was 21 years-of-age when he was killed. In 1977 the IRA was still recovering from the debilitating ceasefire of 1975. The 'conveyor belt' policy, as Bobby Sands would later call it, was in full swing. People were being arrested in large numbers and pushed along the conveyor belt of Castlereagh interrogation centre, the Diplock courts and prison. I would be among them.

I had enjoyed a mere seven weeks of freedom, the last three of which I spent in Turf Lodge. I was busy every day and sometimes at night also. I'm not complaining. It was the life I had freely chosen. My only complaint is that I didn't have longer to make a bigger contribution. The story was the same for many others. The man I felt most sorry for was Sean Coleman, who only enjoyed four weeks of freedom before his return to prison, where he would serve a life sentence. There is always someone worse off than you.

My taste of freedom came to an end after an incident in which a British soldier was shot and wounded on the Whiterock Road. He had been shot by an IRA man firing from the rear of the Ardmonagh Flats in Turf Lodge. Shortly after the shooting, a car in which I was travelling was rammed by a British armoured car on Norglen Parade. Joe McQuillan, a man who I had only met that morning for the first time, was driving. Joe accelerated as the Brits pursued. He managed to get us ahead and out of sight for a short time. I asked Joe to stop the car and alighted to hide a number of items between a hedge and a garden wall. I leapt back in and the car sped off again. We reached Norfolk Way and found two armoured vehicles blocking our way. Our goose was cooked. I attempted to make off on foot but a soldier barrelled me to the ground and placed the muzzle of his rifle to my head. Joe was still in the car with a rifle pushed against his head. The soldiers were shouting and whooping in jubilation. They searched the car and found nothing. A soldier began beating and questioning me. I never uttered a word. That remained the case until I arrived in Townhall Street Court House three days later.

I was charged with possession of a weapon and membership of the IRA. This was on the word of a British soldier who had identified me as the man he had seen coming out from behind Ardmonagh Flats immediately after the shooting. He claimed that I'd been carrying an AR-15 Armalite assault rifle. The rifle used in the shooting that day was a Remington 742 Woodsmaster .30-06, bearing no resemblance to an AR-15. Identification is often an unreliable piece of evidence. Regardless, I appeared in a court, whose jurisdiction I refused to recognise. I was consigned to Crumlin Road Gaol to await trial.

The Old Dog for the Hard Road

What a pleasant return that was to be! Two familiar faces, both of whom I knew well from the days of P.O.W. status, were gleefully waiting to welcome me to 'B' Wing, where I would undergo the usual committal procedure. 'Jackson', shouted one of the screws: 'There are no OCs now, we're in charge. Everything has changed.' I wasn't, if I'm truthful, too pleased to see this pair, but I remained silent. I remembered my first experience in 'B' Wing and wasn't keen to repeat it. Although political status no longer existed we were, nonetheless, asked to choose which organisation, if any, we wished to be housed with. I chose the Provisionals. After my visit to the governor, which passed without incident, I was dispatched to 'A' Wing. I was placed on the ground floor in cell 14 on the yard side. Things were different here too. Loyalists and republicans were housed in adjacent cells.

Each grouping would avail of exercise and association, but on alternate days. We were therefore under confinement 24 hours a day, every other day. There were plenty of altercations when opposing prisoners met outside the cells on visits or during a visit to the doctor. The screws always contrived to ensure that republicans were in a minority. Many received beatings by loyalists. That's how things were to be throughout my period in the Crum. In H-Blocks One and Two, where prisoners were housed after receipt of their committal papers, things were even worse.

In the Crum I was sharing a cell with John Davey from Gulladuff. John was a good bit older than me. He was a veteran republican for whom I had the highest respect. I was only 18 years-old but to me he seemed ancient. John was in fact 49 years-of-age.

I never spent long in the cell with John. He was released when charges against him were dropped. I would get to know him a lot better on my release in the 1980s. But alas John, like so many others, was murdered by a UVF gunman as he drove along the lane-way leading to his isolated farmhouse on Valentine's Day 1989. John was a Sinn Féin councillor at the time of his murder. He had twice been interned. The year before his murder, the DUP's William McCrea had used the cloak of British parliamentary privilege to accuse John of IRA membership, exactly the same device used by the British junior minister, Douglas Hogg, ahead of the murder of human rights lawyer, Pat Finucane, shot dead by the UDA with the active assistance of British security services. Hogg had been given the brief on Pat Finucane by then RUC Chief Constable, Jack Hermon. Pat's best known client had been Bobby Sands.

Settling back into the routine in the Crum was easy enough for me as I'd had plenty of recent experience. I was soon appointed to the role of debriefing prisoners following their time in the interrogation centres. That itself could provide material for a decent book. The work was often sad and dealt with people often at their most vulnerable. Through this work I got to know a lot about the situation in various parts of the country, which would prove useful in the years to come. One case stands out as an illustration of the naivety of many IRA operatives. Six Volunteers had been caught in a convoy of cars, the first containing guns, the second explosives and the third a firing set and bell wire. It occurred to me that putting all the material in one car may have been a better idea. However, the lads were banged to rights. Detectives told one of them that another had indicated that he was the man who would detonate the device. 'I put him straight,' said the lad. The same ploy had been used on three of the others and each in turn had 'put the detective straight!'

Debriefing was an important process. Prisoners were informed they would receive a book of evidence. They were told that a frank and full account of what happened in the barracks was in their best interest, as there could be implications if damaging information was discovered later. What was most important was to ensure that any information which had been revealed in the barracks was communicated to the outside as quickly as possible.

As far as the running of the prison was concerned the screws certainly had a much stronger hand, but IRA discipline was still solid. Prisoners recognised only the authority of the IRA Officer Commanding. There were difficulties in the interplay with the prison regime, as the screws insisted on not recognising the role of the IRA OC. But we had ways and means of ensuring that they were forced to do so. We had the weight of numbers on our side. Eventually for practicality the screws would work the system. The levels of brutality within the prison began to rise. We were also receiving information about the violent regime in force in the H-Blocks. Kieran Nugent, had begun a protest in September 1976, refusing to wear a prison uniform and being forced to cover his naked body with nothing but a blanket.

The Blanket protest had commenced. Kieran, in conversation with the OC before his sentencing, had informed him of his intended course of action. John Thomas was in his third term of imprisonment by this stage. Kieran sought JT's advice. 'Don't put on the prison uniform,' he was advised. That was the totality of the strategy for dealing with criminalisation. The Blanket protest, in spite of its weak beginnings, would go on to bring the story of the Irish struggle onto the world stage by 1981. The Blanket began with Kieran Nugent's defiant reply when told to don prison garb: 'You'll have to nail it to my back,' he said. Others soon joined him. Jimmy McMullan, Alex Comerford, Jim McAuley, Paul McNerney, Tommy Cosgrove and Finbarr McKenna – who would later die on active service for the IRA – had been arrested on a multiple IRA bombing mission in Belfast in 1976. They would remain on the Blanket until it ended. By the time I arrived in the Crum there were 60 prisoners on protest in the H-Blocks. There were also a number on protest in the Crum: Gerard 'Beef' Murray, fiery Joe Maguire, Jimmy Duffy (RIP) and Fra McCann, later an elected member of the Stormont Assembly, were on protest in 'B' Wing. If memory serves me right, Matt Bradley joined them before they were all transferred to the H-Blocks.

During my early days in the Crum I was teaching Irish, reading as much as I could and going over in my mind what had been said to me during my interrogation in the barracks. The first book I read on my return to prison was *Dice Man* by Luke Rhinehart, an intriguing tale of a psychotherapist who decides to base his life choices on the roll of a dice. I don't want to spoil the book for anyone who might want to read it, but there are better ways to make life choices. My second book was *The Ungodly: A Novel of the Donner Party* by Richard Rhodes. This was a story about a group of people who in the 19th century chose the road less travelled. It was essentially a story of the courage and resilience of the human spirit. I got inspiration and some wisdom from each of the books; firstly it was always best to decide actions based on knowledge and analysis. Secondly, one always needed to remember that the human spirit is always more powerful than any hardship or difficulty which we as individuals might encounter. My main preoccupation, however, was unravelling all the clues I had gleaned from what the detectives had said during my interrogations.

They had been aware of too much accurate information. I knew that Joe had admitted possession of an armalite and hijacking. He had also known about the items which I had placed behind the hedge but these had not been mentioned nor captured. So it was obvious that he wasn't their source of information. Besides, they had facts that he wasn't aware of. At first I concluded that it was the work of an informer, the curse and bane of resistance and revolution down through the centuries and across the globe. Some of their facts, however, related to information that pertained to things which had occurred both behind and in front of the flats and no one person was in a position to give them that information. I had been in prison several weeks and was sitting up in my bed late one night reading Graham Greene's *Our Man in Havana* when I had a Eureka[37] moment! There had to have been a concealed spy-post in the flats!

I sent word to the outside giving the reasons for my conclusion. Within a week the IRA had uncovered a hidden observation post manned by two British soldiers. It transpired that an informer had allowed the Brits access to the roof space through a trapdoor in his bedroom ceiling. I won't name the informer, but his father was a veteran republican and prominent in one of the Movement's associated organisations. Rather than suffer the usual and, in my view, deserved fate of the informer, this snake was allowed to go into exile for one year. I was astounded. Looking back now, I can see that this incident had a profound effect on me. I realise that was the first moment in which I began to have doubts about the integrity of some of the people within the Movement. It wasn't to be the last such time for soul-searching. How many other informers, some lesser offenders than this man, had been executed? Yet

---

37 Eureka, a Greek interjection celebrating discovery and invention was famously used by the inventor and mathematician Archimedes 287–212 BCE, when he leapt naked from a bath in Syracuse having discovered how to calculate the volume of irregular objects using displacement of water.

here was this low-life being treated with kid gloves because of who his father was. It was immoral and corrupt. I was to bump into the informer after my release and I simply avoided eye-contact with him. He dropped his head in shame, as well he might.

Because we were remand prisoners, we were allowed to receive parcels of foodstuffs and books. This provided an opportunity to facilitate an escape. Detonators, explosives and other components were smuggled into the prison inside blocks of butter and tubes of toothpaste. These were stored in various cells around the ground floor of 'A' Wing. Early one morning the screws, backed up by British soldiers, entered the wing to carry out a search. Those in possession of explosives felt reasonably secure as we had endured an earlier search in which none of the material had been uncovered. On this morning the prisoners in the first cell shouted out in Irish that the screws were taking the butter and toothpaste and placing it in boxes. The appropriate people began tossing the butter and toothpaste out the window. I looked out my cell window and there were a pair of hapless screws, one with a clipboard and the other running up and down furiously shouting, 'Cell 10, butter and toothpaste.' His mate began writing cell numbers down. An order was shouted by the OC telling everyone to throw the butter and toothpaste out the windows. The escape was clearly thwarted but at least no one would face charges of possessing the explosives.

Although I hadn't seen much of life during my short period of freedom, it was clear that the earth was still spinning on its own axis. Events were happening with their normal frequency, oblivious of me and my petty worries. The world had enough on its plate without having to shoulder the burden of my existence. 1977 had been a seminal year for the Republican Movement. On the one hand significant efforts were being made to ensure Sinn Féin became a serious political force rather than a mere support group for armed struggle. The IRA itself was undergoing significant change. The old system of brigades, battalions and companies was being transformed. Some of the structures would remain for administrative purposes, but armed actions would be the preserve for new tight-knit cells. An Garda Síochana, and thus the RUC, came into possession of the restructuring plan, following the arrest of the IRA's Chief of Staff Séamus Twomey in Dublin in December 1977.

The year had begun with a terrible tragedy when the IRA killed an infant called Graeme Dougan. He died when an IRA bomb, with insufficient warning, had been planted at Harmin Park in Glengormley on January 1st. Another 110 people would die before the year was out. The bombing of England, as always, remained a priority for the IRA. Bombing campaigns in England were as old as the modern Republican Movement. There had been campaigns in 1867 and again from 1881 until 1885. Between 1939 and 1940, the IRA planted 300 bombs in England. Volunteers were again active on enemy soil between 1971 and 1975. With the IRA restructuring, active service was again resumed in England. On January 27th the IRA detonated seven bombs in West London. On February 4th a setback occurred when British police uncovered an IRA bomb-making factory in Liverpool. Momentum was stalled for a period but by October the IRA was again active 'in the belly of the beast' when bombs exploded at boutique restaurants in London's Mayfair and Chelsea areas. These had been well known playgrounds and haunts of the British establishment. The soon to be arrested Chief of Staff, Séamus Twomey, said in an interview: 'By hitting Mayfair restaurants we are hitting the type of people who can bring pressure to bear on the British government.'

Closer to home, prisoners in the Free State's Portlaoise Prison were suffering brutality to rival that being carried out under direction from the abhorrent triumvirate of British politicians James Callaghan, Merlyn Rees and Roy Mason. South of the border another rotten triumvirate, Liam Cosgrave, Patrick Cooney and Conor Cruise O'Brien had given the green light for the Guards and the screws to unleash brutality against republican detainees and prisoners. Things got so bad in Portlaoise that the prisoners saw no alternative to hunger strike. This commenced on March 6th and was led by former Kerry county footballer Martin Ferris, who would later become a TD. In total, 19 others were to join him. The striking prisoners were transferred to the Curragh Camp in County Kildare. The hunger strike ended with Ferris on his 47th day without food. It was shameful that Irish citizens, who were prepared to defend their fellow countrymen, were brutalised to the point of hunger strike by the policies pursued by fellow Irishmen. Since its inception the Free State, and its successive governments of all hues, had always resorted to clamping down on republicans rather than have the courage to face down the British.

My first taste of the H-Blocks

My own turn to receive committal papers arrived and I was both surprised to read the content and felt lucky to be alive to do so. In setting out its case, the Crown had revealed that one of the British soldiers, secreted in the ceiling of the flats, had several times, before and after the shooting, and with increasing urgency, sought clearance to execute me. I would remember his final words and those of his commander for a long time: 'Permission to open fire; he's about to open fire.' 'Don't worry about him opening fire on the patrol. He'll be got,' replied the commander. 'Hold your fire. Don't reveal your position. Hold your nerve and hold your fire. That's an order!' They were quite willing to allow one of their own to be shot, when it could have been prevented. His life was worth less to them than their hidden spy-post.

I pondered those words in my head as I made my way to the H-Blocks. On arrival I was to find that I was in very good company. On my wing there was Gerry McDonald, Seamus Kelly, Joe McQuillan and Séanna Breathnach from Belfast. Tom McElwee (who was later to die on hunger strike) and his brother Benny from South Derry were there, as was Big Joe O'Boyle and Danny Clarke from Antrim. We all knew we would face challenges as the screws had the upper hand, due to low numbers of republican prisoners who were mixing on the wings with loyalists. We had discussed this situation in the Crum and the IRA had instructed Séanna Breathnach to take over command on arrival in H-Block 1 and to end this regime.

For the first few days we spoke with the prisoners already in H1 and Séanna informed them of what we planned to do. We would end integration with loyalists and would undermine the control of the screws. The first objective was easier than the second. We told loyalists we would attack them if they left their cells. They obliged by not coming out the next day. Within the week the screws had removed the loyalists to a wing of their own. Two particularly obnoxious screws were in charge of the wing, one a loyalist with a UVF tattoo, the other a Catholic lackey who made it his business to show he hated us more than his Protestant colleagues. Our first move was to end the practice of prisoners locking up on command and refusing to 'stand by the doors' for a head count before cells were locked. When the screws shouted 'lock up' we all remained seated for 10 minutes before Séanna Breathnach shouted: 'Faoi glas anois, sin ordú ón cheannfort.' He repeated it in English: 'Lock up now, that's an order from your OC.' We proceeded to our cells and ignored the screws command of 'stand by the doors.' Séanna was placed on punishment, so the next night we all shouted the order together.

When the same two screws arrived in the mornings they would constantly tap their keys on each cell door shouting: 'Prisoner, move your blankets and show yourself for a headcount!' We decided not to comply. The screws got angrier as they moved from cell to cell with no one moving. They reached Big Tom McElwee's cell. They told Tom he'd be sorry when they returned with reinforcements. Tom ignored them. They duly returned and we heard them opening Tom's cell. There was a commotion and total silence fell on the wing as was always the case in such situations. After a short pause we heard the Catholic lackey saying: 'Just let us get him out of the cell McElwee, we won't touch you.' Big Tom had knocked out 'tattoo' man. He was taken without incident to the punishment blocks. The key-tapping ended that day. Gradually we broke down the screws' control. It was a good lesson for us all. If we maintained discipline and stood united we could achieve most things. There were others of exemplary bravery like Tom McElwee and the screws always trod lightly around them. There was Tom's cousin, Francis Hughes and Kieran Doherty, 'Big Doc'. Both Francis and Kieran were to die on hunger strike. Men like them were never prepared to bend, despite all the brutality. It was a very special privilege to know them and a great inspiration for all of us.

The 'super' screws had one more card to play. We were allowed to play football and soccer in the yard. In the case of football and, less often in the case of soccer, the ball would go over the fence. Most screws would throw it back. The 'two fools' decreed that the ball couldn't be thrown back without us calling the screws 'sir'. We were prepared to go without sport, rather than yield to that indignity, until Séanna came up with a plan. We, as individual prisoners could seek to see the governor, to resolve issues. So all 50 of us put our names down to see him. We all told him: 'I want you to speak to my OC to resolve a problem.' This went on for quite some time, with the governor growing increasingly frustrated. After meeting more than 20 prisoners, the governor sent for Séanna. 'I'm not recognising you as anything other than an individual prisoner,' he said, 'but what's the problem?' We got our ball back from then on.

With the struggle on the outside only beginning to regain some traction, we engaged in lots of debates and discussions about what was required and what role we, as captured activists, could play in assisting. Myself and others were of the opinion that the British were beginning to contain the efforts of the IRA. In any war of attrition the stronger side will always prevail. In guerilla warfare, if the insurgents fail to establish free zones, or establish political strength sufficient to bring about negotiations, then the struggle becomes one of pure attrition. The guerrilla forces will wither and eventually die. The IRA outside was transforming and embarking on what became the 'Long War' strategy. The need for more and better weaponry was obvious, as was the need for more imaginative military operations. Building confident political activism aside from armed actions was also an imperative. Further politicisation of armed Volunteers was also essential.

The Blanket protest was reaching the conclusion of its first year and there were obvious weaknesses. No protesting prisoner was permitted to wear the uniform for any reason. As a result visits weren't happening, with a consequent lack of communication coming from the prison. Sympathetic priests could be relied upon. But that was far from satisfactory. Prisoners were permitted to put on the prison trousers for Mass, although some wouldn't even do that. It appeared to me and others that if the wearing of uniform could be permitted for such an esoteric purpose as attending Mass, then why not allow it for the betterment of communications with the outside? The struggle in the prison and that outside were badly out of sync. The leadership's view of prisoners was that they were casualties of war. It believed that, beyond giving some measure of support to their families, prisoners were essentially a distraction. I fully understood their position, but didn't agree with it. Prisoners had an effective role to play in the struggle and things would need to change. The debate was in its infancy but would mature over time.

Back in the Crum

My time in court was approaching and, as was customary, I was shifted back to the Crum. This time I arrived in 'C' Wing. It wasn't radically different from 'A' Wing. I was appointed vice OC, a job I didn't relish as it involved responsibility for discipline.

One incident occurred in 'C' Wing, which left me very annoyed. I went to join a lad I recognised from Derry, who was sitting in a cluster of tables somewhat removed from the others. I spoke to him and what he told me left me angry. I went and sat at another table alone and was approached by a former internee from Andersonstown, who said: 'I thought for a minute there that you were going to sit at the touts' table.' I made subsequent enquiries and found out that the 'offence' of our Derry comrade, was to have broken and signed statements during interrogation. Those prisoners, who had instigated this practice on their own authority, had no right or justification for doing so. I encouraged my friend to write to the leadership outside for clarification. He was told that the only status of any imprisoned Volunteer was that of 'suspension pending inquiry on release.' I informed the OC of what had occurred and the practice ceased. I can't imagine how those subjected to this ill-treatment by fellow prisoners felt. I can only repeat the apology of the IRA at the time and say again, it should never have happened.

Another lesson I was to learn which stayed with me concerned a minority of prisoners who were highly critical and disparaging of prisoners who hadn't joined the Blanket protest. I thought they were too harsh and too quick to judge. None of us knew how we personally would face the challenge. I was to discover that a majority of this vocal minority, in fact those loudest in their condemnation, chose not to join the Blanket when their turn came. In my opinion they condemned others because they themselves feared the prospect.

I again taught Irish in 'C' Wing and thoroughly enjoyed it. Our strategic debates and discussions were ongoing. The days in the Crum were peaceful enough and without any untoward brutality from the screws. The courts had picked up pace after a lull. We believed that lull was designed to deliberately keep numbers joining the Blanket low. Overcrowding in the Crum put paid to that. More men began to join the ranks in the H-Blocks. Conditions in the Crum were rough enough on the days when we were locked up 24 hours a day, with three and often four men sharing a cell designed for two. There were lots of books available and I was devouring them, knowing that the days of reading would soon become but a memory.

There was one very funny incident in 'C' Wing, which stands out in my mind. A few Travellers had been remanded for some petty offence and they were lodged on the top landing. They were very supportive of the republican cause. They were the best of craic as well. We would receive our food parcels from home in big brown paper bags so we filled a few with supplies and gave them to the lads. The following day the loyalists were in the yard and the lads were on lock-down with the republicans. A whole uproar started in the yard with the loyalists abusing the Travellers. The lads, it turns out, were throwing stuff out the windows at the loyalists. A short time later the screws landed at their cell and took them to the punishment block. The lads were puzzled as to how they had been caught as they had used the brown bags to cover their heads. They thought they wouldn't be identified with their makeshift balaclavas.

Another major, but not funny incident, occurred in 'C' Wing during this time. One of our prisoners, Gerry 'Blute' McDonnell, would come into the canteen at teatime and would return to his cell after getting a cup of tea. It turns out he was scoffing biscuits and the loyalists had been watching his routine. We were in the canteen as usual one night and Blute left to scoff his secret stash. We heard a muffled explosion. The screws had let loyalists into Blute's cell where they planted a crude booby-trap explosive device in his biscuit locker. He was extremely lucky not to have been seriously injured.

It wasn't to be the last loyalist attack on republican prisoners or their families. The next incident happened in 1991. Loyalists machine-gunned the bus bringing relatives to the prison, injuring two women and terrifying a young child who had been thrown to the floor for safety. Over 60 shots hit the bus. It was a miracle no one was killed. Republicans were furious, but made clear that loyalist relatives had nothing to fear from the IRA. Instead the IRA bade its time. The response came on November 24th 1991. Semtex was smuggled into the prison and a bomb was placed behind a radiator in the canteen in 'C' wing which loyalists were due to use. UDA man Robert Skey (27) was killed in the explosion. Seven other loyalists were injured. UVF man Colin Caldwell (23), died four days later. There were other explosions in other prisons in the 1980s connected to the campaign for segregation in Long Kesh and Magilligan camps. One other major incident occurred on Sunday December 13th 1992 when loyalists fired an RPG warhead at a canteen on the top floor of 'A' Wing, where republicans were eating their evening meal.[38] The rocket hit the roof causing damage but nothing more. That RPG came from an arms shipment which British Intelligence had allowed to enter Ireland.

My day in court arrived. Joe McQuillan and I crossed the tunnel together to the High Court. I met my old 'friend' Tonto Watt in the cells below the courts. Nothing much had changed since my last visit. Before me in the court sat a self-important man in a scarlet cloak and wig. He sat on a red leather chair with the symbols of the 'majesty' of the British Crown behind him. It was, I thought, suitable that 'Dieu et Mon Droit', the motto first adopted by Richard I of England, was above the regal

---

38 Rocket Propelled Grenade, a shoulder held weapon which discharged an explosive warhead.

chair.[39] Richard had died in 1199 of putrefaction, following an injury inflicted by an arrow. Rotten Richard's motto was above the scarlet clad clown, whose court was putrid and rotten. In my eyes it had no writ in Ireland and no right to try me. The screws led us from the holding cells and dragged us to our feet to face the judge. We both refused to recognise the jurisdiction of the court. We took no further part in the farce. I listened impassively as the British soldiers gave their evidence. The main piece of evidence against me was a contention by one of the soldiers that he had seen me '... for less than a minute emerging from the flats with an AR 15 rifle,' which he alleged had been partially concealed below my coat. He told the court of his deep frustration at having been denied clearance to kill me. The trial was over in a few hours. Joe was convicted of IRA membership, possession of a rifle and hijacking a car allegedly used in the attack. This was all on the basis of statements which had been forced out of him in the barracks. The judge ordered that we be dragged to our feet. He gave Joe five years for possession and three years on each of the other counts to run concurrently. He said he was reluctantly acquitting me of IRA membership for 'lack of evidence', but gave me five years for possession of a rifle. It was the maximum sentence allowed under law. We were on our way to the H-Blocks to join our comrades on protest.

---

39 God and my right.

Chapter 3

H-Blocks: 'The Breaker's Yard'

'Learning is never a burden.' (Seanfhocail Uladh 317 Tír Chonaill)

Welcome to the Pleasure Dome

I arrived in the H-Blocks reception area in October 1977. I was 19 years-of-age. I spoke fluent Irish by this stage and was already a veteran of imprisonment. Looking back on it now, I was a mere youth. Of course I didn't see myself as such back then. I'd had a turbulent enough life since my early teens. I'd already lost three of my cat's nine lives. I was again on the verge of another number of turbulent years. Bobby Sands would christen the H-Blocks as the 'Breaker's Yard' shortly after my arrival there. I wore a brown Marion scapular[40] around my neck, the last vestige of my cultural Catholicism. The wearing of the scapular was a custom among republicans. My scapular was given to me by Volunteer Bridie Dolan, an aunt of Dolours and Marion Price, who were serving time in Armagh Gaol with my sister Pauline. Pauline had been part of Bridie Dolan's honour guard on February 10th 1975, the night my granny, Lizzie McNally, died. Bridie had lost both her hands and her sight in a premature explosion, but remained a dedicated member of the Movement until her death.

I was among the more senior prisoners as far as age and experience went. The youngest prisoner was Ciarán McGilicuddy from Tyrone,

---
40 A religious cloth symbol worn on a string around the neck and dedicated to Our Lady of Mount Carmel.

who was just turning 15 years-old when he went on protest. It's hard to describe accurately the physical journey sentenced prisoners made on their way to the H-Blocks. You were placed in the back of a blacked-out van with individual cubicles like miniature horse boxes. You were handcuffed and claustrophobic. There wasn't even space to stretch your legs. Inside this coffin-like space there is no daylight or fresh air. Each prisoner could smell his own and others' sweat. It was the sweat of fear. A prisoner didn't know what awaited him. To survive this he had to go into a state of mental neutrality. Qué sera, sera. The worst feeling was that of helplessness.

On my arrival I wore black Oxford brogues, a Wrangler denim jacket and jeans. The outfit was completed by a white, collarless granda shirt. I was just over eight stone in weight, had long mousy-coloured hair and looked very young. The cops took me out of the van and led me through a number of gates. The sound of keys jangling, gates clanging and screws gabbling filled my ears. I was led into a fairly spacious room. The handcuffs were removed. The cops handed over my paper work. I was left facing a screw seated behind a hatch. He asked my name. I refused to answer. He shouted out: 'Here's prisoner 289; put him in there.' He pointed towards one of a number of grey doors which ran the length of the rear wall. I was taken across to the door and placed inside a narrow cubicle, where I was left to stew. Robbed of sight, hearing becomes accentuated. Every minor sound was sifted for clues as to what was happening or might be about to happen. Detecting danger signals becomes second nature. Some considerable time passed, I imagined, but it was probably no more than half an hour. I heard approaching footsteps and heard one screw ask: 'Where's that scumbag Jackson?' From the footsteps I reckoned there were four or five of them.

The door opened and there before me was the screw I had encountered on my first day of gate duty in Cage 11. All the screws had their batons drawn. 'Strip and throw your clothes out on the floor.' I refused to respond. They fell on me as a pack and forcibly removed my clothes. I was left naked. 'We're in charge now,' said my old acquaintance. They asked for my clothes' sizes. I never spoke. I stared straight at them trying not to show any sign of weakness or fear. Inside I was terrified. Another screw appeared with a grey prison uniform and boots. He told me to take them. I made no response. I was beaten, but not too badly. The screws were telling me I was an animal and would learn respect and manners. They told me they had broken bigger and better men than me. I adopted my old survival strategy, journeying in my mind through my mother's front door, concentrating on every little detail: the colour of the door, the smells, the colour and shape of the little holy water font which hung on the wall inside the door. Every time they broke my train of thought, I returned to the start again. The ordeal ended when they dragged me across the room by the hair and threw me, barefoot and naked, into the back of a van. The prison uniform and boots were slung in behind me. 'They'll put manners on you where you're going, you Provie bastard!', my old 'friend' shouted as he slammed the van doors.

Perhaps some reading this will think that I should have physically fought back and maybe they're right. There were prisoners, braver than me, who did just that. Some fought back just once, others at every opportunity. My view was that I was naked and they were clothed and booted and wielded batons. I would pick my fights carefully. I chose passive resistance and silent defiance. For me the only challenge was not allowing them to break me.

The van brought me to H3. As I alighted all I could see was the inside of the front H-Block yard and the sky above. There was a double fence, topped with razor wire running all around and a big set of double gates, with an intervening airlock, through which the van had driven. There were smaller pedestrian gates with a green watch hut in the airlock, manned by a screw. The fencing was covered all around with corrugated iron. I was in a rectangular space, both sides of which were occupied by rows of cell windows set into a single storey building. I could see a watchtower behind the buildings, but it appeared to sit some distance back from the H-Block itself. Each window had a large pane of glass and two smaller panes above. Behind these I could make out concrete pillars which functioned as bars. The buildings were connected by a central one storey building, slightly taller than the two windowed buildings. It was fronted by set of wooden double doors behind which was a a grilled gate.

We had already heard so much about these H-Blocks. We were all fearful of our arrival there. I was pushed through the grill and doors and found myself in a rectangular room which I estimated to be about 20ft wide and 30ft long. Several doors and three sets of grilles were set into its white walls. The doors were marked: 'Guard Room', 'Governor's Room' and 'Surgery'. There were two sets of double air-locked gates to my left and my right. Turnkeys stood beside each set of gates. Beside one was painted the letters 'A' and 'B' and beside the other 'C' and 'D'.

The gates were painted bottle-green, the colour only broken by an inset brass square which contained the locks. In front of me was another single grille with inset gate, but no mark to indicate its purpose. I was trying to take in all my surroundings but my attention was really fixed on the reception party of five screws with batons in hand. They were eyeing me up with menace.

'Stand up straight, 289. You're only a number here boy and you do exactly what we say when we say it. There are no political prisoners here,' one of the screws announced. I would get to know this individual well over the coming years. He was one of H3's main torturers. This screw, and many others I was to meet, were the worst examples of humanity that I ever encountered. They were filled with hatred and had only one mission: to make our lives hell and break our spirit. They would ultimately fail and when the Blanket protest ended, these craven cowards were putty in the hands of the IRA. I hadn't recognised any of the screws on my first day but it was with deep regret that I was to get to know them all well from that day on.

This motley crew welcomed me in their own perverse, cruel and insulting way. By the time they had finished I was bruised, sore and lying on the floor in my solitary cell. Despite all their efforts I wouldn't lift the prison gear, nor would I call them 'Sir'. The only thing worse than the treatment I received was the feeling of hatred which I felt for these people. In some corner of my mind I was aware, even on that first day, that hatred would do more harm to me than to them. It took me some years to overcome this feeling and to realise that hatred is a cancer and would ultimately be more damaging than any brutality they could inflict on me. I am eternally grateful that, in spite of their worst efforts, I succeeded in not becoming bitter. I would never want to be in their shoes or their heads. I certainly wasn't going to let them have any space in mine.

The following day and other days like it

I awoke the following morning to the chirping of sparrows and had the opportunity, before the arrival of the day guard, to carry out a minute inventory of the concrete box which was to be my world for the foreseeable future. I checked out the furniture: a single black-framed bed with a thin sponge mattress and pillow; three grey, woollen, army-style blankets with red wool edging; two white sheets; a white rough cotton hand towel; a grey plastic basin for washing; a white hard plastic pisspot; a plastic water container; a plastic knife, fork, spoon, plate and cup; a small foot locker containing the prison uniform and boots. On top of this locker sat my old friend, the bible. It was a *King James: New Standard Revised* version.[41] As for the cell itself, it had white walls, a black bitumen floor and a bottle-green door. There were two heating pipes running along the back wall; each was eight inches in diameter and had five inches of space between them. Above the pipes was a window and four concrete pillars, spaced out every five inches, which served as bars. Beside the door was a small metal panel four inches wide and seven inches tall. It contained a light switch and dimmer as well as a small alarm button. These could be overridden by a master switch outside the cell. Needless to say we never got to control the lights. The screws would turn them on when it was bright and extinguish them as soon as darkness fell. A curse in the winter. The cells, however, got illumination from the security lights, which were a constant. Three quarters of the way up the door was a small rectangular window one inch in height and 10 inches wide. This window was covered by a 'Judas' spy flap, accessible only to the screws. If we hit the door hard enough, it would move slightly, giving us the ability to peer out each side along the wing. The ceiling, which was seven and a half feet in height, contained a plastic covered fluorescent light tube. I could take seven paces from the window to the door and four steps from one side wall to the other. We would remain in these cells 24 hours a day until October 1981. We were permitted to go out to Mass provided we wore the prison trousers. I had no problem with that. Not wearing the uniform was a tactic in my view. I always thought the Republican Movement had a tendency to elevate tactics into principles. We caused ourselves a lot of unnecessary grief with such an approach.

Life in the H-Blocks was tough enough and some men suffered mental breakdowns. It happened to a lad next door to me. It was a traumatic and awful experience to witness the disintegration. The mind is an amazing thing. It can raise us to the highest of heights and sustain us in the face of terrible adversity. It can also fail us and cast us down into the depths. On my first day I learned that I'd been joined by Seamus Kelly, Joe O'Boyle, Danny Clarke and Gerry McDonald. I was delighted and heartened by their presence. We were all together and standing our ground against a British policy which sought to criminalise our struggle. It was the

---

41 The King James was the authorised edition in England. The revised standard version was printed in 1885 and was based on the King James version, published in 1611. It was to be our only book until we got the wonderful Bíobla Naofa, edited by Pádraig Ó Fiannachta.

British Labour Party which instigated the policy. That party's record on Ireland was shameful. They instigated most of the oppressive policies which were inflicted on citizens in Ireland. So called socialists like Tony Benn sat on the Downing Street cabinets which devised such repressive measures – clear indication to me that Irish republicans shouldn't place any trust in British political parties of whatever hue.

The biggest challenge facing us was to discipline our thinking, so that the mind didn't become 'the enemy within'. It is extremely difficult to convey the reality of life for a prisoner in the H-Blocks. It is so far outside the norm. Imagine that you go into your bedroom. It is empty of any furnishings. The door is locked from the outside. Beyond the door lies the threat of violence. Sometimes the door will open suddenly and violence will be visited upon you. You are naked, defenceless and afraid. You have no reading material. Nothing to write with. No radio or TV. Your only view from the window is of a grey concrete yard surrounded by high fences. Now, ponder the fact that you won't leave this room for years. This is just the start. Things will get progressively worse.

At 8.30 a.m. on that first day a little pantomime was played out. It would happen every two weeks for each individual prisoner. The screws arrived at my cell door. They shouted for me to stand to attention. I ignored them. They dragged me to my feet. 'Prisoner 289, put on your prison clothes and report for work.' I didn't respond. 'His silence can be taken as a refusal. Put him on governor's report.' Act one of the pantomime was over. Act two would see the governor arrive with a battery of screws. 'On your feet 289, and address the governor as "Sir".' 'Prisoner 289, you are charged with an offence against prison discipline in that you did refuse to obey an order from an officer to wear your prison clothes and report for prison work. How do you plead?' I remained silent and defiant. 'Officer, in the absence of a plea, will you enter a plea of not guilty on behalf of the prisoner?' 'Noted,' the governor would say. 'This morning I asked the prisoner to comply with prison rules,' one of the screws would say. 'Is there any other evidence in this case?', asked the governor. 'If not I will now adjudicate.' A slight pause would ensue before the governor would continue:

> In light of all the evidence before me, I duly find you guilty of said offence against prison discipline. I now make you an award of three days' cellular confinement and a further award of 14 days' loss of remission of sentence, 14 days' loss of free association and exercise, loss of visiting privileges, loss of outside parcels, loss of radio and television privileges. I make a further award of loss of reading and

writing materials, loss of letter-writing privileges and loss of all and any gaming privileges.

They repeated this farce every fortnight for the hundreds of prisoners on protest for five years. For three days after these adjudications our bedding would be removed from the cell from 8 a.m. until 8 p.m. and we would be left totally naked.

At 9 a.m. on my first morning in H3, I heard the screws approaching again. A door opened. 'Slop out, Kelly, and take that fucking blanket from around your shoulders.' We hadn't yet worked out that we could fold the blanket around our waists like a long kilt. We soon learned and also put a hole in a second blanket which we could wear like a poncho. I heard Séamy Kelly's naked feet slapping along the bitumen floor of the corridor. The process would be repeated with each prisoner individually. My turn came and I had to walk naked to the ablutions room to empty my pisspot and then make a return journey to the cell to collect the basin. A second trip to the ablutions and the cell meant I had several inches of water in which I could wash. The whole rigmarole was almost over when I heard the voice of a particularly vicious screw shout out: 'Clarke, stand against that wall and address me as "Sir".' We all remained as quiet as mice. The screws all started shouting that Clarke had struck an officer. The screw who had been hit shouted in a rage: 'Pull the bastard to the grilles and secure him to them.' For 10 horrifying and nauseating minutes we listened to the screams, shouts and the dull sickening thud of batons on bare flesh. There is nothing as soul-destroying as listening to a comrade suffer. You are powerless. You suffer shame and frustration at being unable to help. Every inch of my body would shake with pure anger on such occasions and my stomach would churn.

When our comrade returned and we saw him at Sunday Mass, he was bruised from his neck to his heels. His skin was black, blue, yellow and purple. This wasn't the worst brutality that I was to witness nor endure. That still lay before us. With nightfall and the disappearance of the Day Guard we were largely left to our own devices. We would talk out the doors, speculating and planning. A screw would enter the wing every hour and push a button at the bottom of the wing, which we assumed to be an alarm. Otherwise we were alone. In the early days, with numbers small, silence was enforced by beatings and the threat of beatings. From time to time an overzealous screw would turn on a vacuum cleaner and leave it running all night. These early days were largely ones of rare violence and lots of petty harassment and verbal abuse. The danger in these early days was largely during the early morning slop out. Another flashpoint was the delivery of food to our cells. Prisoners were often assaulted, myself included.

The worst thing was the random violence. A door would be suddenly opened and a prisoner attacked. This frayed nerves and kept everyone on tenterhooks. The unremitting psychological torture was much worse than the actual violence itself. Most prisoners were able to endure whatever was thrown at them. Unfortunately some couldn't and they left silently for the working blocks among the common criminals. They would need to put on the uniform and prison boots, which would make a squeaking sound on the bitumen floor. Thus the terms 'Squeaky Boots' and 'Squeaky Booting' entered our vocabulary. These prisoners suffered the additional trauma of feeling that they had let their comrades down. They hadn't. They were pushed beyond endurance and should hold their heads high as republican prisoners who suffered for their beliefs. They did their best and no one should judge. Each of us has a breaking point and we are lucky indeed if it is never reached.

On the Blanket protest we were never sure what any day would bring. We lived a surreal existence, taking each hour and each day as it came. All prisoners live either in the past, reminiscing on good times, or in the future, which they constantly plan. No one in the H-Blocks lived in the here and now. It was too grim a prospect. Republican prisoners always drew strength from each other. We always maintained discipline and were a collective, as opposed to the prisoners who the screws referred to as 'ordinary, decent, criminals'. These thieves, muggers, rapists, killers and scam merchants were interested only in number one. The screws hated us, because we dared defy the might of the state and remained resolute in our collective loyalty to our cause. To the screws, we were 'murdering terrorists'.

From the Blanket to the No-Wash Protest

Things were changing as 1978 arrived. There was a prolonged and at times heated debate around the direction and what some called the stasis in the protest. Many argued a new approach was needed. Tom McFeely was still the OC, but that changed with the arrival of Brendan 'The Dark' Hughes from the cages. The Dark had been serving 15 years following his capture in an IRA base in Myrtlefield Park in the affluent Malone area of the city. Three years into his sentence there was an altercation between screws and prisoners, which he in fact had tried to break up. All in the vicinity of the fracas were convicted of assault. As this had occurred after the criminalisation date of March 1st 1976, all those sentenced lost their political status and were transferred to the H-Blocks. Brendan was initially in H5. He was appointed OC for all the protesting blocks. He immediately began making changes and creating a structured debate on the way forward. In H5 he got reacquainted with Bobby Sands. He appointed Bobby as Public Relations Officer, a role well-suited to Bobby's talents, as he was well practised with the use of that weapon which English politician and writer Edward Bulwer-Lytton held to be mightier than the sword. Bobby began to write voluminously under the pen name 'Marcella', the name of his eldest sister.

The Dark made a number of immediate decisions. One was telling all prisoners to put on the prison uniform to avail of visits. Communications had been badly hampered by the decision to refuse visits. He also ordered that from Saint Patrick's Day 1978 we would refuse to clean out our cells. Increased brutality forced him to then order that we shouldn't slop out. This led to an accumulation of faeces and urine in the cells. We were ordered to throw the contents of the chamber pots out the windows. The screws retaliated by blocking up the windows and so we were finally told to smear the faeces on the walls and throw the urine out under the doors. Brendan and Bobby were in regular contact with H3, which was the only other protesting block at that stage. The debate went wider than just concerns pertaining to the prison struggle. Sinn Féin was still a largely moribund organisation, acting as little more than a support group for armed struggle. Many of us urged change, arguing that the base of the struggle needed broadened and that the 'primacy of politics' should be recognised. I myself wrote to the leadership urging an accelerated political education programme for all activists and a recognition that the Movement needed to form a broad anti-imperialist alliance.

The Relatives' Action Committees (RAC), *ad hoc* groups of women, mostly the mothers, wives, sisters and girlfriends of prisoners, had just begun touring Europe and North America campaigning on our behalf. They were making little headway in spite of their huge efforts. The RAC started at the end of 1976 when a group of Derry women had protested outside the Bishop of Derry's house clad only in blankets. Others followed their lead and slowly the protests and pickets spread across Ireland.

Bobby Sands outlined a picture of an all-encompassing criminalisation programme by which the British sought to undermine the struggle by breaking the prisoners and their families. We were resolute in our determination that they wouldn't break us, despite their worst efforts. There was, however, an underlying question posed by Brendan and Bobby: how long could we expect prisoners, many of them teenagers, to endure such conditions? There was an even more pressing question: what options did we have to bring things to a head by wrecking the criminalisation policy itself? It was clear that the leadership outside had their own specific priorities and viewed us as nothing more than a distraction from the main business of winning the overall struggle.

As always, with even the worst of situations, the early decision to stop cleaning out our cells brought its own bit of light relief. It also provided a lesson in the benefits of learning Irish. We had ended the practice of shouting from cell to cell in English. All orders and instructions were issued in Irish and verbal messages would be passed from cell to cell with Irish speakers informing English speakers of what was being said. General dirt and dust had been accumulating in the cells due to us not cleaning them out. An order was given to dampen down the dirt with water and to 'rub it round your cell'. The screws returned from lunch break and were doing their customary head count. They arrived first at the cell of two Derry men and burst into laughter. We discovered that the Derry pronunciation for self was sell. Our two intrepid English speakers had misinterpreted the message and had smeared themselves in dirt. The poor lads – they soon learned Irish after that!

The prison leadership's policy on Irish was very progressive. There were beginners, intermediate and advanced classes being taught in all the wings. There were also conversation classes and any news which came in from the visits was delivered out the doors in Irish. Myself and a number of others were delivering lectures on various subjects in Irish. My chosen subject was the history of Ireland from the earliest times. Lectures would last 15 to 20 minutes. Lectures were 'on the air', as we called it, immediately after the Catholics concluded their rosary. My next door neighbour at the time was an Armagh man. He would call through the pipes after every lecture with questions. In the lecture on the Viking raids on Ireland I mentioned the warrior chieftain, Turgesius, pronounced Turgéis in Irish. Turgesius had been raiding the coast of Andalucia before arriving in Ireland and establishing a base at Loch Lene in County Westmeath in 837. He died in 843/844, according to the *Annals of the Kings of Ulster*, as a result of drowning in Loch Owel near Mullingar. My mate called me to the window after the lecture looking to know Turgéis' surname. I was about to explain that surnames didn't exist in Ireland at the time, but I realised this would only invite further questions. I told him it was Lúchair, the Irish for delight. I'm not sure if he ever got it translated into English. If you're reading this now, the nearest English equivalent would be 'Turkish Delight'!

He also had a similar question about Saint Patrick. I had been explaining during the lecture, that Palladius was the first missionary to those Christians already existing in Ireland in 431. We have this from two authorities, *Liber contra Collatorem* and *The Chronicles by Prosper of Aquitaine*.[42] We also have the papal appointment itself from the pen of Celestine I, who made Palladius 'first Bishop to those Irish believing in Christ'.

We don't hear as much of Palladius as we do of another missionary, Saint Patrick, who allegedly arrived in the following year 432. We only have two pieces of writing from Patrick, his *Confessio* and his *Epistola*. In fact we have no certainty about anything regarding Patrick. Regardless of how much of this my mate took in, he was at the window again after the lecture looking Patrick's surname. 'Ó Raghallaigh,' I told him. 'What's that in English?' 'Reilly,' I answered. 'Great – I never knew that,' he said. 'Didn't you see the scene in the film where the Irish are calling Patrick back?' 'I didn't,' he said. 'You must remember the song from the film, "Come Back Paddy Reilly to Ballyjamesduff".' 'I remember the song,' he said, 'but as God's my judge I never knew Paddy Reilly from Ballyjamesduff was Ireland's Patron Saint.'

Throughout 1978 we rarely got a great deal of information about what was happening on the outside. Visits mostly covered events relating to our own situation. We bled new prisoners dry for every scrap of information. Visits only lasted half an hour, although we had a few characters in H3 – take a bow Hector and Geek – who could carry on for 90 minutes at least, telling us what they'd heard on the visit.

Things improved dramatically in 1979 when we received miniature crystal radio sets manufactured by IRA engineers. A big thanks to the 'Magic Man' who oversaw the design and production. He was never properly credited with the work he did due to his self-effacing manner and discrete nature. The radios were contained in small plastic medicine tubes and were equipped with a single earphone and an aerial wire. They came wrapped in 'stretch and seal'. We carried them secreted in our back

---

42 Prosper Aquitanius 390-455 AD. Prosper was a Roman scholar, disciple of Augustine of Hippo and continuator of the Chronicles of Saint Jerome.

passages. They could pick up BBC and RTÉ and with a bit of luck a few other radio stations. They were to be used strictly for receiving news. I have to put my hands up to having broken the rules and having listened to the odd programme on Radio Three and Radio Four.

Radios revolutionised our lives. We learned of the arrival of the first test tube baby, Louise Joy Brown, who was born into the world on July 25th 1978, thanks to Patrick Steptoe and Robert Edwards, not forgetting, of course, the child's parents Lesley and John. We also learned of tragedies as well, such as the loss of Air India Flight 855, which plunged into the sea near Mumbai, killing all 213 passengers and crew on January 1st 1978. The beginning of the end of the regime of Anastasio Samoza in Nicaragua was announced when violence, which had erupted following the assassination of Pedro Chamorro Cardenal in January 1978, reached new heights. By 1979 the Frente Sandinista de Liberación Nacional (FSLN), or Sandinistas, were in power in Managua. Years later I was to meet Nicaraguan President Daniel Ortega when I had the privilege of attending the Foro São Paolo Forum in its eponymous city in July 1990. Daniel's father had been a soldier in the army of César Sandino which drove the Yankees out of Nicaragua in the 1930s. César had been assassinated in January 1933 by Anastasio Somoza at a 'peace summit'. The Camp David Accords, signed in 1977 by Jimmy Carter and Anwar Sadat, were still in the news. They would return to the headlines when Khalid Ahmed Showqi El Islambouli killed Sadat on July 6th 1981, citing the Camp David Accords as his motivation. Among the injured was Irish Defence Minister, James Tully. Khalid's brother, Mohammed Showqi Al-Islambouli, would later narrowly fail to kill Sadat's successor, Hosni Mubarak, in June 1995 as the Egyptian president made his way to Addis Ababa. At least for us, we were all once again engaged in international affairs.

Meanwhile, under the Pleasure Dome

Locked in our own narrow world, we faced the challenge of a lack of books and other essentials, but we always had ingenuity and creativity on our side. We realised that necessity is the mother of invention. We had developed a system whereby we could furnish ourselves with tobacco, writing paper, pens and books (miniaturised copies of dictionaries and Irish language grammars books produced on rice paper). We could also distribute things from cell to cell by wrapping them in a towel which was then swung from window to window.

Cigarettes and written messages could also be transferred across the wing by sliding a button, attached to a string, to the opposite cell. Other necessities were wrapped in layers of cling film and smuggled back from the visits secreted in our bodies. We also smuggled thousands of messages and personal letters out on visits, vastly improving communications. Most prisoners became adept at putting between 150 and 200 legible words onto a single cigarette paper.

    I sent word out to my mother, explaining she needed to put tobacco and papers into cling film and wrap them tightly to form a large suppository. I was successful in getting my 'bairt' (package) back to my cell after a visit and felt very chuffed with myself until I opened it only to discover that Rosie had given me Warhorse pipe tobacco, her father's favourite. Beggars can't be choosers, so the Warhorse was swung up the lines and diluted with ordinary cigarette tobacco. We were able to light our cigarettes using a flint secured in a piece of biro tube. This was struck with a small lighter wheel and the spark directed onto fluffed cotton from our towels. We also fashioned wicks of plaited cotton threads dipped in margarine. On the night of the Warhorse's arrival we all lit up as usual when the day guard had left the wings. A screw rushed down the wing shouting: 'I don't believe it – some of these vermin are after smuggling a pipe in!' They never found the pipe and a corrective letter let Rosie know that only Golden Virginia or Old Holborn was suitable. The Warhorse was a bit too strong, even for the most hardened of smokers. A shortage of cigarette papers would occasionally see us resort to using the thin paper from our bibles for making roll-ups. I only ever used the edges, not wanting to loss any text. Others were not so scrupulous. On one occasion a priest remarked to Kieran Nugent that he was glad to see him reading his bible. Kieran replied: 'I haven't read a word of it, but I've smoked Genesis, Exodus and Leviticus and will soon make a start on Numbers and Deuteronomy.'

    The dispersal of cigarettes was a nightly ritual and could often provide entertainment when an over-zealous screw would try to strike a blow for God and Ulster. The screws had welded angle-irons down the side of our doors to prevent us seeing out on to the wings. Unbeknownst to them we had used a nail, retrieved from the visits and had made small spy holes between the angle-irons and the concrete. We were always able to monitor their every move. One night in H6 in 1980, a true and loyal son of Ulster was on duty. He was moving stealthily along the wing in his socks, holding his breath and moving like a Ninja. The word was given that a line should be shot across at the bottom of the wing and that the screw should be allowed to get within striking distance before the line was withdrawn. Meanwhile behind his back we were busy transferring everything. The idiot would be within inches of success only to be thwarted by the swift action of Rab McCallum and Jackie McMullan, who were operating the line. With all the business completed, Brendan Hughes shouted instructions in Irish to Jackie and Rab. They tied a message to the line and shot it across the wing. With a whoop of triumph, the Ninja clown captured the message, which he must have assumed was top secret. He opened it and read the words: 'Dick Head!' Just then the order was shouted to throw the contents of the pisspots under the doors. Speed wasn't the Ninja's strength, and so dashing up the wing, he slipped in the flood of urine and landed on his back, cursing us to high heaven. He exacted his revenge by soaking all of the cells with the fire hose. We luckily had time to put our bedding on our heads, thus avoiding the worst of the hose. By the time he had soaked all the cells he was exhausted and someone shouted out that we had saved the bedding. He retired with a stream of abuse. The same clown never repeated his Ninja move again, but other idiots did, with the same result.

Some bright spark of a screw came up with a plan to thwart smuggling. He inserted a mirror into a rectangle of sponge, which had a recess cut in it. This was to prove a major source of torture and brutality, but did nothing to disrupt smuggling. Going to and from every visit we would be spread-eagled naked over the mirror. Screws would kick us behind the knees to bend us down. We were held tightly by the outstretched arms and by the hair. Then the most degrading and brutal of searches followed. On quite a number of occasions prisoners were sexually assaulted by three particular screws, known for their perversion. One of them was subsequently killed in an IRA attack. Most screws made a point of inserting their fingers into our mouths to search and would invariably use the finger which had carried out the worst of the body search.

On July 31st 1978 Archbishop Tomás Ó Fiaich came on a pastoral visit to the H-Blocks. He was deeply affected by what he witnessed. He came to the cell which I was sharing with Brendan McFarlane. He asked if we wanted confession. I was delighted that he only spoke Gaelic to us, but I replied that we had no interest in confession. He opened his cassock, revealing packets of cigarettes, saying that we would be interested in this confession. Of course we were interested.

The archbishop was a giant of a man, although short in stature. He and Father Raymond Murray purchased and supplied us with copies of Pádraig Ó Fiannachta's Irish bible, a true gift and a wonderful contribution to our vocabulary in Irish. Ó Fiaich was also the patron of Bunscoil Phobail Feirste, the first Irish Medium School in the Six Counties. He was also a prominent Gaelic scholar. Having emerged from the H-Blocks after his visit, Ó Fiaich said:

> Having spent the whole of Sunday in the prison, I was shocked at the inhuman conditions prevailing in H-Blocks 3, 4 and 5 where over 300 prisoners were incarcerated. One would hardly allow an animal to remain in such conditions, let alone a human being. The nearest approach to it that I have seen was the spectacle of hundreds of homeless people living in sewer pipes in the slums of Calcutta. The stench and filth in some cells, with the remains of rotten food and human excreta scattered around the walls, was almost unbelievable. In two of them I was unable to speak for the fear of vomiting. The prisoners' cells are without beds, chairs or tables. They sleep on mattresses on the floor, and in some cases I noticed they were quite wet. They have no covering except towel or blanket, no books, newspapers or reading material except the bible (even religious magazines have been banned since my last visit), no pens or writing material, or TV, or radio, no hobbies or handcrafts, no exercise or recreation. They are locked in their cells for almost the whole of every day and some of them have been in this condition for more than a year and a half.

The prisoners held the archbishop in the highest regard, unlike Margaret Thatcher, when she came to power in 1979. Ó Fiach's statement came on the heels of a statement by Amnesty International, issued in June 1978 which read: 'Maltreatment of suspected terrorists by the RUC has taken place with sufficient frequency to warrant establishment of a public inquiry to investigate it.' Ó Fiaich joined forces with Father Alec Reid in behind-the-scenes efforts to find a resolution to the prison protest. Things were beginning to move at last and these changes would impact on our planning and strategy.

De Profundis – from the depths

At the end of 1978 I left H3 for personal reasons and put on the uniform for two days, securing a transfer to another block, H4. I was completely on my own in the block and would remain so until the arrival two months later of Mark Hannigan (RIP) from Strabane. I would, at times, feel like shouting aloud the opening line of the 'De Profundis', Psalm 130, but since I didn't believe in God it seemed a pretty silly thing to do. It's always hard, however, to rid yourself of residual Catholicism.[43] During my time alone in H4 the screws would approach my cell wearing only socks so that I wouldn't hear them coming. Silence was their weapon, but prisoners develop acute hearing and I always knew when they were on their way. I didn't know how long I would be alone. H3 still had some spare capacity and the screws would be in no hurry to give me company. The wing filled up rapidly after Mark's arrival and by the time I was moved to H6 in late 1979, H4 had three full wings.

I resolved to live in the moment. Thinking of the future and speculating was self-defeating. I thought of Tom Clarke from Dungannon who had served 15 years in Pentonville Prison under the silence rule. They also had to wear hoods to Mass so they wouldn't see each other. The Brits never broke Clarke's spirit. He came out of prison as defiant as ever and was given the honour of signing the 1916 Proclamation ahead of Sean MacDiarmada, Tomás MacDonncha, Pádraig MacPiarais, Éamonn Ceannt, James Connolly and Joseph Plunkett. I could recite the Proclamation in Irish and English from memory and one of my jobs was to write it out for distribution to every wing at Easter. The seven leaders of 1916 would be our inspiration for choosing seven men to embark on the 1980 Hunger Strike. In prison I would wake first thing in the morning. It was a habit I formed from the days when I would rise to the sound of Radio Éireann being played by my father as he prepared our porridge before going off to his early shift on the buses. I loved to watch the crows as they made their way to raid some farmer's field. I was astonished at how organised they were and at how they would diligently guard their young as they flew in swirling formation. The crows would arrive with first light, flying in pairs in a grid pattern. One pair flying east to west and the other north to south. When the land was gridded by the advance pairs, the main flock would arrive with their wings beating slowly and with outriders chasing their young into the main flock when they strayed. I was mesmerised by the crows. They would repeat the entire performance in the evening, just before sunset. I always regretted that I could never witness their descent to the rookery. In the mornings I would use my imagination to follow the flock. In my mind's eye I looked down on the fields filled with food, where small streams meandered between heather and furze-lined banks. When breakfast came I would eat and then read my bible

---

43 'De profundis clamavi ad te Domine, domine exaudi vocem meum – Out of the depths I have cried to thee o Lord, Lord hear my voice.'

and walk around five miles, pacing out six steps towards the door and six towards the window. I would recite stories in my head and before I knew it lunch time had arrived. The screws, as black as crows, would be standing behind the prison orderly, all as silent as ghosts. I would always save some bread to feed to the sparrows, starlings, yellow hammers, tits and wagtails, which were always in the yard outside my window. It was always a huge treat for me to spot a kestrel hovering majestically over some farmer's field. The wings trembled as it prepared to dive like a missile on some tiny prey.

Bird-watching was a great pastime for prisoners. I remember a great interlude in H6 where Bobby Sands and Ginty Lennon argued over which birds were in the yard. 'Do you see the yellowhammer over at the fence, Ginty?', asked Bobby. 'It is in yer arse; that's a bunting,' said Ginty. 'No, it's a yellowhammer.' So the debate went on for a while, until Ginty asked Bobby to explain why he thought it was a yellowhammer. 'Because they always congregate near streams,' said Bobby. 'I can't see any streams,' said Ginty. Bobby explained that the streams were on the other side of the prison wall. 'How do you know that?', said Ginty. 'Because there are yellowhammers congregating near the wall,' replied Bobby.

As regards brutality, H4 was every bit as much a hell hole as H3. During my time in H4 the screws decided to carry out forcible baths on all prisoners. The process started early one morning and lasted for hours. The first door was opened and we heard the thuds and groans as a prisoner was beaten along the wing from his cell. We were in single cells at the time and I had Séamy Bradley from South Derry on one side and Tommy Gorman from Belfast on the other. We chatted to keep our spirits up. When my turn arrived I was dragged from the cell and was run with my two arms outstretched by screws until they slammed me into a table, which was positioned in the middle of the wing. Screws stood on my feet and I was dragged forward by the hair. One screw forced his finger into me, ostensibly to carry out a search. I was then tossed, head over heels across the table, landing on the floor on my back. From there I was dragged by the feet and plonked down facing a chair on which sat 'Doctor Mengele', as we called him. This excuse for a medical professional and human being inserted a stick in my hair and said: 'Lice-infested, clean and shave this specimen.'

I was dragged around the corner to the wash-rooms and thrown into a cold bath. I was then dragged from the bath and laid out cruciform on the floor, my limbs held in place by screws' boots. Four screws then began to scrub me with yard brushes. Having completed this, they painted me with a paste-like substance and sat me in a plastic chair. Two stood on my feet and others held my arms. A screw with a set of electric shears then proceeded to shave my head, none too gently. They left tufts and lumps, which left me looking ridiculous. Throughout this ordeal one of them would repeatedly slap my face shouting: 'Your number is 289, scum. Say it!' I remained silent. After they finished I was made, like those before and behind me, to run a gauntlet of screws which lined the way to our newly cleaned wing. I was thrown into a cell which already held another prisoner. It was Dean Crossan from Clonard. The screws had left Dean with a clump of hair on the top of his head, which resembled a bird's nest. When everyone had been done, an inventory of injuries was compiled to be sent out in a message informing the outside what had happened. Then the shout went out to get to our doors where we sang in unison 'A Nation Once Again'. It was a tradition established by Martin Hurson from Tyrone, who would later die on hunger strike on July 13th after 44 days without food. We always sang out our defiance after any major onslaught to show the screws that they hadn't dampened our spirit.

It was during my time in H4 that a number of loyalist prisoners came on to the Blanket protest. They never joined the No-Wash protest. There were UVF and UDA prisoners among them. The longest protesting loyalists were Tommy Isaac Andrews and Sam McClean, both UDA men who remained on protest for two years. Along with Sam Courtney, Norman Earle and Bobby Adams from the UDA, and Jim 'Tonto' Watt from the UVF, Tommy Andrews joined the hunger strike in its latter stages in December 1980. Tommy and Sam McClean were, for a time, next door to me in H4. On my other side was a UVF man, Robert James Campbell (RIP). Jimmy, as he was known, had been convicted of the McGurk's Bar bombing, which claimed 15 victims. In conversation with him he told me that he deeply regretted having carried out the bombing and had prayed for forgiveness. He also confided that he hated the Rev Ian Paisley, who he blamed for bringing him into the world of loyalism. Jimmy never remained long on the Blanket. Another UDA prisoner who remained for a lengthy period on the protest was Billy 'Twister' McQuiston. The longest serving UVF man on protest was Victor Hanna. Victor was on the Blanket when the British Army ambushed and killed three IRA Volunteers at Ballysillan. Jim Mulvenna, Dinny Brown and

Jackie Mailey were caught in a killing zone along with Victor's brother William, who was an innocent civilian. Victor was refused parole to attend the funeral. In the early days there were over 30 loyalists on the protest, but they drifted away gradually. They all abandoned the protest after the 1980 Hunger Strike on strict orders by their outside leaderships.

I had respect for those loyalists who spent long periods on the protest, regardless of what had brought them there. They did their bit and were true to their beliefs. At one point the Shankill Butcher Lenny Murphy joined the protest. He lasted less than two weeks. I always thought Murphy to be nothing more than a narcissistic psychopath who had found the UVF and Loyalism a convenient vehicle for indulging his sadistic murderous tendencies. Murphy became an orderly in H6 and when he was about I would never drink the tea for fear of what he'd done to it. The IRA executed Murphy on November 16th 1982. Those UDA men who remained on the Blanket, like Tommy Andrews and Sam McClean, would participate in our political discussions and would endure some of the same brutality inflicted on us. I wouldn't see Tommy again for 39 years. In March 2018 I got a call from Tommy, who was at the time working alongside the wife of my nephew. He asked if I would mind sharing a cup of coffee with him. I told him I'd be delighted.

We met at Cultúrlann McAdam Ó Fiaich. At the time I wrote a short piece about our reunion:

> Yesterday I met for coffee with an old friend and fellow Blanketman. I hadn't seen Tommy since 1980. Tommy spent time on the hunger strike in 1980 called off by the late Brendan Hughes. I was delighted to see Tommy again and certainly won't wait as long to see him again. We met with a very warm embrace, as is customary with those who shared the trauma of the Blanket protest. As Tommy said, there is a depth of connection from the shared experience which will forever be. Texting him after our coffee I added: 'There is a depth of comradeship that binds us all together regardless of the journey which took us there.' We had a great chat, catching up on old times, also filling in, to some degree, on what we'd been up to since. We only had a half hour, as both of us needed to be off to other business, Tommy to the physio and me to an inspiring art and craft project which Forbairt Feirste were facilitating with local company ProGaa and Coláiste Feirste. Tommy, born and raised in Moyard, told me how his journey to the H-Blocks began when his mother ended his childhood idyll of football and fun with the news that her brother had been shot and wounded during disturbances in Hooker Street in Ardoyne and that it was time to flee their home as things were volatile and dangerous. Tommy became a loyalist combatant. It was great to see him again. Thankfully his uncle survived the shooting.

Some time later I met with Tommy again along with Sam McClean. I had brought Tommy back to his old home in Moyard. When we met, Sam said: 'My God Jake, it's great to see you. The last time I saw you was when steam was pouring into our cell through the hole in the wall and you were screaming at the top of your lungs.' That brought me right back to H4 and the day the screws decided to scald us.

Our ordeal began at 2 p.m. when the screws returned from their lunch break. This was always a dangerous time as they would have taken drink and could be volatile. On this occasion we heard noises at the top of the wing, which indicated something new was happening. The noises were not part of the usual routine. The door of the first cell, which housed Gerry Dowdall, was opened. We heard the screws shouting: 'Stay still, you bastard!' Then we heard the splash of water followed by a scream and by Dowdall shouting: 'Jesus Christ, the water's scalding!' The screws proceeded from cell to cell. We imagined the suffering of each prisoner from the intensity of the screams. Those of us who waited were suffering as well as we knew our turn for scalding was coming. I was in a state of fear and anxiety, as were others. Suddenly my door opened. Three screws stood there. One looked at me and said: 'You'll have to wait your turn, scumbag. You're the bastard giving the orders in here and we're keeping a special treat for you till the end.' I didn't respond.

When the screws left I began to mentally prepare myself for what was to come. I pulled the blanket tightly around me to give myself some measure of protection. Inwardly I vowed I wouldn't scream. I would deny them the pleasure. I continued to listen to the torment and suffering of my comrades. Suddenly an uneasy quiet descended on the wing, which was more trying on my nerves than the bedlam which had preceded it. Five minutes passed, although it seemed like an eternity. My door opened and a screw hissed: 'Our friend is up boiling some water so that it's nice and hot and fresh. See you shortly scumbag.' My heart was in my mouth, my body trembled with fear. I again resolved that I would stoically suffer my fate. I tried even harder to pull the blanket tighter around me. The door opened and there stood the three screws, one holding a bucket of boiling water. I turned my back to them. One screw said with a voice full of malice and hatred: 'Pull that blanket off the bastard; I want him properly scalded.' I was left naked before them. A bucket of scalding water hit me on the back, neck, thighs and arms. I let out a scream that would've wakened the dead. I had never experienced pain like it. I was frozen to the spot. I could literally feel blisters rising on my skin. I heard

Sam McClean from next door asking if I was okay. I couldn't speak. Eventually the waves of pain and shock subsided and all I could think of was my good luck that the water hadn't soaked my bedding. At least I would have somewhere dry to sleep. The mind is a strange conundrum at times. I put the incident into its mental box, along with the many others. I wouldn't dwell on it. I would dry my eyes and carry on. We were, after all, men and men don't cry like little 'Jeannie with the light brown hair'. We simply had to get on with things. Trauma, pain and suffering like this can be locked in strong boxes but believe me there isn't a box strong enough; eventually the trauma leaks and has to be faced.

My door opened again and one of the three screws was there alone. He tossed a tube of antiseptic cream on the floor. 'You'd best put that on,' he said. Then he placed three Gallaher's Blues cigarettes in my hand and said: 'Have yourself a wee smoke. You deserve it after what you've been through.' He closed the door and left without another word. I had no words to describe what had just happened and 40 years later I'm still lost for words. I realised at the time, and still believe, that we as members of the Republican Movement shared collective responsibility for all the actions of the IRA. The screws of course hated us and held us responsible for every bombing and shooting. That may well explain their behaviour but I don't think it can excuse grown men for brutalising and scalding naked teenagers. I was sure of one thing. I wasn't going to allow hatred to enter my being where it would only act as a cancer. The screw who scalded me returned to give me balm and cigarettes, so ultimately his humanity prevailed – though he still has to go to bed with what he did. All of us must reconcile with our decisions and actions.

Of all the suffering we endured I think nature became our cruellest foe, when in November 1978 the fiercest winter since 1962-1963 descended upon us. We were in cells with no windows at that stage. We had to break them when disinfectant with the quality of CS gas was poured into the cells. Our noses and throats burned and our eyes watered and so the order was given to smash the glass. The winter was to continue until the end of February. Temperatures plummeted to -13°C. I thought at the start that we wouldn't be able to stick the cold. It got right into our marrow and was impossible to shake off. The blankets were almost useless but I learned with experience that putting them loosely over us rather than pulling them tight was best. Air-flow assisted in allowing more retention of what heat there was. The bitumen floor was so cold that a blanket needed to be put down to make walking tolerable.

We did of course get used to it. Food was never up to much but in that winter I found myself eating even the most inedible and cold fare that the screws served up. We would often wake in the morning with frost in our hair and on our eyebrows. Our feet suffered most. They were impossible to keep warm. Our first job every morning was to shake the maggots from our bedding, bodies and hair. It was worse for those with long beards as the maggots went close to the mouth seeking heat. At least they were smaller in numbers with the piercing cold. But they still multiplied in the rotten food, which sat in the corner of our cells. We got trifles at Christmas. They came in small plastic containers and we were able to fill these with water which provided us miniature ice blocks which we could use to close up the spaces between the bars. Eventually winter gave way to spring.

That winter had also thrown up another biting wind in the shape of Margaret Thatcher. On May 3rd she came to power after a spectacular election victory. The day after her elevation she stood at the door of 10 Downing Street and without a hint of irony mouthed the words: 'Where there is discord, may we bring harmony. Where there is error, may we bring truth. Where there is doubt, may we bring faith. And where there is despair, may we bring hope.' Francis of Assisi must have spun in his grave.[44] Thatcher faithfully followed the policies of the Labour Party as regards Ireland. The media dubbed her the 'Iron Lady' and she often announced that she would never talk with 'terrorists' – that was a patent lie as her government would twice engage in talks with the IRA, once in 1981 and again in 1990. Thatcher would bring nothing but discord, error, doubt and despair to Ireland and Britain. Her poisonous legacy is the rise of neo-liberalism.

---

44 Saint Francis of Assisi 1182–1226. He was born Giovanni di Pietro di Bernardone and never actually said the words widely attributed to him.

Chapter 4

Via Dolorosa – the road of suffering

'It's a long road that has no turning.' (Seanfhocail Uladh 930 (b) Ard Mhacha, Fearnmhaigh)

The future of the movement on our shoulders

In July 1978 a communiqué from Brendan Hughes and Bobby Sands was read out to all the protesting prisoners in the H-Blocks. The statement laid out the position as it appeared to the leadership of the prison: 'We are asking you all to dig deep and hold the line for the Republic, against an enemy who is determined to crush us. In many ways comrades the future of the Republican Movement rests on your shoulders; therefore hold the line!'

It was clear that much more struggle lay ahead of us. We would shoulder the burden. In October the loyalists were moved out of H4. I wouldn't see any of them again until November. By then they would be in a wing opposite us. We would never again be on the same wings.

The screws arrived at my cell one day and took me out without explanation. I was thrown into the back of a van. The truck already contained six or seven other prisoners. We were transferred to H6. The prison authorities had decided to remove what they viewed as the prison leadership and isolate them in H6, well away from the other protesting blocks of H3, H4 and H5. They hoped that with the leadership removed it would be easier to break the spirit and morale of the remaining prisoners. We immediately understood that they had made a huge mistake. They would break no one and had in fact provided the leadership with the perfect opportunity for in-depth and prolonged discussion. In H6 I found myself in a cell with my old mate Brendan McFarlane. Our comrade from the cages, Bobby Sands, was next door to us. On the other side of us were Brendan Hughes and John Chillingworth and next to Bobby were Sean 'Ginty' Lennon and Séanna Breathnach. Séanna was to be made OC of the jail in the aftermath of the 1981 hunger strike. I had also served time with him in the Cages. He was an enthusiastic Irish speaker and a man for whom I still retain the greatest of respect. He was to serve a total of 21 years in prison. He was the first man since 1972 to read out a statement on behalf of the IRA while not wearing a mask. That statement, made in 2005, called a final end to the IRA's campaign.

Our arrival in H6 heralded the most intense discussion and reflection on planning and strategy to date. By mid 1979 we had decided that we would begin a hunger strike. Seven men were chosen: Volunteers Brendan Hughes (Belfast), Tom McFeely (County Derry), Raymond McCartney (Derry City), Tommy McKearney (Tyrone), Leo Green (Armagh), Sean McKenna (South Armagh) and an INLA man John Nixon from Armagh City. Those seven were chosen from more than 100 people who had volunteered for hunger strike. We had decided that the seven should be representative of the areas of highest IRA activity and would symbolically represent the seven signatories of the Proclamation of 1916. Hunger strike was rooted in Ireland's ancient Brehon laws and is referred to in the ancient manuscript the *Seanchas Mór*. It was available by right to anyone who felt they had suffered an injustice. The practice is also in Hinduism and is rooted in the 'Manu Code'. In other parts of Indo-European law it is referred to as 'Acharitan'. A previous IRA hunger strike had ended on April 22nd 1977. It had been led by Martin Ferris of Kerry, who had endured 47 days without food in Portlaoise Prison. Nineteen others had joined the fast. In 1979 we drafted five demands which we hoped would draw the broadest base of support for a hunger strike: 1) The right to wear our own clothes; 2) The right not to be forced to do menial prison work; 3) The right to free association with our fellow republican prisoners and to design our own social activities and education; 4) The right to receive one letter, one food parcel and one visit a week from our families; 5) The right to the restoration of remission of sentence lost during the protest.

The outside leadership was vehemently opposed to hunger strike. Following much intense and at times heated debate we were asked by the outside leadership to defer hunger strike for a year to allow for efforts to resolve the protest. A National H-Block/Armagh Committee was formed, with representatives of various organisations involved. Archbishop Ó Fiaich and Bishop Edward Daly of Derry began a series of engagements with the British authorities. It was clear the British had no desire to move, a fact that became apparent even to the clergy after six months of utterly fruitless talks. In the midst of all our planning we were dealt a heavy blow from within, which would have serious implications for our plans. Two IRA prisoners, Martin Meehan and Séamus Mullen, embarked on a hunger strike, seeking to be granted appeals on the basis that they had been wrongly convicted. Meehan had a well-deserved reputation as a courageous IRA Volunteer. Both individuals left the protest to undertake their hunger strike. Their actions were contrary to IRA orders and were taken despite heartfelt pleas from the prison leadership. The OC explained to them that we were collectively going to launch a hunger strike and that the precipitative action for personal reasons would jeopardise and undermine that strategy. Meehan and Mullen wouldn't be swayed and wouldn't listen to any pleading from the IRA prison leadership. Meehan ended his hunger strike having secured a promise from Archbishop Ó Fiaich that he would get his appeal if he ended his fast. Our view was that the British would interpret this as brinkmanship, which could possibly colour their approach to any hunger strike to the death which prisoners would subsequently undertake. Martin Meehan ended up a Sinn Féin councillor and died of a heart attack on November 3rd 2007 at the age of 62.

Regardless of all these events, we had settled on our strategy before we were returned to the other H-Blocks at the beginning of 1980. Myself and Brendan McFarlane, Bobby Sands and Brendan Hughes were all returned to the same wing in H3. When Brendan Hughes and the others finally embarked on the hunger strike on October 27th 1980, Bobby Sands was appointed OC of the prison. Our collective position on the fast was that it couldn't be ended unless the hunger strikers first consulted with the OC and he agreed that an acceptable agreement was available.

Back in H3

When we were returned to H3 I remained sharing a cell with Brendan McFarlane. Bobby Sands was again next door to us. Jimmy 'Teapot' was on the other side of Bobby. Later the screws would move Bobby to the bottom of the wing into a cell with Malachy Carey from Loughgiel. This took place during the talks with the governor, Stanley Hilditch, which ran from December 19th 1980 until January 27th 1981.

Malachy was some pup. We called him Bobby's suitcase due to the amount of material he could store in his body. At one stage he was carrying two Parker pen refills, half an ounce of tobacco and a miniaturised *Progress in Irish* grammar book. Malachy was a great individual. On his release from prison in 1987 he stood as a Sinn Féin candidate. He received numerous death threats but showed no fear. Sadly he was murdered by loyalists on December 13th 1992. I only got to meet Malachy once on the outside. We met by accident in Ballycastle on a day trip. Myself, my wife Chrissie, Brendan Hughes, Jimmy McMullan and his then girlfriend, Anne Marie, my wife's sister, met him on a glorious sunny day and had the very best of craic with him. He was as full of fun and humour as he'd ever been and we had a great few hours together. He was murdered within six months. I reminded Malachy that day about a visit from Mrs Blackburn from the Board of Visitors during our time in H3.[45] She had spent a bit of time in Malachy's cell and on her departure Malachy had started calling the screws. The screws shouted that he'd better explain himself or they'd thrash him. We were all listening intently. Malachy and the screws shouted back and forth and eventually Malachy shouted: 'Tell the wee woman she's left her tights behind.' Everyone burst out laughing. Malachy called us filthy animals and explained that the tights had fallen from her handbag when she was getting him a bible tract and some polo mints. The level of comradeship which grew up in the H-Blocks has never, in my experience, had a parallel. The bond between protesting prisoners was unbreakable and was reinforced by the shared horrors of life in the H-Blocks.

A consequence of the brutality we faced was the decision by the IRA to target screws for assassination. In all, the IRA would execute 27 members of the Northern Ireland Prison Service; three governors

---

45 A voluntary group of citizens who visited prisons for religious or altruistic reasons but who were totally ineffectual in their ostensible role of upholding the rights of prisoners.

and six principal officers among them. We paid dearly for every attack. Most prisoners despised screws as the lowest form of humanity. Bobby Sands put it best in verse in his poem: 'The Crime of Castlereagh' when he wrote: 'So bury him and let him lie and play your brass tattoo. But write above his marble stone: "Here lies a stinking screw." For if men knew what he had done they'd turn their backs and spew!' This poem of Bobby's was based on the epic, 'The Ballad Of Reading Gaol' by Oscar Wilde. He read it out to us as he did with all his writings. He was a good writer, especially considering that the vast majority of his adult life was spent behind prison bars and that he was to die shortly after his 27th birthday. Bobby also began a practice of reciting books from memory. One of his favourites was *Jet*. It was a travelogue and love story about a young couple fleeing parental disapproval and setting-off on a motorcycle odyssey. I learned later that there was no such book. The only novel called Jet was written by Russell Blake, but that wasn't written until 2012. My own feeling is that he weaved the story from the Wings' song, 'Jet'. He was very fond of Paul McCartney's group, Wings. Whatever the truth, it was a wonderful tale and, if conjured from the mind, an even greater achievement. I remember also the night we had a parade in honour of Commander Tom Barry, leader of the 3rd Flying Column of the West Cork Brigade, who died on July 2nd 1980, the day after his 83rd birthday. Following a minute's silence Bobby rose to his door and read a poem which touched me deeply. It ended with the words: 'And in darkened shadows, 'neath prison bars, the hags of torture wave. But we hear a voice that is of ours, with Barry, boys be brave!' We bade farewell to Barry that night, a brave Volunteer who took on the might of an empire which we felt was facing its final terminal decline.

We 'hags of torture' faced further challenges. It was clear that all the efforts at finding a resolution had been stone-walled by the British. Action was required. Following intense debate inside the prison and intense engagement with outside, the decision was made. After four years of protest and suffering, it was time to bring things to a head. On October 27th the seven chosen Volunteers went on a hunger strike. On December 1st they were joined by three Volunteers in Armagh Women's Prison. Mairead Farrell, Mary Doyle and Mairéad Nugent also began refusing food. On December 15th another 23 prisoners in the H-Blocks joined the strike, and the following day another seven began refusing food.

Mairead Farrell, whom I knew well and greatly admired, was assassinated in Gibraltar on March 6th 1988 alongside Dan McCann and Sean Savage, both of whom I also knew well. They had been unarmed when they were cut down in a hail of SAS bullets. The British called the slaughter 'Operation Flavius' and they were every bit as ruthless as Titus Flavius in his destruction of Jerusalem in AD 70. When the two Maireads and Mary joined the hunger strike in 1980 there were 30 women prisoners on the No-Wash protest in Armagh Prison, although they retained their own clothes. They endured similar suffering to the 400 prisoners in the H-Blocks. On December 12th UDA prisoners Tommy Andrews, Sam McClean, Sam Courtney, Norman Earle and Bobby Adams and UVF man Jim 'Tonto' Watt also embarked on hunger strike. The fast was ended unilaterally by Brendan Hughes on December 18th after 53 days. Sean McKenna had fallen into a coma just as Sir John Blelloch, Deputy Permanent Secretary at the Northern Ireland Office, was preparing to enter the prison with a document which would lay out the British position on prison conditions should the hunger strike end. He had taken possession of the document from Fr Brendan Meagher, who had received it earlier at Aldergrove Airport from British Intelligence Officer Michael Oatley.

All prisoners had already received a shorter document from the NIO on December 8th. As prisoners on protesting wings we knew nothing of what had occurred until Bobby, our OC, was taken to the prison hospital to see the hunger strikers. Bobby was taken round all the OCs of individual blocks to explain the situation. We didn't see him until midnight when he returned to our wing to brief people as to where things stood. He explained that he would be embarking on talks with the prison's main governor, Stanley Hilditch, in an effort to establish if an acceptable settlement could be achieved. Speaking privately to myself and Brendan McFarlane, he confided his belief that a second hunger strike was required: 'I will lead this one myself. Bik, you will be appointed OC, because I know you will have the resolve to let me die, if necessary.' Bobby was rock solid in his resolve but he was also determined to exhaust every avenue for settling the protest, if that was at all possible. We faced into another uncertain Christmas. With the pressure of hunger strike removed, we were very unclear as to what position the British would adopt.

Between a rock and a hard place

On December 19th Bobby informed all the Block OCs that he had embarked on exploratory talks with Hilditch on the basis of the 34 page document which the British had presented to us after the end of the first hunger strike. He also told us that he had informed Hilditch that two wings, ours in H3 and that of Séanna Breathnach in H5, would end the No-Wash protest and move into fresh and furnished cells before Christmas, if the British permitted us to wear our own clothes. As a group we engaged in a minute scrutiny of the document, which the British had also made public. When they met for a second time Hilditch made clear to Bobby that there was no chance of us receiving our own clothes. The regime was adopting a hard line. In Armagh Prison there was even less flexibility, with governor George Scott refusing to meet the OC. Things looked grim.

We hadn't a lot to celebrate that Christmas, but as usual the wing impresarios Jimmy 'Teapot' McMullan and James 'Hector' McNeill stepped up to the plate. You couldn't have asked for two better 'Masters of Ceremonies'. They were in constant battle, trying to outdo each other and taking the hand out of each other. The usual suspects did their favourite party pieces. Seamy 'Doll Head' Kelly was in fine form rattling out 'Old Man' by Neil Young. 'Daydream Believer' by the Monkees was Gerard 'Geek' O'Halloran's offering. I gave a rendition of 'Vigilante Man' by Woody Guthrie and Gerry 'Blute' McDonnell gave us 'Matthew and Son' by Cat Stevens. Aidan 'Insane' Slane from Tyrone, gave us his classic poem 'The Swallow-Tail Coat'. Kevin 'Barrabas' Lynch, who was to die on August 1st after 71 days on hunger strike sang 'The Gem of the Roe', and we got a rendition of poetry from Big Tom McElwee who died a week after 'Barrabas' after 62 days of hunger strike. We sang until the wee small hours. But not a man of us went to bed without thinking of the second hunger strike that loomed. Bobby was in great form. It was his ninth consecutive Christmas in prison. It was my fifth. I would enjoy many more Christmas festivities. This was to be Bobby's last. He would be dead within five months. I knew in my bones that was how it was going to be, but where there's life there's hope. But even with hope on our side it wasn't long until the British tried to dampen it. On January 9th, British proconsul, Humphrey Atkins, told their Westminster parliament that prisoners would not be permitted their own clothes.

Two days later Bobby had another meeting with all the OCs. He informed them that in spite of the regime's procrastination and negativity, he was still going to order the two selected wings to abandon the No-Wash protest, to test for any possible flexibility. As a result of this decision, 96 of us were moved to fresh and furnished cells. The IRA leadership in the prison was making every possible effort to bring the protest to an end on acceptable terms. Meanwhile loyalist death squads continued to target members of the National H-Block/Armagh Committee. On January 16th, despite her house being staked out by British troops, loyalists entered the home of Bernadette McAliskey where they pumped 14 bullets into her body in front of her terrified children. They also shot and wounded her husband Michael. British troops arrested the perpetrators as soon as they withdrew from the house with the dirty deed complete. Thankfully both victims recovered. They were the lucky ones. John Turnley, Miriam Daly, Ronnie Bunting and Noel Lyttle would all die at the hands of British death squads during that period.

In the following days our families arrived at the prison gates with our clothes but the screws refused to accept them. So on a bitterly cold January 27th 1981 we were given the order to destroy our furniture and resume the protest. The screws' riot squad arrived on the wings late that night. We heard them in the central section of the H-Block banging their batons on their riot shields. The threatening rhythm would build slowly from a low tempo to a crescendo, accompanied by the stamping of boots on the floor and blood-curdling cries of 'kill the bastards'. They rushed the cells and we were beaten out in pairs through a gauntlet of screws. We were then thrown into waiting vans, which brought us to H6. We were dumped into entirely empty cells without bedding. We had arrived in H6 in the middle of the night and were frozen to the bone. There were pools of water on the floors, as the cells had only recently been power-hosed. The windows had no glass and there were traces of the most recent snowfall. The night was heavy with a freezing fog. I thought I wouldn't make it through the night. My body was as cold as the hearts of the screws who had dumped us there. An audit of injuries was taken. In total 80 out of our 96 had sustained a variety of injuries. My back, arms and legs were sore from the beating and I knew that I would have at least one black eye by morning. My upper lip was swollen and I entertained myself doing impressions of Marlon Brando as Vito Corleone in 'The

Godfather'. As the bard wrote at the end of the *Book of Leinster*: 'Ad delectationem stultorum' – 'for the entertainment of fools.'

That night was one of the longest I spent in the H-Blocks. It was impossible to get even a wink of sleep. I was totally frozen, as we all were. We lived in hope that we would get bedding at breakfast time. Cold tea and equally cold toast arrived the next morning. We still had not been given bedding or blankets. Lunch arrived; boiled egg, cold hairy bacon and dry bread. No blankets. Dinner arrived and the lads shouted out that it was corned beef and chips but there was still no sign of bedding as yet. My door opened and one of the screws who had scalded me in H4 stood there: 'Here's a wee special dinner for you, scumbag,' he said. When I looked at my plate it contained only a square of corned beef. The door was slammed shut but it was opened again in seconds. The screw put his head round the door and said: 'It's not as bad as you think.' He left again slamming the door behind him. I sat on the floor, which was as cold as a grave. I began to eat the corned beef and discovered four cold chips below it. I almost burst into tears but caught a grip of myself. I ate the meagre ration and began exercising to get some warmth. They would never break me. Nor would they break the brave men who shared these freezing tombs with me. The future of the Republican Movement was riding on our shoulders and we needed to ensure those shoulders were as strong as possible. The blankets and mattresses arrived finally around 8 p.m. We were alone and defiant and ready to face into another night's imprisonment at the hands of our enemies. I reminded myself that it's a long road that has no turning.

On the Threshold of Another Trembling World

Between that frozen night in H6 and February 4th plans were finalised for the second hunger strike. In total 120 prisoners had put their names forward. Each prisoner had to write a personal letter to his OC, setting out why he was volunteering for hunger strike. Each candidate gave a background to his arrest, interrogation and sentencing. I took time to reflect deeply on the situation. Could I see it through? There was no definitive answer. How do any of us know, until we've been proved in fire? Eventually I decided that it was my duty to volunteer. I put my name forward and was rejected on the grounds that I had just over a year to serve before my release. I was disappointed but also relieved. I wouldn't have to face the ultimate moment of truth. I have reflected on this over the years and I still can't say if I would have been brave enough to die on hunger strike. It is a question that no one can answer until they look death square in the face, as those brave souls did in 1981.

After some final arrangements had been agreed, Bobby announced that he would lead-off the 1981 hunger strike on his own. He made the necessary arrangements with Brendan McFarlane, insisting that no negotiations be entered into and that no ending of the strike be permitted unless Brendan and a representative of the outside leadership were involved. He advised Brendan that there would be false efforts made to offer a settlement at moments of crisis, but that Brendan should steel himself and be clear-headed in his approach. He was convinced that elements of the Catholic clergy would try to undermine the hunger strike. He told Bik: 'Don't be worried about me. I will see it through. I think that I at least will have to die. The British want their pound of flesh.' The statement announcing the hunger strike read: 'The British have failed to address the prison crisis and we will therefore begin another hunger strike.' The die was cast; there would be no going back. Bobby was to keep a diary for the first 17 days of his fast. He opened it on Sunday March 1st with the words: 'I am standing on the threshold of another trembling world. May God have mercy on my soul.' He finished the diary on Saint Patrick's Day:

> If they cannot destroy the desire for freedom, they'll not be able to break you. They won't break me, as the desire for freedom and for the freedom of the Irish people, is in my heart. The day will come when this desire for freedom will be shown by all the people of Ireland. It is then we'll see the Rising of the Moon.

It was arranged that hunger strikers would be phased on in groups of four. When one died he would be replaced by a fresh Volunteer. The first four to join the strike were Volunteers Bobby Sands (Belfast), Francis Hughes (Bellaghy, County Derry), Raymond McCreesh (Camlough, South Armagh) and INLA man Patsy O'Hara (Derry City). They were followed by Volunteers Joe McDonnell (Belfast), Martin Hurson (Galbally, County Tyrone), Kevin Lynch (Dungiven, County Derry) and Kieran Doherty (Belfast). These four would be followed to their deaths by Tom Mc Elwee (Bellaghy) and Mickey Devine (Derry City). Brendan McLaughlin joined the strike on May 14th but was removed on May 26th when he developed a perforated ulcer. Between June 15th and the beginning of August four others joined the strike but were taken off by their families. Paddy Quinn (South Armagh) spent 47 days on hunger strike. Laurence McKeown (Randalstown, County Antrim) spent 70 days refusing food. Pat McGeown (Belfast) spent 42 days on fast. Matt Devlin (Ardboe, County Tyrone) endured 52 days without food. Two others would end their strikes themselves. Liam McCloskey (Dungiven, County Derry) came off his fast after 55 days on August 3rd when his mother said she would authorise intervention when he lapsed into a coma. Bernard Fox (Belfast) ended his hunger strike after 32 days on August 24th due to kidney stones. The entire strike lasted 217 days and was ended by the prison leadership on October 3rd 1981.

There were still six prisoners on strike when it was called off. They were: Pat Sheehan (Belfast) who had spent 55 days without food. Jackie McMullan (Belfast) went 48 days without food. Hugh Carville (County Down) went 38 days without food. John Pickering (Belfast) was in his 27th day without food. Gerard Hodgins (Belfast) was 20 days on fast while James Devine (Strabane, County Tyrone) was 13 days into his fast.

Ten of the bravest men in Ireland lost their lives and were to change the face of politics in Ireland. Within three days of the ending of the strike British secretary of state, James Prior, gave prisoners the right to wear their own clothes and within two years all five demands of the striking prisoners had been won. Two years later 38 IRA prisoners broke out of the escape-proof H-Blocks in one of the most spectacular jail breaks of the 20th century. In the statement ending the hunger strike, the IRA leadership in the prison said:

> We are ending the protest because we have been robbed of the hunger strike as an effective protest weapon principally because of the successful campaign waged against our distressed relatives by the Catholic hierarchy, aided and abetted by the Irish establishment, the SDLP and Free State political parties.

During the hunger strike, 61 people were to lose their lives in violent incidents. The IRA killed 13 British soldiers, 13 RUC men and five civilians. The British Army and RUC fired 29,695 plastic bullets, killing seven people, the majority of whom were women and children. It was the bloodiest period since 1972. During the fast, Bobby Sands was elected to the British parliament and two other hunger strikers, Paddy Agnew and Kieran Doherty, were elected to Leinster House.

Bobby Sands' election agent, Owen Carron, was elected in his place with an increased majority. There had been increasing debate among the prisoners on the issue of electoral politics from late 1979. We knew local elections would be held in 1981 and there was a group of us advocating that Sinn Féin should contest those elections. We debated the merits of electoral politics and the objective that should be set for such participation. Some prisoners were vehemently opposed to such a development but Bobby Sands, Pat McGeown, Tommy McKearney, Brendan McFarlane, Séanna Breathnach, Donncha Mac Niallais and myself were fully supportive of such a move and were advocating to the leadership outside that they should drive for the creation of a broad front. We argued that Sinn Féin should enter local councils with a view to making them unworkable and should establish People's Councils in all nationalist areas. Bobby Sands was also pressing for the leadership to throw its weight behind a policy of establishing Gaeltachts wherever possible. He described the establishment of the Shaws Road Gaeltacht in Belfast in 1969 as one of the most revolutionary actions of the 20th century. Some of the lads branded me a 'stickie bastard' during these debates on account of my championing this departure. Things got heated at times, which was only to be expected, given our passion for the struggle. We never fell out, resolving to accept and respect the integrity of each other's positions. The outside leadership took none of our recommendations on board at the time. I concluded that the leadership were wedded to a vanguardist approach and that the IRA Army Council feared any strategy over which they hadn't ultimate control. In the event Peoples' Democracy, a fringe leftist group, and the IRSP, a quasi-Marxist group, contested the local elections and returned four councillors in Belfast. By 1982 electoral intervention had become Sinn Féin policy. However the objective was never to destroy the councils or make them unworkable. Sinn Féin gradually fell into a modus operandi heavily influenced by clientelism.

As regards the hunger strikes, I felt that the tactic was rendered ineffective from the point when Paddy Quinn's mother took him off the strike on July 31st. By the time Mickey Devine died and Pat McGeown was taken off hunger strike, the writing was on the wall. When Matt Devlin and Lawrence McKeown were taken-off on September 4th and 6th, it was time for a serious rethink. Within 20 days Liam McCloskey ended his strike and the INLA announced that he wouldn't be replaced. There were still scores of IRA Volunteers ready to embark on the fast. Indeed, everyone who came off was immediately replaced. The prison leadership knew that a new strategy was required to head-off the intervention of the clergy and particularly the machinations of Father Denis Faul. One decision was taken which didn't work out too well. We knew Faul was abusing his position as chaplain and we decided to neutralise him. We told him that if he insisted on coming into the prison to say Mass that we would order a boycott. Myself and Brendan

McFarlane were holding a discussion at Mass on July 19th, a week after Martin Hurson had died. Faul came towards us red in the face. He looked straight at Brendan and said: 'Where does the buck stop?' There was a heated argument and Bik said: 'I'm the OC, the final word rests with me.' Faul stared at him and hissed: 'Then you murdered Martin Hurson. I'm going to stop you.'

When Bik ordered that prisoners were not to attend Mass if Faul was the celebrant, there were rumblings but no open opposition. We found out that the order had been a mistake when Faul returned the next week and significant numbers of prisoners, especially those from Derry, defied orders and went to Mass. We learned the hard way that it was a mistake to interfere with people's religious beliefs. I think we also realised that we were beginning to lose perspective. Discussion began among a number of key prisoners across the Blocks around the possibility of hunger strikers nominating another prisoner with a lasting power of attorney, which would remove the ability of relatives to intervene.[46] I was asked to take a visit with PJ McGrory to explore the matter. When I explained to Paddy what we were considering, he looked at me as one would on someone who had taken leave of their senses. He explained that it was, of course doable, but advised that we consider very carefully what we were proposing: 'You are asking that British law be used to prevent Irish mothers from doing what they believe to be right.'

Our internal debate went on for another while. Prisoners on the hunger strike were sounded out and some were prepared to take the step of granting power of attorney to other prisoners. We were truly in a hard place. In an interview with *An Phoblacht*, an IRA spokesperson said that while the future of the hunger strike was a matter for the prisoners, 'They [the prisoners] do not have the basis for a permanent settlement and obviously we sympathise.' The time to make hard decisions had arrived. On September 30th a meeting was held at Stormont Castle attended by British Secretary of State Jim Prior, Archbishop Tomás Ó Fiaich and Denis Faul. We now know, given the release of British state papers, that Prior was looking for a way to end the prison crisis. His colleague Lord Gowrie, a minister of state at the NIO, was making regular visits to the H-Blocks and visited the families of some of the

---

46 Ceding the right to an appointee to make decisions on your behalf over your health and care should you lose mental capacity.

hunger strikers.[47] In his meeting with Prior, Denis Faul said: 'They are relatively isolated, are inward-looking and they have a deep sense of loyalty to each other after five years of suffering and ill-treatment, as they do to their colleagues who have died.'

Given all the circumstances, it was clear that our race was run. However, the decision to end the hunger strike was one of the hardest that any prisoner would ever have to make in their lives. At an intellectual level we understood that it was time to end the fast, but at the emotional level we were loath to do so and couldn't process the reality of the situation. In a way we were paralysed and the memory of those who had died was too fresh in our minds. No hunger striker had died since the awful loss of Micky Devine on August 21st. We were now 43 days beyond that and had in effect witnessed the power of the fast diminished by others. Strong leadership was required and Brendan McFarlane was not found wanting. The hunger strike was ended after an epic 216 days of horrendous suffering. I felt, and still feel, that we all suffered trauma as a result. Our pain and suffering is, however, irrelevant when viewed in the light of the suffering of the heroic families who stood by their dying relatives in that watershed year of 1981. They are never far from my thoughts.

Life continues

Even as the horrors of the hunger strike unfolded around us in the awful year of 1981, we still retained our humanity, even if that had been long lost by our jailers. Five days into the fast, the nationalist MP for Fermanagh South Tyrone, Frank Maguire, tragically lost his life. Frank, a former internee himself, had been a great supporter of the prisoners. He was only 51 years-of-age when he died. We were saddened at his untimely loss. Those prisoners who were so inclined recited a decade of the rosary for Frank. We then all held a minute's silence to honour his life and mark his loss. Four days after Frank's death Bobby Sands turned 27. Since turning 18 he had spent every birthday in prison. Bobby was by this stage on his ninth day on hunger strike. We decided to hold a concert in his honour. The memory of that bitter-sweet night still lives with me. I can still feel the emotions of that night, even though 40 years have passed. I was 22 at the time. We were incarcerated in 'A' Wing of H3. I had the role of shouting

---

47 Alexander Patrick Greysteil Ruthven, 2nd Earl of Gowrie, was a hereditary peer of the Scottish clan Ruthven, who served in a number of capacities in the Conservative government of Margaret Thatcher.

between the wings at the time. We were known as 'scorchers' – a corruption of the Irish word to shout. When all the dinner plates had been cleared away and the Day Guard had left the wings we would shout messages and receive updates from all the wings.

I hooked my fingers into the metal grilles which covered the windows, climbed onto the heating pipes at the back of the cell, and commenced my nightly duty. Spotto Devine from Belfast was in the wing facing us and when all his messages were completed he shouted: 'One last thing comrade,' his entire wing then shouted in unison: 'Breithla sona Bobby! – Happy Birthday Bobby!' We all had a lump in our throats. We prepared for the concert we were going to give in Bobby's honour. If truth be told we needed it more than he did. He wrote in his diary that night:

> It is my birthday and the boys are having a sing-song for me, bless their hearts. Braved it to the door, at their request, to make a bit of a speech, for what it was worth. I wrote to several friends today including Bernie and my mother. I feel all right and my weight is 60 kgs. I always keep thinking of James Connolly, and the great calm and dignity that he showed right to his very end, his courage and resolve. Perhaps I am biased, because there have been thousands like him, but Connolly has always been the man that I looked up to. I always have tremendous feeling for Liam Mellows as well. Well, I have gotten by twenty-seven years, so that is something. I may die, but the Republic of 1916 will never die. Onward to the Republic and liberation of our people.

That concert, for a few short hours, took us out of ourselves and out of our cells. We sang, danced and celebrated with our comrades. Jimmy 'Teapot' McMullan and James 'Hector' McNeill took centre stage, as full of craic and life as ever, blowing raspberries at the less accomplished singers and trying to get one over on each other. We could all picture Teapot and Hector behind their doors. Hector was the only man in the prison who was smaller than Teapot. We knew Hector would be standing on his upturned pisspot to put him an inch above his co-host. Brendan McFarlane, gave us the first song: 'Big Yellow Taxi' by Joni Mitchell. It was a favourite of Bobby's, who was an eco-warrior before his time. He loved nature. As Bik sang the line: 'They're gonna take all the trees and put them in a tree museum and charge the folks a dollar and a half just to see 'em,' in our minds we were transported thousands of miles away from the horrors of the H-Blocks for that one night. We were free in spirit. This would be our last chance to spend quality time with our comrade, as we knew he would be removed soon to the prison hospital where he would die. Bobby came to the door and said a few words and then sang 'Back Home in Derry'. It was a song he had composed himself and had it set to the tune of Gordon Lightfoot's 'Wreck of the Edmund Fitzgerald'. It was a heartbreaking moment and the poignancy of the occasion almost swamped us. We all joined in the chorus at the top of our lungs. I will never for the life of me know why, but I chose to sing 'Skibbereen', a lengthy dirge about the horrors of An Gorta Mór. Something lighter was called for after that. So, after giving me the required abuse, Hector and Teapot called for Big Tom McElwee, who would, in his turn, follow Bobby to his death. 'I've no songs,' said Big Tom, 'but I'll give you a dance on the lid of the pisspots and I'll recite a poem.' The dance was a hoot. Tom wasn't much better at the dancing than he was at the singing. After taking his dose of abuse Tom began reciting his poem. It was wonderful. Both Tom and his poem were rooted in the soil of Ireland. His big, rough country voice held us spellbound as he spoke lovingly of the beautiful flowers blooming among the mists from the sea. It would have been impossible to call it a concert, without a touch of Neil Young from Seamy Kelly. Neil Young was another of Bobby's favourites.

When all the usual suspects had been given their place and with Teapot and Hector flagging, Brendan McFarlane agreed to close out the concert. First he sang 'McElhatton', a song co-written by Bobby and Colm Scullion from Bellaghy, a close neighbour of Tom McElwee and Francis Hughes. The song would become famous after it was recorded by Christy Moore. What a birthday, what a night and what an escape from our grim reality! We did the only thing we could – our very best under the circumstances. We would have a few other causes for celebration that year, one at the start of April when Bobby unseated the unionist bigot, Harry West, a former leader of the UUP and another in June when Kieran Doherty and Paddy Agnew won seats in Leinster House and helped boot Charlie Haughey from power. Haughey had played cynical games all through the hunger strike and never took the action which any taoiseach worth his or her salt would have taken in the face of the death of Irish citizens on hunger strike. We didn't have our sorrows to seek as ten comrades went to their deaths. Their sacrifice smashed Britain's criminalisation policy, reinvigorated the republican struggle, internationalised the struggle, radicalised nationalism and paved the way for the endgame in Ireland. We will never see their likes again and their revenge is the laughter of our children.

After the 1981 Hunger Strike

Our lives changed entirely after the hunger strikes. We had our own clothes and furnished and clean cells. We could associate and exercise together within the wings and in the prison yards. We had televisions, showers, pens, books and radios. We still hadn't resolved the question of education and work; that would be sorted in time. The screws were extremely nervous but we were under strict orders not to attack any of them. A small group at the heart of the prison leadership had already begun planning the 1983 prison break. The screws were so relieved at being 'safe' that they gradually let their guard down. The only type of prison work we would engage in was the upkeep of our wings. The prison governor announced that any prisoner available for work would regain 50 percent of their lost remission. Some succumbed to the offer and headed into the general criminal population. The most prominent prisoner to do so was the former PRO, who would later profit from a highly contested account of the hunger strike which did nothing other than wound the families. He severed all his connection with the Republican Movement in the aftermath of the 1981 fast and has since written two books, neither of which I will ever read.

I was due for release in April 1982, at which point I would have served my entire sentence. I would have been eligible for release in January of that year had I chosen to do prison work. A screw arrived and offered me a job maintaining our own wing. He was a particularly mean specimen who was in the habit of clanging his baton off the wing gates during the hunger strikes and shouting: 'H3, bring out your dead.' I had been in two minds about availing of the early release but the sight of this lowlife made up my mind. I told him I wasn't interested. 'You'll get out early,' he said. I told him that I would wait until April and would hopefully meet him after that. As it happened I only met him once and that was when I was visiting my brother Rab in 1986. I looked him in the eye and asked him quietly if he was still driving his Renault car.

Life was strange after the hunger strikes. Everything had changed but those days of horror were still fresh in our minds. I couldn't pass any of the cells from which the lads had departed for the prison hospital without seeing them and thinking of their families. It was hard and it was also difficult when I met those who had survived the hunger strike. I concentrated on reading and planned to return to education on my release. I happened to read an account in the media of a revolutionary community school at Saint Louise's College run by a woman named

Pauline Murphy. I wrote to Pauline and told her I would be in touch on my release. I did and would get to know her well over the years. She ended up in a long tenure in the University of Ulster and remains one of my heroes. I would also discover that she was a sister of Pádraig Ó Snodaigh, the owner of Coiscéim Publishing, an author of many works, a poet and a champion of the Gaelic language. Pauline drove her initiative forward, giving education to many adult learners. She persevered in face of constant obstruction from Sister Genevieve O'Farrell, a right wing Catholic from Offaly, who was head of the college and who would, on the success of the initiative, have the audacity to claim credit for the very thing she had tried to destroy. I attended Saint Louise's for two years, completing my 'O' Levels in year one and my 'A' Levels in year two before heading to Queen's University.

In the H-Blocks we had a lot more opportunity for debates and discussions. We hotly debated domestic and international affairs. Irish classes and a whole range of other learning opportunities opened up for us. Discussions were held on the establishment of a Gaeltacht within the prison. This would eventually happen and it was named Gaeltacht na Fuiseoige – The Gaeltacht of the Lark – a bird close to the heart of Bobby Sands. I began writing regular pieces for the Belfast Irish language paper, *Preas an Phobail*, which had been set up by Eoghan Ó Néill and Gearóid Ó Caireálláin. I would continue to write for the paper after my release and for its successor *Lá*. It is a matter of huge disappointment that Foras na Gaeilge, the Irish language body, would withdraw funding from *Lá* in spite of a commitment in the European Charter for the provision of at least one Irish language paper. I hardly noticed my last six months of imprisonment fly by. Before I knew it the day of my release was upon me. I was finally returning to my family and to the struggle. I had served every day of the sentence imposed on me. My spirit and my politics were as solid as they'd ever been, if not stronger. I was ready for the challenges ahead.

Chapter 5

Back in the world, back in the struggle

'Don't break your shin on a stool which isn't in your way.' (Seanfhocail Uladh 972 Uladh/Roibeard Mac Ádhaimh)

Back in my mother's, for a time

The day of my release had finally arrived. I had waited so long for this day, but it was to be one of bitter-sweet feelings. I didn't experience the happiness which I had anticipated. I recalled my first release and the sadness I had felt of leaving people behind. This time I was leaving behind ten of the bravest men it had ever been my privilege to have known. They would never follow me out the gates. It broke my heart. My throat was constricted. I was fearful that the emotions would get the better of me. We said little, taking refuge in the joking, teasing and small talk which was always a defence in such situations. I knew I was leaving for another world, not just another place a few miles down the road. I spent my last few days going quietly into the cells which the hunger strikers had left to go to the prison hospital and then their early graves. I thought of each one of them but I especially thought of the grieving families. I was sad, hurt and full of grief. I solemnly swore that I would never forget them or their sacrifice, which had changed the course of the struggle and reinvigorated the Republican Movement. I wandered the wing and the yard in my final days like a man in a trance. I dearly wanted to leave this hell hole which had been my world for five years. I was extremely anxious and full of hope for what freedom would bring. I couldn't properly explain how I felt. I was, in the end, determined to look to the future. I would usually end my periods of introspection with a firm resolve, to do my best never to betray the sacrifice of my ten comrades.

The moment of truth arrived. I began the long walk from the wing to freedom. The lads all shouted good wishes. I couldn't speak for fear that tears would flow. I clamped my jaw tight and raised my fist defiantly in the air in a final salute. I dropped my head and walked to the gates. A van took me to reception where I had been stripped and battered five years before. The smart talk from the screws and the governor hardened my resolve. I spoke not a word, nor answered a single one of their inane questions, simply avoiding all eye contact with them. I was sure where my path led and what I envisaged for the future. I hoped that screws would play no part in it.

A huge homecoming party had been prepared for me. The craic went on for three days and nights, with precious little sleep. My brother Rab and his mates had been buying in supplies for months. All of them were in their teens and early 20s. All were solid members of the Republican Movement and passionate, dedicated and decent human beings. The majority of them, Rab included, would see the inside of a prison cell themselves in the years that followed. Hundreds of people visited my mother's house during those celebrations. On the first day of that wonderful homecoming I laughed, joked and had one of the best days of my life. At some stage during the madness I got a quiet moment with an old comrade and informed him that I wished to play an active role in the Movement as soon as I could. He told me not to be in any hurry back as there was a long road ahead of us still. I understood that and I wasn't going to go breaking my shin on any stool that wasn't in my way. However I was determined to play my part.

During my first month of freedom it was clear that the war was still raging. Four British soldiers, an RUC man and a UDR man were killed. Two civilians died in Magherafelt when an IRA bomb had exploded prematurely. The IRA executed one of their own, Patrick Scott, as an informer. He was the brother of a prisoner on the Blanket. The IRA also killed a civilian, Raymond Devlin, who they accused of serious criminal activity. 'Devil', as he was known, had been a few years behind me in school. Another brother, Damian, who had been one year below me in school, would also die in 1988 during a UVF attack on the Avenue Bar, which also claimed the life of another young Catholic, Paul McBride. The IRA in Armagh killed an innocent Protestant civilian, William Morrison (42), without any explanation. He was shot dead on his farm near Middleton. On the 19th of the month an 11 year-old, Stephen Óg McConomy, died in hospital three days after a British soldier shot him at close range in the head with a plastic bullet. He was one of eight children murdered by plastic bullets, fired by British soldiers and RUC men in a blatant policy aimed at cowing nationalist resistance.

One of the things that made my blood boil after my release was that so many of our own people were buying and reading the filthy gutter papers from England. I learned not to allow this to get under my skin but when I was newly released it infuriated me. I had other things to learn to fill in gaps in my knowledge. Skills for coping with the heavily increased traffic were a must. Styles of clothing had also greatly changed. The lower Falls, which I had known well, was being totally transformed, as the old housing stock made way for new style streets and cul-de-sacs. Another thing that I found both off-putting and challenging was that prices had almost tripled during my time in prison. I was nervous about offering anything under a £5 note in shops for fear of making myself appear foolish. One of the most debilitating traits my father had inculcated in me during my childhood was an almost morbid fear of appearing foolish. I have only rid myself of this fear in recent years. I believe that nurture is as strong as nature. I was free now and I would have to overcome the challenge of my shortcomings, along with many other challenges.

I resolved that it would be best for me and my parents if I found myself somewhere to live. I was fully intent on playing an active role in the Republican Movement, so I therefore managed to get myself a flat quite quickly. It was a one bedroomed flat on Lenadoon Avenue and I invited my brother Rab to join me. It would be good to be able to split the bills and to get to know each other a lot better than we had already. It was also useful in that we only had to say 'I'm going to be busy' and there would be no questions asked. We also knew to only expect each other when we saw each other. It was our habit to go to my mother's house every Saturday, provided we were free. All our sisters, their husbands and children, would also gather in Rosie's. My mother would make us all an Irish fry. It was a habit we all kept up until she died. I treasured those Saturdays dearly and miss them still.

It's a rare man that doesn't benefit from advice

I understood that many things had changed and a new dispensation ruled. As a result of this I kept my own counsel and did lots of listening. I also made it my business to visit a lot of other people to seek out their counsel. I spoke to people I trusted in the community, the Movement and Irish language community. I knew these people would give me straight answers in confidence, knowing that I wouldn't betray their confidence. It's a habit I've maintained to this day. Accurate knowledge is strength. The best answer I received to my questions came from an Irish language activist, a man for whom I had and still have, the greatest of respect. He gave me the minutiae and a run-down of the who's-who, but added one crucial piece of advice. He advised me that I wouldn't go far wrong in Irish circles if I remembered that community had more lunatics per capita than the wider community. Strangely I was to be pleasantly surprised that I found these eccentrics to be very good company. If I enjoyed the company of the eccentrics, there was another group in the Irish community whom I found intolerable. These self-appointed 'great and good' I called the 'UberGhaeil'. They had a number of traits in common besides snobbery. They believed it essential to cultivate a fake Donegal accent but only in Irish. They were intellectual snobs with a compunction to correct other people in conversation, before launching into a boring lecture on Irish grammar. One other trait I found among the majority of these snobs was their aversion to Irish Medium education. Most chose elitist Catholic grammar schools for their off-spring. Their last common denominator was their disrespect for what they termed 'Jailge' or jail-Irish.

I began teaching two classes, one in Gort na Móna GAA Club and the other in the Felons' Club on the Falls Road. I first met Robin Dunwoody (RIP) through my class in the Felons'. I would get to know Robin well. I was in and out of the house he shared with his partner Una Marron. Their daughter would become one of the first pupils in the Irish Medium secondary school. I would later work with Robin in *An Phoblacht* and found him not only great company but also a dyed-in-the wool Marxist. I learned a lot from Robin and was deeply saddened at his loss. I also became active in the Sinn Féin cultural department, although I never joined Sinn Féin itself. It was there I met some very dedicated activists such as Máirtín Ó Muilleoir and Pádraig Ó Maolchraoibhe, one of the few people I would describe as a close friend. I also met Bairbre de Brún, who would become a teacher in Coláiste Feirste and later a minister in the Stormont assembly. I also met Gearóid Ó hEara from

Derry, who would lead the revival in his home town. There were lots of others I met, particularly at the annual republican Gaelic congress known as An Slogadh. Two people in particular that I had great respect for were Pádaí Dubh Ó Donnchú and Seán Savage, both of whom would die young – Pádaí, carried away by ill-health, Seán killed in Gibraltar by the SAS. Pádraig Ó Snódaigh had established his publishing company Coiscéim in 1980. He has published more than 1,500 books in Irish since then. Pádraig is himself an author of many fine works and I would get to know him first through his son Aengus, a member of the Republican Movement, now a TD in Leinster House. I remain a member of Clubleabhar Choiscéim Feirste, the Belfast-based Irish language book club. I also wrote in my early years of freedom for both *Preas an Phobail* and *An Phoblacht* under the pen name 'Síle Nic Gearailt'.

Keeping the eye on the ball

Electoral politics became a fierce topic of debate from 1981 onwards. The question of electoralism was very prominent at the Sinn Féin Ard Fheis of 1982, where the 'Éire Nua' policy was debated and rejected. A year later in 1983, Ruairí Ó Brádaigh declined to stand for the presidency of Sinn Féin, citing the rejection of 'Éire Nua' as one of his reasons. Gerry Adams succeeded him as president, a post that he held for 35 years before handing over to Mary Lou McDonald who, until 1998, had been a member of Fianna Fáil. The night before the Ard Fheis in 1983 I met Martin Ferris to give him a copy of the speech which he would deliver to a closed session of the Ard Fheis. Less than a year later, on Saturday September 29th, Martin would be captured by Free State troops on board the 'Marita Ann' ferrying seven tonnes of arms to Ireland.

The abstentionism debate rumbled on in the Movement until an IRA convention voted to remove the ban on taking seats in Leinster House in 1986. The Sinn Féin Ard Fheis in November of 1986 also endorsed the move. Other debates were also ongoing in the Movement in the years between 1981 and 1986. In 1983 a new IRA Chief-of-Staff was appointed following the imprisonment of his predecessor, who had only held the position for a year. He was to remain in post until the late 1990s. He was a solid republican and a very decent human being. I admired him greatly for his discretion, humility and judgement. Unfortunately he died from cancer, robbing his family of a treasured father and husband. In 1984 tensions had arisen within the IRA after its former Chief-of-Staff had been released from prison and began with others to oppose any further expenditure on electoral politics and the general direction of the struggle. He was subsequently summoned before an IRA court martial. A senior IRA woman and three other men were also charged with treason. He refused to attend the court. All were found guilty. However, instead of imposing the usual sentence of death, the IRA Army Council directed that all involved should be dismissed from the Army. The underlying tensions which had led to this turn of events were to rumble on in the IRA until 1997. I deliberately stayed out of the controversy and cautioned others to take no part in it. My firm opinion was that there had been an IRA before these events and there would be one after. All the dismissed Volunteers applied to be allowed back into the IRA, but the woman Volunteer and the former Chief-of-Staff were denied re-admittance. One of those others readmitted was to die at the hands of the British Army in 1988.

Between 1982 and 1986 I was principally active in the Falls, Clonard and Lenadoon areas. I was learning new skills as well as brushing up on old ones. My mentor was Seán Savage, a nephew of IRA veteran Billy McKee, who died in June 2019. Seán shared neither his uncle's Catholic fundamentalism or political conservatism. Seán's mother and father were devout Catholics. He had a brother Robert who had Downs Syndrome and from whom Seán was rarely parted. I learned a lot from Seán, who was dedicated, driven and as straight as a die. I worked alongside Seán for two years and treasure the time I spent with him. Seán was six years my junior and was to die aged 24 in 1988, cut down by the SAS with Mairead Farrell and Dan McCann.

I was also to become active as an election manager. I fulfilled this role at various times in West Belfast, north and south Derry, Upper Bann, Roscommon/Longford, County Meath and Westmeath, Kildare, Laois and Offaly. It was useful in many ways as I was able to forge close relationships with people across the country and I was often able to double-up carrying out various duties for the Republican Movement. I ended my role as an election manager after the successful retaking of the West Belfast seat for Sinn Féin in 1997. That was a tough assignment as there were lots of strong personalities surrounding the candidate. I made clear to the person who appointed me to the job that authority came with responsibility and accountability. I insisted that one condition of my taking the role was that I alone was in control of the campaign and not others. I entered the role in late 1995 and worked at it on-and-off with a tight team which we dubbed the Committee for the Re-Election of the President (the Creeps). At the first meeting of the group, to which neither the candidate nor his PA were invited, I laid out the strategy we would follow. We would run the campaign on a collective basis but in disputes I would be the final arbiter. I also organised another small group who would undertake intensive training with local area managers and key individuals. I explained that it was my opinion that the loss of the West Belfast seat had been a self-inflicted disaster and had been largely due to complacency. Gerry Adams had first been elected in 1983 with 16,379 votes and had lost the seat in 1987 with 16,862 votes. I believed the election team had been blind to the threat of unionist tactical voting, even though it had been well flagged-up. There was I felt, an over-confidence and a general complacency. I laid down a target of 24,000 votes, which would be an insurance against even the largest possible tactical voting by unionists. I confidently told Sinn Féin on the night of the election that I was sure we had reached the target. At the count on election day Sinn Féin reclaimed the seat with 25,662 against 17,753 for SDLP candidate, Joe Hendron, an increase of 338 on his previous vote.

I met Chrissie Keenan in 1982. She was beautiful and still is. I was smitten with her straight away. She had a very strong personality and still has. She was a very capable republican, who would work with myself, John Livingstone, Goretti McDonnell, Martha McCann, Charlie Rodgers, Kate Finucane and Sally Elliot to perfect our electoral system. We took a scientific approach, categorising voters in our system as green (Sinn Féin), yellow (SDLP) and white (non-committed or anti-republican). We created targeted canvassing notes and trained electoral workers in how to process and record data. Our strategy became widely embedded in Sinn Féin's election system. In 1990, Sheena Campbell (RIP), who was going out with an old comrade of mine, Brendan Curran, was to take our system and use it in the Torrens by-election in County Tyrone. After that Sinn Féin dubbed it the 'Torrens' strategy, but in reality the approach had originated with the Lenadoon crew. With minor updates, the same system of fighting elections is still in use by Sinn Féin. Loyalists were to target Brendan and Sheena's house for attack in 1987. The following year they attacked the home of Brendan's parents, badly injuring him. In 1992 Sheena was attending Queen's University in Belfast when the UVF attacked and murdered her. She was a talented, committed and lovely woman. I was very fond of her. Sheena was one of 17 members of Sinn Féin murdered by loyalists during the 1980s and 1990s. There were more than 100 attacks on members of Sinn Féin, their homes and families. Loyalists also murdered the son of Sinn Féin councillor Bobby Lavery, who was shot dead on the day the first ever republican march reached Belfast city centre. Sean Lavery (21) was gunned down in his father's home on August 8th 1993.

I first met Chrissie at a social evening in the Green Briar in Andersonstown. I didn't know at the time that she was a daughter of Brian Keenan, who was something of a legend within republicanism. It wouldn't have mattered had I known. It was Chrissie and not Brian I was interested in. I never held any truck with hero worship or the cult of personality. I think both are stupid notions and feel the cult of personality is a curse and can be very damaging to any movement. Chrissie was 18 at the time and I was 24. I later found out that she was attending St Louise's College, where I myself was a mature student. Chrissie and I started dating. She always had a very strong personality and shared many traits with her father. However she also had her mother's heart and caring nature. I was very fond of her mother. 'Big Chrissie', as I called her, was very small in stature but she had the heart of a lion. She had done a wonderful job of raising her six children, largely on her own, as Brian had been on the run or in prison since the 1970s. 'Big Chrissie' never gave advice to us and never interfered in our lives. She was a very understanding and wise woman and would constantly give us food that she had 'left over'. We greatly appreciated it as we lived in relative poverty until I began my first paid employment in 1997. She was also a discerning woman when it came to people. I remember when Robert Lean called to her house looking for me. She advised me not to have him near her house again: 'He's a wrong one. I can feel it in my water,' she warned. Within six months of that conversation Lean was in RUC custody and naming people he accused of IRA activity. 18 people went to prison as a result of his allegations and 15 others were being sought by the RUC. Many people fled across the border but I refused to flee. I wasn't arrested on Lean's allegations until two days before Christmas 1983, by which time he had withdrawn his evidence. I spent three days in silence in Castlereagh interrogation centre speaking not one solitary word to my interrogators.

The British policy of paid informers or 'supergrasses' was being employed more and more in the early 1980s. The first of them had been Chris Black from Ardoyne. I knew Black in the cages of Long Kesh. He had become a Crown witness against republicans in 1981 before my release. There would be others. I was arrested during a visit to Derry on the night the RUC began rounding up people on the word of informer Raymond Gilmour. I didn't know Gilmour and thankfully he didn't know me. I was released late the following evening when it became clear that he had nothing to say about me. The bottom was to eventually fall out of the paid perjurer policy, but not before many people had spent long periods in prison. It was but another British method to ensure the 'removal of unwanted members of the public'. On one occasion I had been out of prison several weeks and found myself working overnight with a guy called Bobby Brown. I never introduced myself to him and this was the first time he'd ever seen me. I sensed the man was under huge stress and mentioned this to the appropriate people. Within days Brown was in the hands of the RUC and had turned state's evidence.

I felt in the early months after my release that republicans needed to review and refine their tactics. The IRA had been at war for 12 years. It was clear that the British, through the use of technology and informers, both within and outside the IRA, was capable of frustrating many military operations. Looking back, I can now clearly see that such a review was ongoing at leadership level. Back then, working at a local level, it was hard to assess these things properly. What was clear at that time was that more emphasis was being put on military actions in England. Republicans always understood that one bomb in England was worth 100 bombs in the Six Counties.

On the cusp of marriage

Myself and Chrissie decided that we were committed to spending the rest of our lives together. All that remained was the setting of a date for the wedding. I tried to get a visit with her father, who was serving 16 years in Leicester Prison at the time. The prison governor refused me permission to visit. I spoke with a solicitor and he thought we had a very strong case against the prison authorities for refusing a prospective son-in-law a visit with his father-in-law to be. The governor was back in touch and said that he had made a mistake and that I would be welcome to visit. I received a visit from the RUC Special Branch within two days informing me that I had been served with an exclusion order from Britain. So I could visit Brian but couldn't enter the country where he was being held.

We went ahead and organised our wedding for July 11th 1985. We picked a Thursday because many of our friends were unemployed and received their benefits that day. We also decided that we would marry at 6 p.m. so that the day would be less costly for people. A night out with a dinner thrown in. What we didn't think of was that July 11th was the annual Orange bonfire night and most of my close friends would be on defensive duties that night guarding nationalist areas from possible loyalist attack. Many wouldn't get 'leave' to attend the wedding. My brother Rab, my best man, could attend the wedding but wasn't allowed to have a drink. The best laid plans of mice and men!

Our ceremony took place in St Agnes' Church with our reception afterwards in Gort na Móna GAA club. We were lucky all went to schedule. On the morning of the wedding myself, my brother Rab and a lifelong friend, Brian McDonald, decided to chill out with a trip to the beach. We spent a wonderful day at a beach in Ballygally. Brian collected a bucket of crabs that he intended letting loose in the women's toilets in Gort na Móna, just so that he could listen to the screams from the poor women. At 3 p.m. we headed for home. Brian's car unfortunately broke down on the M2 motorway. After two nervous hours and with the help of friends, we finally arrived back in Belfast. My poor mother was in a state but I managed to settle her down. We arrived at the church suited and booted with time to spare. We needn't have worried as Chrissie and the bridal party exercised the time-honoured tradition of arriving late. We were due to go on honeymoon to the south of France. We had paid our deposit for the trip but unexpectedly ended up getting a house. We decided to defer France to allow us to get our new home in shape. France would end up being deferred until our 25th wedding anniversary.

The day after the wedding we headed to Kerry to enjoy the beautiful summer sunshine. We travelled with Chrissie's sister Jeanette and her boyfriend in a seven-seater car owned by our friend Ian Catney. Ian was a brother of Tony Catney, whom I had served time with in prison. 'TC', as he was known, was to die from cancer while still in his 50s. I worked with Tony following his release from prison in the 1990s. He was to resign from the Republican Movement following the second IRA ceasefire. During our drive to Kerry we listened to the 'Live Aid' concert. The road to Kerry was much longer in those days before the arrival of the EU money, which completely transformed infrastructure in Ireland. I have great memories of our trip to Kerry but they are always tinged with sadness as Ian would later be murdered by the UVF at his mother's shop on January 18th 1989. Ian was never involved with republicanism. He was murdered cold-bloodedly by loyalists, like so many other innocent Catholics, to send a message to nationalists that we were all targets and all at risk.

Our early married life wasn't easy from a financial point of view. Chrissie worked full-time and I was a full-time republican activist, and as anyone who has had the privilege will tell you, the pay was non-existent. We hadn't two pennies to rub together. However Chrissie always kept an immaculate home and ensured that we had the best that our meagre finances would stretch to. Chrissie's mother lived in the same street as us and she was very generous with us in every way. We were nine months and 21 days married when our first child arrived. Her arrival on May 2nd 1986 changed my world view and I have never known a more exhilarating moment than holding her in the palm of my hand for the first time. I fully understood unconditional and limitless love as I cradled that tiny miracle. She was 5lbs 15 ounces and stretched from my finger tips to my wrist. I felt the same intense feeling of love at the birth of all my children.

Chrissie had chosen a natural birth. Towards the end, when she was completely exhausted, the attending midwife encouraged me to whisper encouragement into Chrissie's ear. Wasn't I the fool to take that advice? Chrissie caught a grip of my cheek between her teeth. This of course was immediately forgotten, along with Chrissie's terrible pains, the moment a healthy baby girl was placed in her arms. The midwife, who hailed from south Armagh, was a Gaelic speaker and therefore the first conversation our baby heard was in Irish. Chrissie hadn't been willing to take my name when we married so we had decided to take each others. As a result when it came to registering the baby she got the unwieldy name of Orliath Áine Alanagh Ó Chíanán MacSiacais.

I couldn't wait to take her out in the new pink baby sling that I'd bought for her. It was a habit that wasn't as fashionable in the 1990s. A few of the more 'manly men' frowned on it. I didn't give a damn. I had my daughter and I was determined that the world would see her and she would see the world. She was only three months old when I first took her to the Black Mountain, overlooking Belfast. She has been on it countless times with me since and in her turn with her own children.

At the time of writing we are 36 years married and have five wonderful children, Orliath, Conchuir, Eimear, Fionnghuala and Tiarnán. We also have five grandchildren, Séadhna, Eithne, Dualta, Luisne and Caragh. We also lost a baby between Orliath and Conchuir and experienced great difficulties during the birth of our youngest Tiarnán, who was lucky to survive an emergency section delivery. All our kids are Gaelic speakers and have made us very proud. They are solid adults now. We were conscious not to force our values and beliefs on them, seeking only to instruct by example and never asking anything other than they do their best in whatever they decided to do. We reminded them as needed that no one was better than them and that they were never to think of themselves as better than others. We always took people as we found them, whatever their background, politics or lifestyle and we encouraged our children to do the same and to never become judgemental.

With hand on heart, I can say that Chrissie and the children which she brought into the world were the best things that ever happened to me. I wasn't always the easiest of husbands and have more than my fair share of faults. However Chrissie stood by me through everything and I am deeply indebted to her that she did.

By the end of 1986 we had our own home and family but I can't say that everything was right in the world. Conflict still raged all around us. On September 14th, a friend and comrade was shot dead by British soldiers as he returned from an IRA operation. Volunteer Jim McKernan was shot in the back as he left the scene of an ambush. He was the fourth IRA Volunteer to be killed that year by the British Army. Francis Bradley (20) had been killed on February 18th in south Derry. Anthony Gough (24) died in Derry city on February 22nd and Séamus McElwaine (26) was killed in Fermanagh on April 26th. The IRA also executed three of their own members and a civilian, for informing. Colm McKevitt (30) died on May 20th, Francis Hegarty (45) on May 25th and Patrick Murray (30) on August 15th. The civilian, David McVeigh (41) was shot on September 10th. During that year the IRA killed 12 British soldiers, 11 RUC men and five civilians accused by the IRA of collaborating in rebuilding British Army bases. They also killed three innocent civilians by mistake. John McCabe (25), who was working in a pub where RUC man Derek Breen (29) was killed, Kenneth Robinson (30), who died when a booby-trap bomb placed under his UDR father's car exploded and Desmond Caldwell (44), targeted by a booby-trap bomb in the mistaken belief that he was an RUC man. The IRA also executed leading loyalist gunman John Bingham (33) for 'direct involvement in sectarian murders'. Loyalist gangs also killed 14 innocent Catholics and one innocent Protestant. She was Margaret Caulfield (30), murdered because she had married a Catholic.

Chapter 6

Things are not always what they seem

'Only the dead have seen the end of war.' Plato (423–347 BCE)

A good start is half the work

Before moving on, we need to go back to 1984. At that time I was working locally but I had always had a keen interest in matters of strategy. I was never shy about speaking my mind no matter what the forum or what the prevailing wisdom. I was given the privilege of delivering an address to a closed session of the Sinn Féin Ard Fheis in 1984. I was aware that strategic questions were being discussed at leadership level. It was known that efforts were underway within the IRA to ensure they were equipped and in readiness for a sustained escalation of armed action.

The world would witness the out-workings of this when the IRA detonated a huge bomb on October 12th in the Grand Hotel Brighton where Thatcher and many of her key people were staying during the Conservative Party conference. Thatcher and other key figures narrowly cheated the death which the IRA had planned for them. Five were to die: Sir Anthony Berry MP, Lady Jeanne Shattock, wife of the Tory chair in the south-west region, Lady Muriel Maclean, wife of the chair of Scottish Conservatives, Roberta Wakeham, wife of the Tory treasurer, and Eric Taylor, chair of the Tories in the north-west region. Two people were left in wheelchairs, Walter Clegg MP and Margaret

Tebbit, whose husband Norman was a key figure in the Thatcher government. As many as 30 others sustained varying degrees of injuries. In its statement following the bombing the IRA said:

> Mrs Thatcher will now realise that Britain cannot occupy our country and torture our prisoners and shoot our people in their own streets and get away with it. Today we were unlucky, but remember we only have to be lucky once. You will have to be lucky always. Give Ireland peace and there will be no more war.

To give credit where it is due, Thatcher entered her party conference, six hours and 24 minutes after surviving the bomb attack. She was in combative mood telling conference the attack was an attempt to cripple Her Majesty's democratically elected government:

> That is the scale of the outrage in which we have all shared, and the fact that we are gathered here now – shocked, but composed and determined – is a sign not only that this attack has failed, but that all attempts to destroy democracy by terrorism will fail.

Towards the end of that year I had the privilege of visiting Euskal Herria (the Basque Country) for the first time to meet with members of the Basque Freedom Movement. I would be back in Euskal Herria on business in 1987 and again in 1989. I would visit the country often after that in a personal capacity and developed friendships with many people there over the years. I have a real fondness for the country and its people, who have valiantly resisted Spanish occupation and oppression for generations.

In January 1985 things were moving in a political direction which wouldn't become apparent for almost another 10 years. During the course of a radio interview that year Gerry Adams, the leader of Sinn Féin, challenged John Hume of the SDLP to engage in talks. Hume dismissed his suggestion of talks with Sinn Féin, insisting that he should talk to the IRA who were, in his opinion, the dominant partner in the Republican Movement. The IRA took Hume at his word and three senior members agreed to meet with him. The IRA insisted on the meeting being recorded. Hume refused and the meeting didn't go ahead. The then Taoiseach, Garret FitzGerald, strongly and publicly condemned Hume but behind the scenes the leader of the opposition, Charles Haughey, welcomed the intiative. Adams was also at this time working on his book *The Politics of Irish Freedom*. It was clear that the most appropriate description of what was appearing in public was summed up in the old adage: 'Ní mar a shíltear a bítear – things are not always what they appear to be.' This dog had legs and it was going to run and run. A new strategy was being formulated and change would flow from it sooner or later. FitzGerald and his conservative, anti-republican lackeys in Dublin were also focusing on strategy. The rise of Sinn Féin had caused alarm and was being perceived as a potential threat to constitutional nationalism. Dublin's Minister of Foreign Affairs, Peter Barry, started a concerted engagement with Geoffrey Howe, Tom King and Margaret Thatcher to persuade them of the merits of a joint governmental approach. Barry was an old-style Cumann na nGaedheal nationalist, who would describe his objective as to end the nationalist 'nightmare'. FitzGerald had given his blessing to Barry but was much more interested in the anti-republican potential of the approach. Thatcher was eventually persuaded to sign the Anglo-Irish Agreement on November 15th 1985, although she later said she regretted having done so. Unionists reacted with fury. The media was filled with headlines and sound-bites about 'unionist fury' and 'unionist anger'; sure what was new? Unionists were, and remain, 'furious and angry' about something every day. It makes an easy job for editors and headline writers, who need only add a few words to get a good strap-line. We could run a competition asking people to fill in the blanks: 'unionist outrage at ...'

On November 20th 1985 unionists physically attacked British pro-consul Tom King as he arrived at Belfast City Hall. Three days later a huge rally was held outside City Hall which gave a platform for Ian Paisley to bellow his impotent rage:

> Where do the terrorists operate from? From the Irish Republic! That's where they come from! Where do the terrorists return to for sanctuary? To the Irish Republic! And yet Mrs Thatcher tells us that that Republic must have some say in our province. We say never, never, never, never!

Paisley would bellow variations of the same theme through the days of the Third Force, Ulster Resistance, 'Ulster Says No' and 'Smash Sinn Féin' campaigns. He propelled loyalist cannon fodder into the front-line time after time and washed his hands of them just as regularly until he got what he had wanted all along: himself as the prize cock crowing on the pinnacle of the unionist dung heap.

Sinn Féin went into Stormont with Paisley, despite having vowed as late as 1997 that they were committed to 'No Return to Stormont Rule'. It would take another 10 years for Sinn Féin to take the next logical step in signing up to policing. By the time it bit that bullet they had allowed the Police Service of Northern Ireland (PSNI) to settle nicely into the old ways of the RUC. Since Sinn Féin had accepted the Northern institutions as far back as 1998, it should have, in my opinion, wholeheartedly embraced the Patton Report in 1999 and endorsed the PSNI as quickly as possible, instead of prevaricating and allowing the policing controversy to drift for eight years. The 'Punch and Judy' show which Martin McGuinness appeared in with Ian Paisley, Peter Robinson and then Arlene Foster, stumbled on until Sinn Féin's base forced them to collapse the charade in 2017. The return to Stormont, engineered by British pro-consul Julian Smith and Dublin's Foreign Affairs' Minister Simon Coveney, came in 2020. At the time of writing the dumping of Arlene Foster, the arrival and swift departure of Poots and co and the rise of Jeffrey Donaldson to the DUP leadership have thrown fresh doubt on its long-term sustainability. Donaldson in his turn was to throw Stormont into crisis when in February 2022, after months of threats, he finally pulled Paul Givan out of the First Minister's role in protest at the Northern Ireland Protocol which resulted from his party's pursuit of Brexit. The DUP's nightmare was to be added to with the results of the 2022 Assembly election which saw Sinn Féin become the dominant party in Stormont – a seismic result which saw unionism reduced to a minority with a total of 37 seats in the new 90 seat Assembly, in which they refused to participate.

As far as republicans were concerned in 1985, the IRA had made clear that they were opposed to the Anglo-Irish Agreement. Sinn Féin leader Gerry Adams said it was a disaster: 'It formally recognises partition, copper fastens partition, is a disaster for the nationalist cause and this far outweighs the powerless consultative role given to Dublin.' By 1993 Gerry Adams would show much more interest in the machinations which had led to the Anglo-Irish Agreement when he conducted private talks with Michael Lillis, the first ever joint secretary of the Inter-Governmental Secretariat from 1985 to 1987. By 1993 Adams was well down the road with what would become known as the Hume-Adams initiative.

There were also other developments between 1984 and 1986. The IRA took possession of the first tranche of 120 tonnes of arms, which came into the country in four consignments delivered in June 1985, October 1985, July 1986 and September 1986. The success in importing the arms was a hugely positive development from the IRA's perspective, particularly in light of the loss of the materials which Martin Ferris and

Things are not always what they seem

his comrades had been captured with aboard the Marita Ann off the coast of Kerry in 1984. These things would all come to light in the wake of the capture of the Eksund ship in the Bay of Biscay on November 1st 1987 with the loss of another 120 tonnes of armaments.

The British and the Dublin regime got their first hint of this massive IRA operation in 1986 with the capture of three arms dumps in Counties Sligo and Roscommon on January 26th. The Gardaí captured five Volunteers and recovered 130 guns, among them 60 Kalashnikovs. It emerged that a British agent known as '3018' had been the ultimate source of the Gardaí operation. Shortly after the seizure, IRA man Frank Hegarty fled to England, where he remained for a time under British security services' protection. Hegarty had originally been dismissed from the IRA in 1982 and many questions were raised about his re-admittance into the ranks of the IRA. When the arms' seizures occurred in 1986 questions quickly multiplied. Hegarty was lured back to Ireland and on May 25th 1986 his body was found on the border at Cavan Road, Donegal, just across the border from Castlederg in County Tyrone. The IRA said Hegarty was an informer and had been responsible for the capture of arms dumps. Senior members of the Army were still raising serious questions about the Hegarty affair in the late 80s and questions are still being asked. Who let him back into the Army when he had been dismissed under a cloud of suspicion in 1982? Who promoted him to Northern Command Quarter Master? Who lured him back to his death? Was he sacrificed to protect someone else? Like so many other questions, we will probably never know the answers. All we know for certain is that agent '3018' was recruited by the FRU, that it was under the control of Brigadier James Gordon Kerr, and that agent '3018' was allowed back into the IRA by a very senior figure in the IRA's Northern Command.[48] The whys and wherefores will remain forever in the realms of speculation. However I and others were unsettled by it all.

The parting of the ways, again

The second stage to remove the long-standing Sinn Féin policy of abstentionism was mounted at the 1985 Ard Fheis. Back in 1983 the Ard Fheis had passed a motion allowing for discussion of the subject, but the ban remained enshrined in both the Sinn Féin and IRA constitutions. The intervening years had witnessed serious discussions

---

48 The Force Research Unit was a branch of British Military Intelligence established in 1982. It ran agents within the IRA and loyalist gangs and was accused of heavy involvement in collusion with loyalist murder gangs.

and an attempted tilt against the IRA leadership which had come to nothing. In 1985, a motion from the Dublin Chomhairle Limistéir asked that the Ard Fheis look at 'abstentionism as a tactic and not a principle'. Seán Crowe from Dublin, who would later become a TD, along with Tom Hartley and Danny Morrison from Belfast, spoke in favour of the motion. The Sinn Féin president remained silent and the Ard Comhairle declined to back the motion. The motion was defeated by 181 votes to 161. 342 delegates had attended the Ard Fheis, representing Sinn Féin's 171 cumainn. The waters had been tested, the arithmetic assessed. The following year the coup-de-grace was delivered to abstentionism at the Ard Fheis, which was held at the beginning of November. Motion 162 sought three substantive changes to the Sinn Féin constitution, which would require a two-thirds majority. The substance of the motion read:

> That this Ard Fheis drops its abstentionist attitude to Leinster House. Successful Sinn Féin parliamentary candidates in 26-County elections:
> a) shall attend Leinster House as directed by the Ard Chomhairle.
> b) shall not draw their salaries for personal use. (Parliamentary representatives shall be paid a Sinn Féin organiser's subsidy and the Leinster House salary shall be divided at the direction of the Ard Chomhairle to defray national and constituency expenses.)

The contentious motion was debated over November 1st and 2nd. There were 590 delegates in attendance, representing 295 Sinn Féin cumainn, a rise of 124 cumainn on the previous year. Sinn Féin made it clear in the course of debate that the IRA had recently held an Army Convention which had removed the ban on candidates taking seats if elected to Leinster House. A small number of Volunteers had left the IRA over the decision. Sinn Féin Vice-President, Martin McGuinness spoke in favour of Motion 162 saying:

> I can give a commitment on behalf of the leadership that we have absolutely no intention of going to Westminster or Stormont. Successful electoral strategy in the Six Counties is testament enough of that government's inability to overcome the resistance of a new generation of IRA freedom fighters supported on equal terms by articulate and committed Sinn Féin freedom fighters. It will be a sad day for this movement that the record of the present generation of republican soldiers and Sinn Féin activists needed to be defended on this platform. Sadly, the inference that the removal of abstentionism would lead to the demise of military opposition to British rule has indeed called into question the commitment of the IRA to pursue the struggle to a successful conclusion. I reject any such suggestion, and I reject the notion that entering Leinster House would mean an end to Sinn Féin's unapologetic support for the right of Irish people to oppose

in arms the British forces of occupation. That, my friends, is a principle which a minority in this hall might doubt, but which I believe all our opponents clearly understand. Our position is clear and it will never, never, never change. The war against British rule must continue until freedom is achieved.

I was standing at the rear of the hall during the debates, listening intently to all that was said and was convinced that the stance of the leadership was healthy and correct and that those representing that position to delegates were honest and sincere in what they said at the time. Perhaps they were. I would change my mind over time in relation to some of them. My change of mind came alongside a diminution in my confidence in certain figures. During these debates I happened to be standing beside the then IRA Quarter Master General. He has long since died. It was clear that opposition to the removal of abstentionism was being led by the former Sinn Féin President, Ruairí Ó Bradaigh, and Dáithí Ó Conaill, former Vice-President of Sinn Féin. Both were former Chiefs-of-Staff of the IRA. I had great respect for both, although I didn't agree with them on this question.

The Sinn Féin leadership knew that the opposition had already booked space in a hotel in Chapelizod in anticipation of losing the vote on Motion 162. When Ó Brádaigh stood to speak to delegates, a smiling Gerry Adams rose half way out of his seat behind the podium. He tapped Ruairí on the shoulder and shook his hand. Adams then clapped him on the shoulder and stood applauding along with other delegates. It was obvious that Ó Bradaigh was tense and emotional. He spoke briefly in Irish saying, 'Croitheann mise lámh le gach éinne, I shake hands with everyone and at every time, not just in front of the media.' In an oration full of passion, Ó Bradaigh told delegates he was opposing Motion 162. He said that Motion 162 and the Sinn Féin constitution couldn't live in the same house. He went on:

> I want to ask the Ard-Fheis this: where are our revolutionary socialists? How do you expect to build a democratic socialist republic out of Leinster House? How can serious social change come out of Leinster House? How can the fundamental change in property relations come out of Leinster House? No way can it do that. What we are asked to do today is to tip the scales that little bit in favour of parliamentary, constitutional and reformist action. What about Stormont and Westminster? If you raise that, you'll be told they're not an issue. But naturally people want to know what's down the road. Are they in doubt or are they also for consideration in due course? People want to know and they want to know now, and they have not been told.

Motion 162 was passed by a majority of 429 against 161. At the following Ard Fheis the number of delegates fell from 590, present at the historic vote on abstentionism, to 340, a massive fall of 250 in the space of a year. Ruairí Ó Brádaigh led a group from the Ard Fheis in protest. They headed to Chapelizod and then on to the City West Hotel in Dublin where they announced the formation of Republican Sinn Féin. I was concerned as I watched delegates from Limerick, Cork and Kerry leave in significant numbers. I turned to my friend and pointed this out: 'There are a few leaving alright,' he said, 'but I haven't seen as much as a single arms dump go past yet.' Unfortunately, as always, there were enough people on both sides of the political division who would end up with less respect for their former comrades than they had for the common enemy.

At a personal level I fell out with none of my former comrades over political differences. I think it is a disaster when former comrades start insulting, denigrating and attacking people's integrity. Worse still are those minority who spread rumours or indicate with 'a nod to the wise' that a former comrade is in some way suspect. I believe that people do what they think to be right and we should all be mature enough to respect the integrity of differing political positions. I feel sorry for those former Republican activists consumed with corrosive anger against those who they fought side by side with for years. As Mark Twain said, 'Anger is an acid which causes much more damage to the vessel which contains it than it ever does to the objects upon which it is poured.' Following the splits from 1994 and 1997 and beyond, it is extremely difficult for anyone to recite, let alone understand the alphabet soup of republican groups who each claim sole legitimacy as regards orthodoxy. It is a tragedy; as Karl Marx said, 'History repeats itself first as tragedy and then as farce.'

By the end of 1985 I was working at national level. It was to be a busy time. Before I moved from local activity I was to be engaged in one last undertaking. I was working through the night with an old and trusted comrade who has since died. He parted ways with the Movement following the second IRA ceasefire in 1997. We both started our overnight stint of work on Sunday September 15th at around lunch time. Around breakfast time on the following morning we headed to a flat, showered, changed clothes and sat down to eat a sandwich and drink a cup of tea. We were about to head home when we learned of significantly increased British Army and RUC activity in the area. We decided to wait for a time. Around lunchtime a huge contingent of armoured vehicles flooded the immediate vicinity of the flats complex in which we were sitting. Behind the flats was a building housing a day centre for people with special needs. I slipped out the back of the flats and asked the driver of the centre's bus when he would be leaving. I told him he would have two extra passengers. At 3 p.m., with myself and my comrade on board, the bus left and passed, without incident, through the British soldiers and lines of RUC men who had swamped the area. I reached the house which I had departed from the previous day and was told that three IRA Volunteers had been captured with a huge bomb in Andersontown. It turned out that the captured men were 'Big Jim' Crane from Ballymurphy, 'Monty' Montgomery from North Belfast and my brother Rab. They all got 20 years in prison. I was only to see Rab over the next 10 years on the occasional visit.

Family affairs

My daughter Orliath arrived less than a year after I began working nationally. I was as busy as I'd ever been. Orliath brought a lot of joy to our lives. Both myself and Chrissie are so proud of her. She was a very settled, happy and loving child. We were lucky to have secured a house at the bottom of Chrissie's mother's street. Many people didn't have the luxury of a house. Ours was a small two bedroom affair which sat right next to the Henry Taggart British Army barracks, the most frequently attacked military installation in the North. We may have had a house but financially we were poor. Sometimes we didn't have enough money to buy dinner beyond beans and toast, but we were happy. My father babysat for us only the once. It was June 11th 1987 and we were both busy the entire day due to the holding of a Westminster election. A soldier was shot and seriously wounded in our front garden. When we returned home my father said: 'The other cowards in his patrol ran off and left him screaming in his own blood.' Neighbours had to cover the wounded man with a blanket and his colleagues only returned with the arrival of an ambulance.

Chrissie was the breadwinner due to my full time activism. We lived on the poverty line but we weren't any exception. The vast majority in West Belfast were in the same circumstances. By the beginning of 1987 Chrissie was again pregnant but disaster was to strike us when she lost the baby in June of that year. I knew that miscarriage was much more grievous for women. I keenly felt the loss and knew that Chrissie was obviously beside herself with grief. But she was always a strong woman and carried her burden with dignity. We found out that Chrissie was pregnant again just before Christmas 1987. Our second child, a boy, arrived on July 7th 1988. We christened him Conchuir and he brought us as much joy and pleasure as Orliath had. Orliath had been gentle as a lamb and she still is an easygoing, gentle adult. Conchuir was anything but gentle. Like his namesake, Conchuir MacNessa, he was as strong as a bull and as fierce as a hound.[49] Both children shared one trait from an early age, they couldn't stand injustice. As they grew up to be adults they despised hypocrisy and wouldn't tolerate sanctimony, either in their personal or later their working lives. I read to them at every opportunity and made sure that they developed a love for the outdoors and nature. I made it my business to take them walking on the Black Mountain from their earliest days, carrying them until they could make their own way. I maintained these habits with all my children. I also ensured they could swim by putting them into the swimming pool from the age of six months. Our weekends, when I was available, were spent swimming, walking and taking day trips.

Conchuir was to have an awful accident in 1993. Himself and Orliath were playing in a hay barn while I was talking to the owner of the farm. They had accidentally disturbed a wheaten terrier, which was tethered to a chain and hidden behind bails of hay. The dog grabbed Conchuir by the head. Orliath began shouting and it was only with extreme effort that we managed to prise the terrier off the child. I rushed him to Magherafelt Hospital where he had to have multiple stitches inserted in his head wounds. He was extremely lucky not to have suffered worse damage. The dog had initially gone for his face but he was protected by his glasses.

By the time our third child, Eimear, arrived in 1991 we had moved to a three bedroom house in Moyard. The area had the reputation of being a rough spot but I have to say that we were blessed with great neighbours. Eimear was a great child and from an early age we knew she was very intelligent and capable, despite the fact that she never spoke until she was three. Apparently her two older siblings were talking for her and she was able to get exactly what she wanted by relying on them. She was a very inquisitive child and had a great interest in medicine and science. I wasn't in the least surprised when

---

49 The fabled king of Ulster and uncle of Cuchulainn.

she chose a degree in medicine and biomedical science, instead of the youth work degrees pursued by Orliath and Conchuir.

Things were extremely difficult as regards security when the kids were growing up. We had to install steel security gates in the house along with reinforced drop-bars on the doors. The threat of assassination by loyalists was a constant danger for all active republicans. I hated the security as it made our home feel like a prison. I also resented having to check constantly below my car for booby-trap bombs. It came with the territory and we got used to it after a fashion.

In 1994 we moved house for the last time, to Springhill. The area was much more difficult for loyalists to penetrate. It is often referred to as the 33rd County of Ireland. We decided our days of steel gates and heavy security were over. By 1997 we were blessed with a fourth child. Fionnghuala turned out to be a complete tomboy. She was a wild child and an absolute pleasure. She had a very caring nature from her earliest days and always identified with children who she felt to be disadvantaged. I wasn't in the least surprised when she chose to do a teaching degree in Irish. We are as proud of Fionnghuala as we are of the other three. She takes great delight in life and is blessed with a great sense of fun. The millennium brought us our last child, Tiarnán. He is a very loving child and has a wonderful sense of humour. Like his brother Conchuir he is a keen sportsman. He managed to win medals in football and hurling at county and provincial level but hasn't as yet bagged an All-Ireland medal like Conchuir, who holds an All-Ireland Under-16 hurling medal. The hurling and the competition keep them sharp. Tiarnán's birth was a nightmare. Chrissie had a last minute emergency section and both she and Tiarnán were lucky to come through. Tiarnán, despite his rocky start, is today as fit as a fiddle and enjoys robust health. Now the grandchildren have started appearing. Eimear and Tony gave us Séadhna, Eithne and Dualta. Orliath and Phil gave us Luisne and Caragh. I am immensely proud that they have all, like their parents, been raised Irish speakers.

Chrissie and her sisters – Anne Marie, Jeanette and Bernadette – are extremely close with each other. We get to spend most time with Anne Marie as she lives quite close to us. Jeanette lives in south Armagh and Bernadette in America. I'm very fond of them all. They are all good company and enjoy a laugh.

My children gave me a different perspective on life. They brought home to me the preciousness of life. When I think of them, and of all that they have brought to our lives, I can't help but feel an overwhelming sadness for those who have lost children or close family members as a result of the conflict which ravaged our country and left so many bereaved. Anyone who doesn't feel empathy for the grief and loss of families must be lacking something in their own humanity. I regret that Fionnghuala and Tiarnán never got the chance to meet my parents, who died before they were born.

A people's victory – a peoples' celebration

In mid-1988 with horrors occurring all around us and with the people of West Belfast being savagely attacked and vilified by the establishment's running dogs in the gutter press, it was decided to launch Féile an Phobail, the People's Festival. There was a crying need for just such an initiative in that grim year of 1988. Things were dire throughout the North but Belfast was to bear the brunt. There had of course been festivals in West Belfast over many years but the launch of Féile an Phobail was something new. I was more than willing to lend a hand when asked to do so by Jimmy 'Teapot' McMullan.

Between January and the festival week in August that year 66 people had lost their lives in the conflict. The IRA had killed 32 members of the Crown forces. They had also shot two civilians, William Hassard (59) and Frederick Love (64), accusing them of being 'collaborators who were assisting the building programme of the British Army', as well as a UVF gunman Robert Seymour (35), who they accused of 'waging war on the innocent Catholic population'. 17 innocent Catholic civilians had lost their lives. Pro-British proxy death squads murdered 15 of them and two, Elizabeth Hamill (60) and Eamon Gilroy (24), died in an IRA bombing on the Falls Road which was aimed at a British Army patrol.

The IRA also killed three Protestant civilians. Married couple Robin and Maureen Hanna and their young son David were killed when their Shogun Jeep was destroyed in an IRA landmine explosion in the mistaken belief that it carried High Court judge Malachy Higgins. Nine IRA Volunteers also lost their lives, among them my old friend Hugh Hehir, who was killed by the Free State Special Branch. Another, whom I had known in prison, was Anthony McKernan, executed for informing. I knew seven of the nine Volunteers and had spent time in prison with four of them. One of them, Kevy McCracken, had been my last cell mate before my release. I felt Kevy's loss very keenly.

I had been with Kevy in my house on Sunday March 13th and had arranged to meet with him the following Thursday on my return from Dublin, where we were going to bring home the bodies of the three IRA Volunteers killed by the SAS in Gibraltar.

Kevy was shot dead by British soldiers near the home of Volunteer Seán Savage as the bodies of the Gibraltar Three were on their way home. Witnesses to the shooting said that Kevy had been shot in the back and then beaten on the ground by soldiers who prevented an ambulance reaching him until he passed away. 1988 was a dark year and one in which the British media would vilify West Belfast's people as 'the terrorist community' and brand people as 'savages'.

Féile an Phobail was an attempt to show the positive energy and creativity of the community and to replace the annual August bonfires, which were nothing more than an excuse for the British Army and RUC to unleash attacks on young people. Féile an Phobail was shining a light in the darkness which surrounded us. Féile provided a platform for a whole array of local talent and was generously supported by many artists who deserve high praise for going against the tide and coming to celebrate our community. From the outside Féile prided itself on being an open house which welcomed people from all backgrounds. It provided a platform for those who diametrically opposed republicans and offered a platform for debate and discussion. I was part of the debates' sub-committee, and involved in the Poc Fada committee which was begun by Ger Rogan and Éamonn Mór Ó Faogáin (RIP) to raise money for Irish Medium schools. I also co-hosted the Féile Radio morning review of the newspapers and media with my friend Danny Morrison, who was one of the stalwarts of Féile's impressive literary programme. Féile Radio was an important initiative which kept the community updated under the very capable hands of Mart Holland. Mart was one of the funniest, most creative and most positive people you could hope to meet.

Féile can't be mentioned without reference to Springhill. It was nothing more than a piece of waste ground containing a stage and surrounded by a fence erected by Hector Heath, Dessy Cush, Ginger McCoubrey, Blue Kelly and the entire Springhill crew. It was the beating heart of the Féile. Crowds were packed in for some of the best music gigs seen in West Belfast. I'll never forget the night of Shane McGowan's visit. That night his carry-out arrived at our house while Pat 'Beag' McGeown, Brendan 'The Dark' Hughes and Paddy

Molloy searched for the missing Shane at Aldergrove Airport. Shane arrived several hours later to join his carry-out in our kitchen. Shane was a hero to my Orliath, who couldn't wait to meet him. As they say, however, you should never meet your heroes. Orliath met a very drunk Shane in our kitchen and never quiet recovered from the disappointment. West Belfast people always knew that idols had feet of clay but it was the clay between the toes of Shane's bare feet that put paid to Orlaith's illusions.

I remained involved with Féile an Phobail until shortly after the arrival of a new director, Caitriona Ruane.

Chapter 7

'Fere libenter homines id quod volunt credunt'

'Men readily believe what they want to believe.' Gaius Julius Caesar
(100–44 BCE)

The politics of Irish Freedom

By 1986 I was fulfilling a new role at national level. I, along with other comrades, was making a strong argument for an agreed, cohesive ideology which could be drafted and disseminated throughout the Movement. It appeared to me that the Movement was still little more than a broad alliance which was agreed on one vague objective: a united Ireland. This ideological imprecision had been a perennial problem for republicans. Irish history was awash with examples of the tensions between nationalist militarists and revolutionary socialists, often co-existing under one organisational banner. James Connolly had tried to bridge the tensions with his observation that: 'The cause of labour is the cause of Ireland, and the cause of Ireland is the cause of labour. They cannot be dissevered.' The ideological tensions were never satisfactorily addressed. Connolly, the most forthright socialist thinker of his generation, led his Irish Citizen Army (ICA) out with the nationalist forces of the Irish Volunteers and the Irish Republican Brotherhood on Easter Week 1916.

The proposals I was making were generally accepted. This led to myself, a man from Donegal, a woman from Dublin and another woman from Kildare being asked to draft and circulate a series of core lectures which could be disseminated throughout the Movement. These were published as the 'Republican Lecture Series' and they were put out in the name of Sinn Féin. These lectures would be used side by side with the updated and revised IRA training manual, 'The Green Book'.[50] The lecture series was made compulsory for every member of the Movement. I have to say that this wasn't fully endorsed by all members of the Army, some of whom had a deep, and for me confusing, mistrust of politics. The mantra 'I'm a soldier not a politician' was heard with depressing regularity. It was a constant watching brief to ensure that these lectures were being delivered alongside all the other necessary training. The years from 1986 (when Sinn Féin ended abstentionism) to 1988 were important ones for the development of policy and strategy. At the end of November 1986, immediately following the momentous Ard Fheis decision, Gerry Adams published his book *The Politics of Irish Freedom*. He also entered into correspondence with British Secretary of State Tom King. The contact was intermittent for most of 1986 and 1987. In October 1988 three people were accused and later acquitted on appeal for an alleged conspiracy to kill Tom King near his home in Wiltshire.

A major conference was also held in the Carrigart Hotel in Donegal, attended by key figures from across the Movement and the island. Policy and strategy, as well as the current state of the Movement, were discussed. There were key plenary sessions and a series of focussed workshops. As a result of this conference the Sinn Féin publicity department was set to work on producing a discussion document entitled *A Scenario for Peace*. This document was first published and circulated in May 1987. Later it was redrafted in light of discussions and with some changes it was republished in November 1989. The discussion document emphasised three main points: (1) that the document wasn't a definitive statement of Republican Movement policy but a discussion document; (2) that it was imperative that the British government announce its intention to withdraw from the north of Ireland within the life of one parliament and (3) that a constitutional conference be convened in the context of a cessation of hostilities by all sides. The document was clearly preparing the ground for possible talks. A committee was formed at national leadership level to co-ordinate

---

50 The Green Book was first published in 1956 with a second updated version being produced in 1977. It was again updated and revised with new additions in the mid-1980s. It has since been published by a number of sources online and was included as an index in Martin Dillon's 1991 book *The Dirty War*.

this new phase of struggle. Representatives of the Movement were in contact with senior officials from the Dublin government and there was tentative contact with British officials. By 1990 there was direct contact with British officials with the approval of Margaret Thatcher. One of the key public faces of these policy initiatives was Sinn Féin Director of Publicity Danny Morrison. Danny was to be arrested in a house in Lenadoon along with Anto Murray and Gerard Hodgins, a former hunger striker. Five others were also arrested in the same raid. The British agent Sandy Lynch was allegedly being held captive in the house. It was clear also that at least one other British agent was in the house. A number of serious questions were raised about the affair and two IRA men were stood down as part of the fall out. One of them, Freddie Scapaticci, the alleged head of the IRA's Internal Security unit, was dismissed and remained for a time in the South. He is currently in protective custody in England and faces investigation over his alleged role in a number of killings. All seven of those arrested were given long terms of imprisonment. Danny Morrison wasn't released until 1995. In the Appeal Court in 2009 all had their convictions overturned. The court quashed the convictions, stating that if the hearing was to proceed, the court would have to grant the publication of secret documents, which hadn't been furnished to defence teams in 1990. In 2016 the eight who were acquitted shared damages of £1.6m.

As 1987 drew to a close an invitation, which had come through Father Alec Reid of Clonard Monastery in Belfast, led to talks taking place for the first time between delegations from Sinn Féin and the SDLP. This invitation came after a series of exchanges between the Republican Movement and Taoiseach Charles Haughey. Haughey had requested that the point of contact should be through the SDLP leader John Hume, although Haughey would remain within the circle of knowledge. The Sinn Féin/SDLP talks lasted between January and September of 1988. The objective of the talks was to see if it was possible to arrive at an agreed nationalist strategy to achieve justice and peace in Ireland. Sinn Féin was represented by Gerry Adams, Martin McGuinness, Danny Morrison, Tom Hartley, Mitchel McLaughlin and Seán McManus, whose son Joe died on IRA active service on February 6th 1992 at 21 years-of-age. I had known Joe since he was a child. His loss was a heavy blow to Seán and his wife Helen and to their surviving son Chris. The SDLP delegation included John Hume, Seamus Mallon, Eddie McGrady and Denis Haughey. Following the conclusion of the talks Sinn Féin released the papers which both sides had exchanged. Sinn Féin emphasised that the fundamental disagreement between the two parties was on the question of British interests and British policy in Ireland. Sinn Féin contended that this was the principal problem and the SDLP insisted that it wasn't. The Sinn Féin delegation also highlighted the 'unionist veto' on reunification and democratic change, which had been given to them and was underwritten by the British government. Although the talks failed, senior members of the Republican Movement knew that Hume and Adams were continuing their engagement in private. It was clear that Hume didn't share this information with any of the other key figures in his own party. Mallon and McGrady in particular were known to be vehemently opposed to any contact with Sinn Féin.

In December 1988 the Sinn Féin leader published his book *A Pathway to Peace* which basically reiterated what had been said in the Sinn Féin submissions to the SDLP. One point which was given particular attention was the Sinn Féin contention that it was unreasonable of the SDLP to hold that Irish self-determination should be dependent on unionist consent. Sinn Féin made it clear that it was the party's position that there could be no internal settlement. It was a point stressed repeatedly by Gerry Adams. Sinn Féin also stated that it was 'completely opposed to a power-sharing arrangement at Stormont. We say clearly that there can be no internal, partitionist settlement. Stormont cannot be a stepping stone towards unity in Ireland.' That's how things were left publicly in 1988. The talks had failed and the positions of both parties and their leaders were clear, at least in public.

By 1990 I was, as part of my role at national level, sitting on a body whose task it was to oversee and have stewardship of Movement policy, strategy and activity. I was also forming my own analysis of all that was being said publicly and internally. I was growing uncomfortable with the way the process of change was gathering pace without the bulk of the Movement being kept inside the loop. I was, however, bound by silence and collegiate responsibility. The armed struggle continued apace. In the years from 1988 until 1990, a major bombing and shooting campaign was in full operation in England whilst armed actions continued without any reduction in the Six Counties. During May and June of 1990 the IRA bombed three British Army barracks in England, killing two British soldiers and injuring 30 others. The IRA also shot dead a British soldier and wounded two others in Staffordshire. On June 25th a bomb exploded at the Carlton Club, the exclusive reserve of the Tory Party establishment.

The explosion injured 21 people. Donald Kaberry, Baron Kaberry of Adel, later died from his injuries. Following the attack the IRA said:

> Like Brighton in 1984, the IRA has brought the war directly to those who keep the British Army on the streets and in the fields of Ireland. While such occupation continues, and the nationalist people face daily oppression, the policy makers and their military arm will not be safe.

On July 20th the IRA detonated a bomb at the London Stock Exchange causing considerable damage. No injuries occurred as the British authorities acted promptly on the IRA warning. In separate incidents in the Six Counties in June the IRA targeted the British Army in two devastating attacks at Lisburn in County Antrim and at Ballygawley in County Tyrone. 14 British soldiers lost their lives and a further 22 were injured in those attacks. 1988 also saw the British secret services facilitate the importation of the biggest cache of weapons ever to have reached their loyalist proxy gangs. The British agent Brian Nelson had previously been placed into the heart of the UDA, where he was directed and controlled by the Force Research Unit (FRU), to ensure that loyalists were able to kill with more efficiency.[51] In that bloody year loyalists killed 20 people. Three of those killed were members of loyalist organisations and one an off-duty British soldier, mistaken for a Catholic. The IRA killed 20 members of the British Army, two of whom were killed in Germany in a new theatre of operations. The IRA also killed seven members of the RUC and four civilians who they accused of being 'collaborators engaged in building and maintenance work for the Crown Forces'. In addition the Movement killed eight innocent civilians. In October the IRA killed a member of the prison regime. Brian Armour (48), known to prisoners as 'The Red Rat', was accused of being one of the main torturers of naked prisoners in the H-Blocks. The IRA also lost three of its members to accidental explosions and six to undercover British operations in Gibraltar and at Loughmacrory in County Tyrone during that period. In all the British Army killed 10 people in 1988. One of those killed, Aidan McAnespie (24), was murdered on his way home from a GAA

---

51 Brian Nelson was a member of the British Army regiment the Black Watch and a member of the UDA in the early 1970s. He was sentenced to seven years for the kidnap and torture of Catholic man Gerald Higgins. Although Higgins died within weeks of his ordeal, Nelson was never charged in relation to his death. Nelson fled to Germany on his release. In 1985 he was recruited by the Force Research Unit and placed as the chief intelligence officer in the UDA. Here he was directed to target people the British wanted removed and was supplied with updated British and RUC intelligence files and a complete data base on suspected republicans.

match at Aughnacloy on the Tyrone/Monaghan border. By year's end 104 families were left mourning their grievous loss.

When they murder Civil Rights Lawyers there are no Civil Rights

In total 76 people lost their lives during 1989. This included civilians, members of the Crown Forces and members of the IRA. One killing stood out among the slaughter. On January 17th in the British parliament Conservative minister, Douglas Hogg, levelled serious accusations against solicitors who he claimed were 'unduly sympathetic to the cause of the IRA'. Hogg made those allegations based on information given to him by the RUC. The year had only begun when human rights lawyer Pat Finucane was murdered on February 12th. In the six weeks before Pat Finucane's murder seven other people had been killed. One of the dead was a friend of mine, Ian Catney. Ian was gunned down by the UVF at his mother's shop in Smithfield on January 18th. Less than three weeks later the UVF murdered another innocent Catholic, Anthony Fusco, as he made his way to work in Smithfield. Hogg's inflammatory accusations had lit the touch paper and on February 12th Pat Finucane was gunned down in front of his family as they sat down to their Sunday lunch in their Fortwilliam home. Pat's wife Geraldine was also injured in the hail of bullets, which saw a gunman pump 14 rounds into the solicitor. Loyalists in the direct employment of the British security services were involved in every aspect of the murder from planning, supplying intelligence and weapons to the actual killing. Pat Finucane's murder and that of another solicitor, Rosemary Nelson, on March 15th 1999, were the most direct attacks by the British state on human rights protection in the North.

The murders were the most significant examples of state collusion with loyalist killers, many of whom were paid agents of British Military Intelligence and the RUC Special Branch. By 2011, British Prime Minister, David Cameron, was finally forced to apologise for state collusion in the murder of Pat Finucane. However Cameron fell short of allowing an independent public inquiry into the killing. At the time of writing this remains the British position. Another headline-grabbing attack came on March 20th when the IRA's South Armagh Brigade ambushed and killed two senior RUC men at Edenappa, near Jonesborough. Chief Superintendent Harry Breen and Superintendent Bob Buchanan were returning from a meeting with Gardaí in Dundalk when they were intercepted by an IRA Active Service Unit. Another RUC Superintendent, Alwyn Harris, died when the IRA targeted him

'Fere libenter homines id quod volunt credunt'

with an under-car booby trap. Harris' son Drew was himself to rise through the ranks of the RUC and was a key go-between in British counter-insurgency and intelligence. Incredibly, he was appointed Commissioner of the Garda Síochána in September 2018. It was a move which shocked many and was akin to the Palestinian Authority appointing a former Zionist Mossad agent to the most important policing post in the West Bank. Attacks by the IRA continued in England with the bombing of a British barracks in Deal, County Kent, on September 22nd, which killed 11 Royal Marines and injured 22 others.

Sinn Féin suffered an electoral setback in the Local Government elections on May 17th when they lost 16 council seats. I was managing the electoral campaign in South Derry and Sinn Féin lost a seat to the SDLP in every electoral area apart from Moyola and Magherafelt. Sinn Féin candidates had agreed to take a new pledge of 'non-violence', introduced under the Electoral Authorities Act of 1989. Republican Sinn Féin (RSF) refused to take the oath and withdrew their 23 candidates from the race. They were not to contest any elections again until 2007. In the Assembly elections that year RSF put forward six candidates as independents to avoid registration with the Electoral Commission. They were dealt an electoral bloody nose, receiving a derisory 2,522 votes, an average 450 votes per candidate.

By 1989 myself and Chrissie had our first foreign holiday. We went to Bulgaria, which was a relatively cheap break. My sister Collette had kindly agreed to mind our two children. At the airport we met a friend of mine from Derry and his wife who were heading to the same destination. As we waited on our flight I noticed a screw from H3 some distance in front of us. I whispered in Shorty's ear, naming the screw and pointing him out. On board the plane the screw sat at the front while we sat at the rear of the plane. After take-off I mentioned to an air stewardess that we had a number of empty seats beside us and that a 'friend' of ours was at the front of the flight. I gave her his name and asked her to mention that 'Shorty' Donnelly and Jake Jackson wanted to know if he wished to sit beside us. His reaction was to glance round and then turn white in the face. On arrival in Bulgaria the screw headed straight for the police and was escorted away. I don't know if he enjoyed his holiday as much as we did ours.

The screw wasn't the only worried man behind the 'Iron Curtain' that year. A revolt had begun which would eventually sweep away the Union of Soviet Socialist Republics (USSR). It had kicked-off in Poland but before the year was out, regime after regime had toppled in the face of popular unrest. Hungary, Czechoslovakia, East Germany and Romania all fell with amazing rapidity. We all watched in shock at the peaceful fall of the Berlin Wall on November 9th. Things were very different one month later in Romania, where the regime of Nicolae and Elena Ceaușescu fell to a violent purge. It all began when the Securitate and sections of the Romanian Army attacked demonstrators in Timișoara on December 17th. By December 21 the world watched Ceaușescu and his wife flee the roof of their palace on a helicopter. Both were captured on Christmas Eve in Targoviste. They faced a military court on Christmas Day. It lasted one hour and they were immediately taken out and executed in front of a firing squad in Bucharest. We all watched their demise on TV. Elena shouted and cursed her executioners while Nicolae sang 'The Internationale'.

Ceaușescu was gone and the USSR would follow shortly afterwards. The beginning of the rot had come with the ignominious withdrawal of the once mighty Red Army from Afghanistan on February 15th 1989. The Red Army, which had almost single-handedly ended the scourge of Nazi fascism, with some very belated help from the British and the Americans, had fought and lost a costly 10 year war to Mujahideen, armed and trained by the Americans.[52] According to the Soviet government they had lost 13,310 soldiers and suffered 35,478 casualties. More than one million Afghans lost their lives. The CIA-trained Mujahideen were by 1986 in possession of American Stinger anti-aircraft missiles which would turn the tide of the war in their favour. The Americans would rue their anti-Soviet intrigues when the Jihadists turned on the West and humbled America with the attack on New York's Twin Towers. The American warmongers with their British lapdogs would subsequently be dragged into costly wars in Afghanistan, Iraq and Syria.

While the USSR had fallen, things were to be very different in China. Trouble began with the expulsion of Hu Yaobang from his position as General Secretary of the Chinese Communist Party. He had been leading liberal reforms but was turned against by Politburo colleagues following a series of student demonstrations. Hu resigned his position but remained on the Politburo. Things calmed down but with his death on April 15th 1989, renewed demonstrations began seeking a redress of the 'slander' against Hu Yaobang. Things deteriorated when students occupied Tienanmen Square in Beijing on April 22nd, the day of Yaobang's

---

52 A Muslim guerilla force engaged in Jihad (Holy War). A Mujahid is a warrior fighting in the cause of Allah.

funeral. Their demands were extended to include moves towards a Western-style democracy. Thousands openly challenged the authority of the state. During a visit by Mikhail Gorbachev on May 15th more than one million protesters occupied Tienanmen Square. A fierce debate was raging inside the Politburo about how to deal with the demonstrations. Yaobang's successor, Zhao Zhiyang, argued for talks with the student leaders. But he was bitterly opposed by Li Peng, premier of the People's Republic, who advised that the Red Army should be deployed to disperse the crowds. On May 3rd the die was cast when Deng Xiaoping, the chairman of the Central Advisory Commission and de facto supreme leader, sided with Li Peng. The Politburo ordered the clearing of the square. The Red Army was deployed and over two days they crushed opposition in Tienanmen Square, Shanghai and in Changsha. Students, who stood in front of oncoming tanks, were simply crushed to death. The Red Army opened fire on protesters and by May 5th it was all over. According to the Chinese authorities 241 were killed with a further 7,000 injured. Other sources placed the death toll at nearer 4,000.

Iran was to experience difficulties of a different kind with the death of Ruhollah Khomeini. Known by his official title of Ayatollah (The Enlightened one of Allah), the leader of the Iranian Revolution died on June 3rd at 87 years-of-age. His death brought two million Shia Muslim devotees onto the streets of Tehran. The scenes of zealotry, grief and hysteria got so out of hand that 10 people died and 400 were injured in crushes. If the day of the Ayatollah's death was bad, the day of the first attempt to bury Khomeini, June 11th, was worse. His coffin was making its way on a 20 mile journey to Behesht-e Zahra Cemetery with 10 million people lining the route.[53] The crowd were so zealous to see their leader that the coffin was swarmed and smashed apart. The remains were then airlifted by helicopter, with mourners hanging off the landing gear. The burial finally took place five hours later with the Ayatollah's remains encased in a steel coffin.

The wild and undignified scenes reminded me of our own difficulties in burying our republican dead in the face of gratuitous state violence. In the late 1980s we witnessed two years of desecration and sickening scenes as the RUC and British Army were ordered to prevent republicans being buried with honour. Funerals had been attacked in the past, as was the case with my neighbour Terry McDermott in 1971. However, beginning with the funeral of Larry Marley in 1987, the onslaught

---

53 'Paradise of Zahra', named after Zahra, the daughter of the Prophet Muhammad.

against republican burials began in earnest. Larry had been murdered by the UVF on April 3rd. It took three days and fierce hand-to-hand fighting with riot-clad RUC men to finally lay Larry to rest. Funerals were to be repeatedly attacked by the Crown Forces in Belfast, Derry, Tyrone and Armagh. The British abandoned this ghoulish policy at the funerals of Volunteers, Dan McCann, Mairéad Farrell and Seán Savage. Even when the RUC had withdrawn from these funerals, one of their proxy agents, UDA man Michael Stone, attacked the funerals with guns and grenades leaving three dead and up to 60 wounded.

Beginning of the endgame in Ireland

By 1990 I was responsible for all material being published in *An Phoblacht*, the national weekly newspaper of the Movement. I was Northern editor and also had other duties associated with publicity. Rita O'Hare, a Belfast woman based in Dublin, was editor of the paper. I had a great fondness for Rita, a formidable woman who tolerated no nonsense. I admired her and still do. We both worked well together and would continue to do so right up until the second IRA ceasefire in 1997. Rita recently retired from her role as Sinn Féin's representative in Washington and across the USA. She is a very capable and loyal comrade and was to be a central figure in many aspects of the unfolding peace process. We often locked horns on a range of issues. However we never fell out and shared a sense of humour, which allowed us to laugh at quite serious situations. I had sole responsibility for editing and overseeing the production of the Six County input into the paper. It was an onerous job for me as I had other responsibilities. Often I would find myself in the Sinn Féin offices in Sevastopol Street in Belfast until the wee hours of the morning, cramming a week's work into one very long day. Newspaper and magazine deadlines are cruel taskmasters. I also had a young family. I could never have made the contribution I did without the selfless support of Chrissie. I would often be away from home for extended periods and I can't but admire her loyalty and effort. It was never easy.

When our newly born son Conchuir was only a few weeks old I had to go away for a week on business. Chrissie, Orliath and Conchuir accompanied me to Dublin, where they would stay in Rita O'Hare's house to await my return. As I made my way back one week later I was arrested by the Free State Special Branch in the Finglas area of Dublin. I was taken to the main holding centre at the Bridewell. Two branch-men left me at the sergeant's desk and disappeared. The sergeant questioned me, asking for name, address and other particulars. I didn't respond. He asked another Garda if he knew what the story was with me and was told I'd been brought in by Special Branch. They were sent for and the sergeant asked them what was going on. One of the branch-men disdainfully caught hold of the shoulder of my jacket by his fingertips and said: 'This boy has offended the state,' a reference to the anti-republican Offences against the State Act, which had been introduced by Fianna Fáil in 1939. He gave my details to the sergeant and told him to place me in the cells. I was in the cells for two days being interrogated for lengthy periods. During one session on the second day, a detective entered the interrogation room and told me I had a phone call. I ignored him. Eventually he wheeled in a telephone, similar to one you would see in a hospital. He placed the receiver to my ear. It was Chrissie on the other end of the line. She asked if I was OK. I confirmed I was fine. Chrissie explained that she had managed to get the call by telling the Gardaí that she was going to tell me to answer their questions. When I got released the next day we had a good laugh at her trickery.

By 1990 the IRA had opened a direct line of communication with the British government. Talks were also taking place between the IRA and Free State officials. Within the Movement knowledge of this was limited to a small number. This included the Army Council,[54] the chairperson of the Army Executive[55] and a small committee under the direction of the Chief-of-Staff, the Adjutant General and the Officer Commanding the Northern Command.[56] Others at a senior level were later briefed on the process in 1992. By 1993 all those at a national leadership level were made aware of the dialogue.

The upgrade in weaponry and ordnance at the Army's disposal at that point meant the IRA was able to bring down British Army helicopters. This happened at Clogher in County Tyrone in February of that year and the following month the IRA used a Barrett M80 sniper rifle for the first time. The Army was active across the Six Counties, in England and on continental Europe. There were more standing battles with British troops. Semtex explosives had also boosted the IRA's capabilities with engineers in a position to manufacture bombs of up to 8,000lbs. One such bomb, the biggest ever deployed by the IRA, narrowly failed to reach its target, a British border fortification at Annaghmartin near

---

54 The seven-person ruling body of the IRA.
55 The twelve-person constitutional watchdog of the IRA.
56 An IRA command structure established in the late 1970s, covering the nine county province of Ulster plus Counties Louth, Sligo and Leitrim.

Roslea in County Fermanagh. The tractor carrying it became bogged down in soft ground in a field close to the intended target. Other attacks on border fortifications were much more successful and claimed significant enemy casualties. In one such attack at Derryadd in south Fermanagh in December 1989 the IRA deployed flame-throwers when armed units overran the British position just north of Roslea. Volunteers in an armoured lorry using heavy machine guns and grenade launchers killed two British soldiers and wounded two others before placing a van bomb inside the base and withdrawing. The bomb failed to fully explode, sparing the lives of the other troops trapped inside the base.

Ian Gow, a British politician and close friend of Margaret Thatcher, was assassinated by the IRA in July 1990. Gow, who had been a central figure in Thatcher's regime, died when a booby-trap bomb exploded under his car outside his home in East Sussex. His demise was a personal blow to Thatcher. Gow was the second figure close to Thatcher to be assassinated. Airey Neave had died in an INLA booby-trap bombing near the British Houses of Parliament as Thatcher was coming to power in 1979. In other developments in 1990 the British Secretary of State Peter Brooke made a number of significant statements. On November 3rd Brooke stated publicly that a military victory over the IRA wasn't possible and that talks could commence with republicans, if 'violence' was to end. On November 9th he stated that Britain had no 'selfish, strategic, or economic interest' to keep them in Ireland and should it be the will of the people the British government would legislate for a united Ireland. Brooke ended his statement by saying: 'It is not the aspiration to a sovereign, united Ireland against which we set our face, but its violent expression.' Many in the media and in Sinn Féin left out the comma which the British had inserted between 'selfish' and 'strategic'. British officials would draw attention to this mistake in January 1994.

At the behest of Michael Oatley, the main British contact, a three hour long meeting was held in October 1990 with IRA negotiators. During the course of the meeting Oatley gave notice of Brooke's impending speeches. Copies of Brooke's speeches were forwarded to the IRA leadership. On October 24th, in a series of coordinated attacks, the IRA forced civilians working for the British Army to ferry bombs into British bases. The targets were the border installations at Cloghoge in South Armagh, Coshquin in Derry and Lisanally barracks in Omagh, County Tyrone. One of those, accused by the IRA of being a collaborator, was Patsy Gillespie (42), who died along with seven British soldiers:

Stephen Burrows (30), Paul Worrall (23), Vincent Scott (21), Cyril Smith (21), Stephen Beacham (20) and David Sweeney (19). Twenty other British soldiers were injured. I believed the style of attack was a tactical mistake. The British press was gifted a propaganda bonanza. I wasn't, however, going to be taking any lectures on morality from British leaders, who were at the same time dancing to George H Bush's tune in the dropping of huge quantities of bombs on Iraqi civilians. The bile being spewed by the British gutter press was also not going to cut any ice with me or with other republicans. Like every other member of the Republican Movement I shared collective responsibility for all IRA actions but, unlike the British and their unionist allies, I was prepared to accept and shoulder that responsibility. Unionists and their British masters, on the other hand, were quick to avoid any culpability for the actions of their forces and were more than happy to publicly wash their hands of any responsibility for the atrocities of loyalist proxy killers.

The British had other difficulties to contend with in relation to their position in the European Union. Tensions within the Tory Party over Europe led to the ousting of Margaret Thatcher, who had been in power for 11 and a half years. Thatcher fought to the bitter end to retain power but was forced to face reality on November 28th when she yielded to unrelenting pressure and gave her blessing to John Major as her preferred successor. Thatcher, in my opinion, had been the most repugnant British leader since Oliver Cromwell. She destroyed and divided British society and crushed so many of her own people. Her malign policies caused untold suffering in Ireland. She was a bigoted and ruthless right-wing ideologue, who coined the mantra 'greed is good'. She was also personally responsible for the slaughter of 323 young naval cadets aboard the Argentine ship the General Belgrano, torpedoed as it sailed outside the self-declared British exclusion zone around the Malvinas Islands. In Ireland, and among many sections of the international community, Thatcher would always be remembered for her role in the deaths of 10 men on hunger strike in 1981 and for the cold-blooded murder of women and children with plastic bullets.

Regardless of Thatcher's departure, there was no let-up in IRA attacks in the Six Counties or in England. Thursday February 7th witnessed an audacious IRA attack on the British cabinet, which had gathered to discuss the Iraq war. An IRA active service unit positioned a van containing three mortar bombs at the corner of Whitehall and Horse Guards' Avenue. The mortars were launched shortly after 10 a.m.

One struck a tree in the back garden of 10 Downing Street, just yards from the room where John Major and his cabinet were forced to dive under tables to take cover. The Tory elite had a very narrow escape. The IRA said: 'Let the British government understand that while nationalist people in the Six Counties are forced to live under British rule, the British cabinet will be forced to meet in bunkers.' Speaking in the aftermath of the attack, Peter Gurney, head of the Ordnance and Anti-Terrorist Branch of the British military said:

> It was a remarkably good aim, if you consider that the bomb was fired 250 meters across Whitehall with no direct line of sight. Technically it was quite brilliant and I'm sure that many, many army crews, if given a similar task, would be very glad to drop a bomb that close. You've got to park the launch vehicle in an area that is guarded by armed men and you've got less than a minute to do it. I was very, very surprised at how good it was. If the angle of fire had been moved about five or ten degrees, then those bombs would actually have impacted on Number 10.

The British did not make contact again with the IRA until April 1991, when they informed the republican leadership of the intention of the Combined Loyalist Military Command[57] to call a ceasefire for the duration of talks which had been announced at a meeting of the British/Irish Inter-Governmental Conference in Belfast on March 26th. The loyalist ceasefire lasted until July 3rd. However during this period, on May 25th, the UDA crossed the border to murder Sinn Féin councillor Eddie Fullerton (56) in his home at Buncrana in County Donegal. Shortly after his killing an RUC file, with all Eddie's personal details, was found in possession of the UDA in Derry. The Brooke/Mayhew talks, as they became known, would last until November 1992 when they finally ran out of steam. Sinn Féin had been excluded from 'all-party talks' which laid the framework for all future negotiations. This was to be known as the three-stranded approach which addressed (1) internal matters in the North (2) North/South matters and (3) East/West and inter-governmental issues.

The IRA's armed struggle continued unabated. However on November 15th tragedy struck when a bomb exploded prematurely when it was being planted on a British military transporter at St Albans near London. Volunteers Patricia Black (18) and Frankie Ryan (26) were killed. I had to accompany my friend, Pádraig Ó Maolchraoibhe, to the home of Frankie's mother, Margaret Ryan, to inform her of his death. This was always one

---

57 An umbrella grouping of the UDA, the UVF and the UVF-linked Red Hand Commando.

of the saddest duties any republican had to perform. Unfortunately I had to perform it on more occasions than I care to remember. There is nothing as heart-breaking as having to break the news to relatives that a mother, father, sister or brother has lost their life. The emotion, raw grief, shock, suffering and pain stays with you. During 1991 representatives from all sides had to perform this onerous task 97 times, informing IRA, RUC, British Army and civilian families that they were there to deliver the worst possible news. Tears and pain know no allegiance. Everyone's blood runs red and there is no hierarchy in grief and loss.

A new primary contact between the IRA and the British was appointed by the Major government in June 1991. The British were in contact with the IRA again in August and September, checking on rumours which they had heard of an extension by the IRA of its customary Christmas ceasefire, and to give pre-notice of a number of planned speeches by key British politicians. The British were also experiencing political difficulties with John Major requiring the support of unionists in key Westminster votes. It is a scenario which is never helpful to Ireland's interests. You play the cards you are dealt and always must be conscious that strategy can't be constructed or conducted on wishes. Facts on the ground and concrete realities are what govern. No one outside of a select group on any side knew of the gathering pace of negotiations, nor did they know that the following two years would be the most important with regards to the new IRA strategy which would replace the Long-War Strategy which had been in place since the late 1970s. 1991 was to finish with a fresh IRA offensive. The IRA's active service units placed 30 bombs across England from Manchester to London, costing the British £100 million in compensation costs. In the Six Counties huge bombs were also placed at the Opera House in Belfast and at British Army barracks in Derry and Craigavon. Moves towards peace may have been gathering pace but as Yeats noted in his poem 'Lake Isle of Inishfree', 'peace comes dropping slow'.

Quis custodiet ipsos custodes? – unpublished messages

The Roman poet Juvenal's words, 'Who will guard the guardians?', were very much in my mind as the republican peace initiative gathered pace.[58] Who could be trusted with power? By the beginning of 1992 the British were again in contact with the republican leadership. On January

---

58 Decimus Junius Jevenallis was a first century Roman poet who penned the famous 'Satires'. Juvenal wrote in dactylic hexameter, the rhythmic style of epic Greek and Roman poetry. This line is from 'The Virtues'.

7th the British committed their thoughts on the peace initiative to paper and shared this with the IRA leadership. A written reply was dispatched to the British side on January 29th. Even when Sinn Féin placed their record of exchanges with the British on the public record on January 5th 1994, these two communiques and two other documents sent by the British on October 26th 1992 and June 14th 1993 were withheld from publication, on the grounds that they contained 'sensitive material'. These key documents have still not been published at the time of writing. On February 17th Sinn Féin produced their discussion document, 'Towards a Lasting Peace in Ireland'. Sinn Féin adopted this as policy at its Ard Fheis held in Killinarden Community Centre, Tallaght, Dublin on February 22nd. The traditional venue for the Ard Fheis had been moved when the Dublin authorities refused Sinn Féin the use of the Mansion House. In July, Northern unionist politicians from the UUP agreed to meet with the Dublin government, something they had vowed never to do after the Anglo-Irish Agreement of 1985. The meeting itself didn't take place until September when unionist leader James Molyneaux ended his dithering and prevarication and eventually followed through on his commitment to lead a party delegation to Dublin for talks.

Outside of secret talks and political manoeuvring the conflict continued to rage. The British, in an attempt to thwart IRA attacks on Belfast's commercial core, had erected what they called a 'ring of steel' around the city centre. It failed. A huge bomb detonated on January 4th causing widespread destruction in Bedford Street. The following day High Street was devastated by another huge IRA bomb. On January 10th a 300lb bomb was detonated at Downing Street in London. Other commercial bomb attacks were directed at Ballymena, Derry and Dungannon. At the end of January 1992 the IRA killed eight people they accused of being British collaborators, including a member of the Royal Irish Rifles, at Teebane in North Tyrone. The youngest victim was 22-year-old Nigel McKee and the eldest was 61-year-old Robert Irons. Six others were seriously injured when the van in which they were travelling, from the British barracks in Omagh, was destroyed by a roadside bomb. That night on RTÉ, the chat show host, Gay Byrne, goaded British secretary of state Peter Brooke into singing. It was abundantly clear that Brooke was extremely uncomfortable but he sang a little of the song 'Oh My Darling Clementine'. Unionists were furious and it was to cost Brooke his job.

February brought fresh IRA bomb attacks which caused widespread destruction at Adelaide Street and Botanic Avenue in Belfast. The cost of compensation in the first months of the year ran into tens of millions of pounds. Four significant bomb attacks also rocked England in the same month. Britain's proxy gun gangs were also active. February began with the UDA murder of Pádraig Ó Cléirigh (53). Pádraig was an old friend of mine and an Irish language activist. On February 4th, an RUC man entered the Sinn Féin press office and advice centre at Sevastopol Street. He killed two members of Sinn Féin, Paddy Loughran (61) and Pat McBride (40). He also murdered Michael Dwyer (21) who was visiting the advice centre. Michael was the second member of his family who died in the conflict. His mother Sarah (47) died when a loyalist bomb ripped through Sheridan's Bar in the New Lodge area of Belfast on January 17th 1976. Two others were injured in the attack on Sevastopol Street.

I was in the *An Phoblacht* office at Monagh Parade and was contacted as soon as the shooting started. I sent our photographer, recently released prisoner Peadar Whelan, to the scene. I myself raced to the scene as well. When I entered the room where the shootings had taken place a cloud of gun-smoke was still hanging in the air. There was a smell of cordite mixed with the metallic odour of spilt blood. It was a nauseating scene. The sounds of the wounded filled the air, along with the sound of a woman who seemed to be keening. I took in the scene and saw Louise McManus, a friend of republican prisoners and daughter of Volunteer Eugene McManus (RIP). Louise was reciting an Act of Contrition to Paddy Loughran, who was clearly dead. I asked her to get an ambulance. I looked at the casualties, along with others who had entered the room. Pat McBride, a former blanketman lay slumped against a wall. He had been shot in the abdomen. He directed my attention to Pat Wilson who, he said, was in a more serious condition. There was a confusion of noise and groans. However, through all the mayhem I could hear a sound from my rear which I couldn't quite understand. It came from where the body of Michael Dwyer lay slumped on a bench. It was then I noticed a pair of tiny shoes sticking out from below the body. It turned out to be Michael's infant son, who thankfully was uninjured. One of the injured women tended to the child as I headed to the bookshop next door to see what was happening with the ambulance. Inside the shop I could see the RUC arriving in force. A knock came to the door and a man in civilian clothes asked for me by name, introducing himself as Inspector Derek Martindale of the RUC. Outside things were getting out of hand with the RUC beating people with batons and people bravely fighting back. I asked Martindale to pull his men back and myself and others restored calm. The casualties were being evacuated and Pat McBride spoke to me from his stretcher telling me he would be okay. Tragically he died on his way to hospital. Pat Wilson, who had been evacuated first, was to survive.

Belfast was preparing to bury the three dead when news came through of the death of IRA Volunteer Joe McManus (19). Joe had been killed on active service on February 6th. One day later UDA killers entered a bookmaker's shop on the Ormeau Road and gunned down three men and two teenagers. Jack Duffin (66), William McManus (54), Christy Doherty (51), Peter Magee (18) and James Kennedy (15) died in a hail of machine-gun bullets unleashed in the confines of the tiny betting shop. On the 16th of the same month the SAS ambushed an IRA active service unit at Clonoe in County Tyrone. Volunteers Kevin Barry O'Donnell (21), Sean O'Farrell (23), Peter Clancy (19) and Daniel Vincent (20) were killed. Two other Volunteers were injured but managed to escape. The IRA unit had just mounted an attack on Coalisland barracks in which they used a 12.7mm DShK heavy machinegun which had been mounted on a lorry.

The British prime minister, John Major, sought to strengthen his hand by going early to the polls on Thursday April 9th. Despite media predictions to the contrary, Major trounced the hapless Neil Kinnock's Labour Party and secured a victory of proportions which hadn't been seen since the post-World War Two victory of Clement Atlee, who had secured 47.7 percent of the vote. Three big names in politics lost their seats. They were Gerry Adams (Sinn Féin), former Labour leader Michael Foot and Tory MP Chris Patten, who would later return, first as the last governor of Hong Kong and then to oversee the disbandment of the RUC and its replacement with the Police Service of Northern Ireland. Adams would also return to elected office, first as West Belfast MP and then as a TD for County Louth. The following day as Major and his Tories planned their new strategy and as Sinn Féin began its election post-mortem, an IRA active service unit drove a huge bomb into place at the Baltic Exchange in St Mary's Axe, London. Certain media and political figures would claim the bomb was revenge for the loss of Adams' seat. It showed yet again how poor their grasp of logistics was and how confused and pathetic the analysis of 'security experts' was in regards to the thinking of the IRA. Despite the IRA giving a 90 minute warning, there were still people in the area when the bomb detonated at 9.20 p.m. Danielle Carter (15), Paul Butt (29) and Thomas Casey (49) died, while another 60 civilians were injured. It was the largest explosion in England since World War Two. The damage was estimated at £800m – just over £1.6bn in today's money. A plaque bearing the names of the dead was placed on the iconic Gherkin building, later designed by Ken Shuttleworth to replace the destroyed exchange. In total, 88 people would lose their lives due to the conflict in 1992.

At year's end the British would again make contact with the IRA. A meeting between the two sides explored the potential for an IRA ceasefire. The British representative was told there was no chance. He then enquired if the IRA would ease back in the context of agreed talks. He was told an answer would be forthcoming after reflection on the issue. Before the meeting concluded the British representative gave an advance copy of a speech which the new British secretary of state, Patrick Mayhew, would deliver in Coleraine on December 16th. In the speech Mayhew declared that Sinn Féin would be welcome to join talks, should there be an IRA ceasefire.

Many a boat sank within sight of safe harbour

Meetings between representatives of the British government and the IRA Army Council continued throughout January and February of 1993. Exchanges of written material passing between the two sides picked up pace. In essence the British were offering exploratory talks with the Movement which would be held in secret and which would require an unannounced IRA ceasefire of between two and three weeks duration. The British suggested that the talks could take place in Sweden, Denmark, Norway, Scotland or the Isle of Man. The British delegation would be led by Quentin Thomas, Deputy Permanent Secretary at the Northern Ireland Office. Thomas would be later joined by the Permanent Secretary, John Chilcott.

Journalist Eamonn McCann, was selling his *Socialist Worker* newspaper as usual in Derry one Saturday in April when a neighbour told him he had just seen Gerry Adams leaving John Hume's house. McCann gave the story to the *Sunday Tribune*, which published it in the name of another journalist. The hitherto secret Hume/Adams talks were now the subject of media speculation. On April 23rd Hume and Adams released a joint statement saying:

> We are not acting as intermediaries. As leaders of our respective parties, we accept that the most pressing issue facing the people of Ireland and Britain today is the question of lasting peace and how it can best be achieved... We accept that an internal settlement is not a solution because it obviously does not deal with all the relationships

at the heart of the problem. We accept that the Irish people as a whole have a right to national self-determination. This is a view shared by a majority of the people of this island, though not by all its people. The exercise of self-determination is a matter for agreement between the people of Ireland. It is the search for that agreement and the means of achieving it on which we will be concentrating.

The day after the statement the IRA drove a huge bomb into the British financial centre at Bishopsgate. The devastation caused by the bomb was estimated at £1 billion pound (£2bn in today's values). The IRA said:

> The British establishment should seize the current opportunity and take the steps needed for ending its futile and costly war in Ireland. We reiterate that they should pursue the path of peace or resign themselves to the path of war.

By May 10th a formula for proceeding to talks had been agreed between the British officials and the IRA interlocutors. The IRA indicated its willingness to observe an unannounced ceasefire for the requested two weeks. According to the British officials, the agreed formula was put forward for consideration at a meeting on Monday May 17th attended by John Major, Douglas Hurd, Patrick Mayhew, John Chilcott and Rodric Braithwaite, chair of the Joint Intelligence Committee. The meeting was indecisive, with Patrick Mayhew demurring on the grounds that the agreed approach held too much risk for the British government. Major reconvened the group the following day. This time the participants were joined by Kenneth Clarke. On May 19th Sinn Féin increased its vote in local elections in the North winning 51 council seats. The SDLP won 127 seats on a reduced vote. It was clear that the intra-nationalist electoral battle had begun in earnest. In the four days after the election the IRA detonated four huge bombs, two in Belfast with the others in Magherafelt and Portadown.

It was difficult for any of us to know exactly what was happening in all of the negotiations, talks, side talks, secret discussions and exchanges of information. Often large pieces of the jigsaw remained hidden from view. It wasn't only Henry Kissinger who was given to 'constructive ambiguity'. We do know for certain that the proposed formula agreed between the British and the IRA failed to result in the proposed talks. On June 14th however the British did send a communication to the IRA leadership. It has never been published and we still don't know precisely what it said. On July 4th the IRA responded in writing to the British stating: 'We can only presume from the failure by your side to follow up on your proposal and our May 10th response that you do not wish to proceed or that you underestimate the importance, seriousness and significance of May 10th.'

On June 18th Mary Robinson, Ireland's first female president, was on her way north to meet women's groups in West Belfast. She used the opportunity to meet and shake hands with Gerry Adams. Her visit had been vehemently opposed by the British but the Dublin government claimed it was a private visit over which they had no control. Another piece of the jigsaw had been slotted into place. On July 11th, a message was sent by the IRA to the British complaining that stories were appearing in the press which were causing them concern. It appeared that each side was preparing a defence in advance and placing that position on the, as yet, secret record of exchanges. On July 17th the British responded to the IRA in writing, stating that it fully understood and appreciated the importance of the understanding reached on May 10th. The British explained that they were in the process of preparing a comprehensive response and that, with no malice intended, they needed to be very careful and comprehensive and needed to ensure that there were no misunderstandings. They added: 'Events on the ground shortly after the election of 19 May, however, made it impossible to proceed with this response. Events on the ground are crucial as we have consistently made clear.'

The contact between the sides continued for another few months but it was clear that neither trusted the other and were becoming increasingly suspicious of each other. There were lots of questions being raised by senior republicans and others. On September 25th Hume and Adams released their second public statement. They let it be known that a joint position, agreed between them, had been forwarded to the London and Dublin governments and that they were suspending their talks to allow both governments to reflect on what they had said and to indicate what the governments proposed to do. Hume and Adams issued their last joint statement on November 20th, stating that the best ever opportunity now existed to bring the peace process to a successful conclusion. The media was awash with speculation. The speculation went into overdrive on November 28th when the story of the secret talks between the IRA and the British government was revealed in the press. There were two principal questions around how the story reached the media. Was it from a republican source or a British source? And what was the motivation of those who leaked it? The smoking gun was a speaking note from Patrick Mayhew which had been leaked to the DUP's William McCrea.[59] But who had supplied the 'smoking gun' to McCrea? It was surprising that Mayhew's speaking note had found its way into the public domain. The most discerning puzzle however was the famous question first posed by the Roman consul, Lucius Cassius Longinus Ravilla: cui bono? – to whom is it a benefit?

Other things were also emerging around the role of a group operating under the title 'Americans for a New Irish Agenda'. The key figures in the group were Tipperary-born American publisher, Niall O'Dowd, a brother of Fine Gael TD Fergus O'Dowd, Bruce Morrison, a politician and advisor to Bill Clinton, President of Mutual of America Bill Flynn and Chuck Feeney, Director of General Atlantic, better known as the 'Duty Free Billionaire'. Also central to the group were Joe Jamison and Bill Lenahan, key figures in the Irish American Labour Coalition. Feeney had supplied Sinn Féin with the money to open and staff an office in Washington. Sinn Féin's Denis Donaldson and American Larry Zaitschek worked there together in 1993. The pair would later be in the eye of a media storm in 2002. Donaldson had brought Zaitschek to Ireland where the American surprisingly got a job as a chef in the RUC's main interrogation centre at Castlereagh. The storm began on St Patrick's Day 2002 when the IRA broke into the RUC base, stealing secret and sensitive Special Branch files. The plot thickened when the RUC raided Sinn Féin offices at Stormont, claiming to have broken up a spy-ring headed up by Denis Donaldson who was at the time Sinn Féin's most senior administrator in the Stormont Assembly. Donaldson was arrested and charged alongside others on October 4th. The Stormont power-sharing executive collapsed as a result. It would emerge in December that Donaldson had been a Special Branch agent for more than 20 years.

Bill Flynn had entered the equation in 1992 when he sponsored a conference in Derry entitled 'Beyond Hate'. At the conference Flynn met with Martin McGuinness and then travelled to Belfast to meet Gerry Adams. Flynn, O'Dowd and Morrison were back in Ireland in September 1993 to meet an IRA delegation and to persuade them to consider a ceasefire. The IRA observed an unannounced ceasefire for the week which the Americans spent in Ireland. I was very unsettled and opposed to the Americans being given a role in the unfolding process. I was certain a heavy price would be exacted from republicans sooner or later for their involvement. The Americans' role, which was given the blessing

---

59 A written communication which had the authority of the sender but which, because of its sensitivity remained with the official carrying the message.

of the IRA leadership, would without doubt stymie and hamper the IRA's ability to freely decide what was in the best interests of the republican struggle from a strategic point of view. I was opposed to their role from the outset. None of these unfolding events were happening in a vacuum. Serious tensions were developing at national leadership level within the IRA as 1993 drew to a close. I strongly suspected that at least two senior figures were already preparing the ground for a coup against the incumbent leadership should the leadership opt for a unilateral ceasefire. I was firmly of the opinion that the efficacy of the armed struggle had virtually run its course. I was also deeply uncomfortable with the manner in which the leadership was handling the conduct of the struggle and avoiding an open and frank debate on where the struggle stood and how they planned to advance the republican position as we approached an endgame. The majority of IRA Volunteers were blind-sided completely by the media revelations and the increasing 'constructive ambiguity' which surrounded much of what was unfolding.

Events on the ground, as the British had noted in their July 17th response to the IRA, 'remained crucial'. Whether those events were the loyalist attack at Castlerock on March 25th which claimed the lives of four men, or the IRA bomb which exploded prematurely on the Shankill Road on October 23rd claiming the lives of the bomber, Volunteer Tomas Begley, (23), and his nine victims, the youngest of whom was Michelle Baird (7). The slaughter continued at the Rising Sun bar in Greysteel where the UDA killed eight people and wounded another 19. The UVF also got in on the act when they entered a secluded farmhouse at Bleary near Tullylish in County Down on October 29th to murder two young Catholic brothers Gerard (22) and Rory (18) Cairns. When John Hume broke down at the Greysteel funerals it was clear that he was a broken man.

I met with Hume in a house in Andersonstown directly before he and Adams issued their statement on November 20th. He was broken in spirit. He did, however, carry on with his efforts to bring the conflict to an end. I profoundly disagreed with Hume politically but I had great respect for him, despite his post-nationalism nonsense. During 1993 the British proxies in the various loyalist gun gangs murdered 43 innocent Catholics. They did it with arms and intelligence supplied by their masters in the British intelligence services. Direct British political control of the loyalists had been clear from the instigation of the Combined Loyalist Military Command (CLMC) in 1992. The oldest victim of the violence in 1993 was James Moore (81), who died at Greysteel. The youngest was Johnathan Ball (3), who died with Timothy Parry (12) in an IRA attack on March 20th in Warrington, England. The last victim in 1993 was Daniel Blinco (22), a British soldier killed near Crossmaglen in south Armagh on December 30th. A comrade of Blinco's, Paul Garrett (23),was similarly shot by an IRA sniper on December 2nd at Keady in south Armagh. Blinco was the last British soldier to die before the IRA ceasefire of 1994.

On December 15th 1993, after much prevarication, Taoiseach Albert Reynolds, who had inherited an oven-ready peace deal, joined British Prime Minister John Major and signed the Downing Street Declaration. It was the two governments' bottom line and no one was left in any doubt about their position. In section four the governments stated:

> The prime minister, on behalf of the British government, reaffirms that they will uphold the democratic wish of a greater number of the people of Northern Ireland on the issue of whether they prefer to support the union or a sovereign united Ireland. On this basis, he reiterates, on behalf of the British government, that they have no selfish strategic or economic interest in Northern Ireland.

The two governments at section seven of the declaration stated:

> Both governments accept that Irish unity will be achieved only by those who favour this outcome persuading those who do not, peacefully and without coercion or violence, and that, if in the future a majority of the people of Northern Ireland are so persuaded, both governments will support and give legislative effect to their wish. But, notwithstanding the solemn affirmation by both governments in the Anglo-Irish Agreement that any change in the status of Northern Ireland would only come about with the consent of a majority of the people of Northern Ireland, the Taoiseach also recognises the continuing uncertainties and misgivings which dominate so much of the Northern Unionist attitudes towards the rest of Ireland.

The ink was barely dry when the wrangling began over clarification of the Declaration's provisions. This would continue until May 1994 when the British finally responded to 20 questions which republicans had put to them via the office of Albert Reynolds.

Chapter 8

A new era, an unsettling era.

*'The end of the day is a good guide' (Seanfhocal Uladh 467 (a)
Roibeard Mac Ádhaimh)*

T.U.A.S. or T.UA.S. – it depends on who's asking

The proverbial blind man on a galloping horse would have been able to read the runes as regards an IRA ceasefire as 1994 unfolded. Seamus Mallon, the embittered anti-republican deputy leader of the SDLP, however, was still saying with 'certainty', as late as early August, that there would be no ceasefire. John Hume was clearly not keeping Mallon in the loop. Then again why would he? Mallon would be involved with the Good Friday Agreement but he had consistently, since 1989, opposed any efforts to engage republicans. In a 2015 interview he vented his spleen stating: 'I mean they used John, John Hume, like you'd play a three pound trout, and he gave them the thing that they were looking for – and that was a respectable image in the United States.'

1994 opened with Bill Flynn, Bruce Morrison and Niall O'Dowd showing they had clout with President Bill Clinton, who granted a temporary visa for Gerry Adams to attend a conference organised by Flynn in America. Adams was admitted to New York for 48 hours. Clinton announced his decision on January 29th, two days before the Sinn Féin leader was scheduled to land on American soil. It came just two weeks after Albert Reynolds had scrapped Section 31 of the Free State's Broadcasting Act which had denied republicans any access to broadcast media. People could for the first time hear Sinn Féin representatives speak on air. The architect of censorship, Conor Cruise O'Brien, had finally been rebuked. O'Brien would end out his days as a member of Bob McCartney's United Kingdom Unionist Party (UKUP), the place he should have been from the beginning. O'Brien had said in 1976 that it was his aim 'to cleanse Irish republicanism from the culture'. He failed.

Under the terms of his visa, Adams was not allowed to raise money for Sinn Féin nor could he travel more than 25 miles from the Sheraton Hotel conference venue. Clinton was supported by Ted Kennedy, US Ambassador to Ireland Jean Kennedy Smith, Taoiseach Albert Reynolds and many in the Irish diaspora. Opposition came from the US State Department, the CIA, FBI and from the US Speaker of the House, Tom Foley. The British government was livid. Major wouldn't even take a phone call from Clinton for three weeks after the decision to grant a visa to Adams. I felt the visa would come with a hefty price tag for republicans, even if many didn't see that at the time. Clinton had taken a huge step against fierce opposition. Those seeking an IRA ceasefire were getting their ducks in a row.

At a conference held in Letterkenny republicans dismissed the Downing Street Declaration as 'totally unacceptable'. No public pronouncement was made on the basis that time was needed to reflect on the way forward. The IRA made it clear in authorised briefings with selected journalists that this was the case. The Declaration was unacceptable. Some individuals were briefing to the contrary. It was difficult for anyone outside the movement to understand what exactly was happening. Contradictory briefings were being given by 'official' republican sources and by 'senior but unattributable sources'. There was also confusion and uncertainty within the Movement. How could it be otherwise? Certain senior figures were saying one thing in one breath and the contrary with another. There was a great degree of debate and heated discussion about the differences between the Declaration and the Hume/Adams document. While both governments and the Americans had been given sight off this document, no one outside a tight circle in the senior republican leadership had been given access to scrutinise it. There was also the unseen correspondence between Gerry Adams and Tom King and the dialogue that Martin McGuinness had held with senior figures in the British Tory establishment in June 1992. That was before consideration was even given to the IRA's authorised communications with the British government and Dublin officials.

During this period the IRA embarked on its TUAS strategy – sold internally as a Tactical Use of Armed Struggle but outwardly by certain individuals as a Totally UnArmed Strategy. Deliberate tactics were being employed to delay making a firm public pronouncement rejecting the Downing Street Declaration. The rules of the game however had been changed and in that changed situation republicans would sooner or later have to show their hand and play their cards. Things would never be the same again. The ground had shifted, even if many in the Republican Movement hadn't absorbed or understood this new truth. Despite the confusion and uncertainty one thing was crystal clear to anyone with eyes to see: regardless of what the Hume/Adams Agreement contained, both governments, with the support of America and Europe and the mainstream media, had moved to a new policy approach. The Downing Street Declaration had established the underlying principles and these wouldn't change and would indeed be developed and enshrined in the Frameworks document, which was issued by the two governments in February 1995.

That Declaration set out that the consent of the governed was an essential ingredient for stability in any political arrangement; that agreement must be pursued and established by exclusively democratic, peaceful means, without resort to violence or coercion. It stated that any new political arrangements must be based on full respect for, and protection and expression of, the rights and identities of both traditions in Ireland and even-handedly afford both communities in Northern Ireland parity of esteem and treatment, including equality of opportunity and advantage.

A few years later the same principles would be confirmed in the Good Friday Agreement, which stated:

> We reaffirm our total and absolute commitment to exclusively democratic and peaceful means of resolving differences on political issues, and our opposition to any use of threat or force by others for any political purpose, whether in regard to this agreement or otherwise.

The Agreement stated that parties

> recognise that is for the people of the island of Ireland alone, by agreement between the two parts respectively and without external impediment, to exercise their right of self-determination on the basis of consent, freely and concurrently given, North and South, to bring about a United Ireland, if that is their wish, accepting that this right must be achieved and exercised with and subject to the agreement and consent of a majority of the people of Northern Ireland.

That definition of self-determination was a far cry from the statement in the 1916 Proclamation, which republicans had held to for generations. It stated unambiguously: 'We declare the right of the Irish people to the ownership of Ireland and to the unfettered control of Irish destinies to be sovereign and indefeasible.' Be that as it may, the road to Good Friday was now framed within the context dictated by the two governments.

The first sign of moves towards a ceasefire came in an IRA Easter video of armed Volunteers in combat gear released in 1993. A female IRA woman read a statement announcing a three-day ceasefire. The statement warned: 'We call on our enemy to pursue the pathway to peace or resign themselves to the inevitability of war.' On the streets things remained unchanged despite all the smoke and mirrors. Within the Republican Movement, at leadership level, intense, and at times fractious debate on the way forward was ongoing. Across the Movement there was discussion and speculation about where the struggle was headed.

From January to August 31st conflict continued with 64 people losing their lives. The IRA killed 18 people during that period including two informers, five loyalist gunmen and two criminals. It killed three members of the RUC and four British soldiers, as well as one civilian accused by the IRA of being a British Army collaborator. Two other civilians died at the hands of the IRA: Nigel Smith (19), who was shot for having undergone training with the Territorial Army, and postal worker Frank Kerr (53), who died during an IRA robbery in Newry. British proxy killer gangs murdered 38 people. One was the oldest victim of the conflict, Barney Green (87). He was murdered by UVF gunmen on June 18th, with five others, as they watched a soccer match in the Heights Bar in Loughinisland, County Down. That attack came the day after the UVF had murdered two Protestant workmen in the mistaken belief that they were Catholics. William Corrigan (32) and Cecil Doughtery (30) were slaughtered as they ate lunch on a building site in north Belfast. Loyalists also murdered four innocent women during the year: one was Margaret Wright (31), who was mistaken for a Catholic and shot dead in a loyalist den at Meridi Street in south Belfast on April 6th. Margaret was stripped to her pants and beaten with snooker cues and brush handles before being shot four times in the head and dumped in a wheelie bin. Teresa Clinton (33), the wife of a Sinn Féin election candidate, was shot 23 times as she sat in her Ormeau Road home on April 14th. Rose Ann Mallon (76) was murdered at the home of a relative near Dungannon on May 8th. The last woman murdered by Britain's proxy killers died on August 7th. Kathleen O'Hagan (38) was seven months pregnant when she was gunned down in front of her five children after having been held captive for several hours by UVF gunmen, who were believed to be intending to kill her husband, Paddy, a former prisoner in the H-Blocks.

Besides the attacks which resulted in enemy casualties, the IRA also carried out 76 mortar, bombing, rocket and gun attacks on British Army and RUC bases. The last British soldier to die before the IRA ceasefire was Trelford Withers (46) shot at Crossgar in County Down on August 8th. The last attack on a British Army base was a mortar attack on the Henry Taggart barracks in Belfast. I lived less than 100 yards from the Taggart from 1983 until 1995. It was the most frequently attacked British installation in the North.

Another incident occurred just months before the IRA ceasefire which left me questioning the stupidity or cynicism of the British. On June 2nd a British Army Chinook helicopter, containing most of the British intelligence establishment, crashed into the Mull of Kintyre in Scotland. It was en route to Fort George near Inverness. It had just crossed the Sound of Moyle in bad weather when it went down, killing 27 intelligence operatives and two crew. The pilots were blamed for human error, but this was later withdrawn following two inquiries. When the relevant state papers were released in 2018, only two flimsy folders were made public. The bulk of the files had been withheld and won't be released until 2094. I won't get to read them unless I outlive French woman, Jeanne Louise Calment, who died in 1997 in her native Arles aged 122.

Some of the key figures in the British intelligence community perished in the crash, taking with them to the grave many of the secrets of Britain's 'dirty war' in Ireland. A key figure who escaped the fate of his intelligence colleagues was Ronnie Flanagan, who became head of RUC Special Branch before going on to become Chief Constable.

Aside from the headline grabbing conflict and tragedy of death, the political intrigue and machinations continued as the IRA edged ever closer to ceasefire. In February 1994 Gerry Adams was granted a second visa to tour the USA, visiting key groups in the Irish diaspora. On May 16th Downing Street issued a statement which said that Sinn Féin didn't have to accept all parts of the Downing Street Declaration. On May 19th the Northern Ireland Office published a 21 page document as a response to the questions posed by Sinn Féin in January through Albert Reynolds. Sinn Féin was attempting to use this clarification process to place the Hume/Adams document back on the table. However the British were having none of it.

Everyone was waiting patiently, or in some cases impatiently, on the IRA's response to the Downing Street Declaration. They would have to wait. Things within the IRA leadership were fluid and differing views still prevailed. The first view was of whole-hearted support for the 'Republican Peace Initiative' which had been ongoing since the late 1980s. Those members of the leadership felt a ceasefire should be called to allow Sinn Féin to enter talks on the basis of an amended Downing Street Declaration, with the threat of the IRA still in the background. However the second grouping felt armed struggle had run its course and that the IRA should dump arms and instruct all Volunteers to engage in strategic political activity in pursuit of the Army's objectives. They held that Hume/Adams was a dead letter and that the Downing Street Declaration was totally unacceptable. They felt it underwrote the unionist veto and could only lead to a process where the underlying causes of conflict wouldn't be addressed. This group felt that republicans should adhere to the IRA constitution and the previously stated positions of not accepting any internal solution. They were against any attempt to resurrect Stormont or to accede to any unionist veto. They felt that if the Movement united behind these principles it could help develop a proper peace process in the years ahead, which could comprehensively deal with the root causes of the conflict. There was a third view which held that no ceasefire should be contemplated and that continuation of the armed struggle was the only option. Among Volunteers on the ground rumours of an impending ceasefire were rife and general confusion reigned.

On July 14th, the Combined Loyalist Military Command (CLMC) issued a statement announcing that it would call a ceasefire, on the condition that the IRA called its own cessation beforehand. It was clear that the CLMC was being kept abreast of developments and that someone was steering its response. August 26th saw the return of Bruce Morrison and a delegation from the USA who held a three hour meeting with Gerry Adams. On August 28th Hume and Adams issued a joint statement, declaring that: 'If a lasting settlement is to be found there must be a fundamental and thorough-going change, based on the right of the Irish people as a whole to national self-determination.'

The following day Adams issued a statement saying he had met with the IRA Army Council and had told it he believed that the conditions existed which would allow the 'peace process' to carry on. The IRA issued the following statement on August 31st:

> Recognising the potential of the current situation and in order to enhance the democratic process and underline our definitive commitment to its success, the leadership of the IRA have decided that as of midnight, August 31, there will be a complete cessation of military operations... We note that the Downing Street Declaration is not a solution, nor was it presented as such by its authors...

The wording of that statement was a revelation to the media and to the people of Ireland, IRA Volunteers, activists and supporters included, but there were many in the establishments in Dublin, America and London who would be familiar with the gist of the statement and in some cases with the entire statement in various iterations. There was jubilation in many quarters. In west Belfast a celebratory cavalcade was organised. I was driving back from Dublin and was frankly in no mood for celebration. Nothing was certain, other than we had entered a new era and that the Movement was not united as regards the road ahead. Certain individuals were playing others like three-pound trout, but no one knew where it would all end up. John Major immediately said that the IRA hadn't used the word permanent in relation to the ceasefire. The nonsense, prevarication and downright bad faith would continue until the patience of the IRA leadership was stretched to breaking point.

Running out of wriggle room

The government in Dublin under Albert Reynolds' leadership moved quickly to build confidence with republicans. Reynolds, who had done relatively little heavy-lifting for peace, had the ultimate goal of ensuring that the ceasefire would become permanent. He had of course abandoned the Hume/Adams Agreement which had been the basis for the ceasefire, when he climbed into bed with Major and signed the Downing Street Declaration. Reynolds had stood on the steps of Government House in Dublin with Adams on April 6th when he was trying to bring about an IRA ceasefire. Now in September 1994, with the ceasefire in the bag, he stood with Adams and Hume on those same steps shaking hands with both of them and hoping against hope that the ceasefire would soon be declared permanent. It was a powerful image. It was obvious however that John Major, now heavily dependent on James Molyneaux's UUP, was less enthusiastic.

December 16th saw the inauguration of the 27th Dáil and the accession to power of the 'Rainbow Coalition'. It was a rag bag of

John Bruton's Fine Gael blueshirts, Dick Spring's virulently antirepublican Labour Party and the sad remnants of the Official IRA in the guise of Prionsias De Rossa's Democratic Left. Bruton was Taoiseach and Spring became Tanáiste. The London government was in serious difficulties and was now heavily dependent on unionists. It wasn't a situation conducive to progress.

UUP leader James Molyneaux made clear that he would have no part in any talks until the IRA ceasefire was declared permanent. The beginning of the end of the IRA ceasefire began at that point having been effectively undermined by the deliberate introduction of questions over the permanency of the cessation and a demand for decommissioning. It would be 17 long months before the ceasefire finally collapsed.

As 1994 gave way to 1995, there was a sense of hope and optimism, particularly in the media. There was a growing sense of relief among the population. However events on the ground didn't look so promising. The British government decided to deploy the two most despised British Army regiments to the two most hard-line republican areas, the Parachute Regiment to west Belfast and the Royal Green Jackets to south Armagh, a move clearly not intended to build confidence among nationalists. Inside the IRA tensions mounted and the leadership found itself between a rock and a hard place. A minority of senior figures was far from happy with the situation. Among the most disgruntled were the Quartermaster General and the Director of Ordnance. They were supported by a small grouping surrounding them who were openly hostile to the prevailing strategy. This grouping wouldn't finally reveal its hand until the end of 1997.

I believed in 1995 that the Movement was stymied and the strategy unequal to its task. Both governments, with significant international support, were absolutely wedded to the unionist veto over the future of the failed northern statelet. I firmly believed, despite protestations to the contrary, that Sinn Féin was headed into a revamped Stormont. It was a foregone conclusion as far as I could see, despite Sinn Féin's sloganising that there would be 'No Return to Stormont Rule'. I felt very frustrated by the difficulty of being overly critical in a volatile situation. There was a serious danger of the Army splitting from top to bottom, as had happened so often in the past, in times of transition. The very last thing I wanted was to be party to a split and I was determined that I would do nothing that would contribute to the disaster of republicans turning against each other. At the same time I felt the leadership was losing control of events and that things were being contemplated which were clearly against the IRA's own constitution.

If things were to be progressed within the context of the Downing Street Declaration we were making huge mistakes. I felt that we would gain nothing other than a flawed process and that unionism, which had been brought to its knees by the valiant 25 year struggle of the IRA, would be given access to power which they clearly didn't deserve and were incapable of exercising with justice or equity. The two things which republicans had set their face against – the unionist veto and an internal settlement – would become a reality sooner rather than later. That, in my view, would be shameful, especially at a point in history where unreconstructed unionism was at its weakest point ever. I didn't want to see this come about, but like so many other republicans in Ireland, especially those within the Movement, I was very guarded in what I said.

The British removed the ban on interviews in the media with Sinn Féin on September 16th 1994. The party began meeting with British civil servants in December but it would take until May 10th 1995 before any British minister would deign to meet with Sinn Féin. A delegation from Sinn Féin met British security minister Michael Ancram for a three-hour exploratory meeting. Afterwards Martin McGuinness, said: 'We have made a request to the British government for a meeting with Sir Patrick Mayhew and expect an answer in due course.' 'Wasn't he pushing the boat out?', I thought in my more cynical moments. Ancram for the British, would only say that he had pressed Sinn Féin on IRA decommissioning. Patrick Mayhew wouldn't meet anyone from Sinn Féin although in March 1995 he and Adams found themselves in attendance at Bill Clinton's Investment Conference in Washington. Mayhew used the occasion to enunciate his 'Washington Three' statement, which added to a statement he had previously made in the British House of Commons. Mayhew declared:

> Everybody knows, and the Provisional IRA and Sinn Féin know, that the government require that there shall be confidence that the ceasefire is intended to be for good. That is why substantial progress must be made on the issue of the decommissioning of arms in this exploratory phase. As a matter of reality, we cannot move from that phase unless that happens.

Mayhew was trying to exert pressure on Sinn Féin in the belief that his advisors were correct in telling him that such pressure would yield results. He clearly had forgotten that those same advisors had told him there would be no IRA ceasefire in 1994, and that even if there was, it would last no more than three to six months. Mayhew declared that Sinn Féin would have to agree in principle that decommissioning had to happen. Republicans would have to come forward with practical modalities for decommissioning and some actual decommissioning would have to occur before any all-party talks.

He was sadly mistaken in his approach. All that happened between March and September of 1995 was that the Dublin government became very uncomfortable with Mayhew's approach.

Although Taoiseach John Bruton met with Gerry Adams on January 27th 1995, it was clear that the rapport wasn't as good as it had been during Reynolds' tenure. Bruton's coalition was as weak on the national question as any blueshirt government since the inception of the southern state. Dissatisfaction was building in public, but within the IRA the pressure for decommissioning coming through Sinn Féin was creating bigger and more serious problems. The prevarication, delays and bad faith were tilting things away from the prevailing strategy. Pressure began to build for the Army Executive to take a clear view on the constitutionality of Sinn Féin putting forward a position paper on the potential modalities for decommissioning, as was being contemplated and suggested. The IRA Constitution was unambiguous on the question.[60]

An ongoing debate was addressing these issues and seeking to have an assessment carried out across the entire organisation and for the Chief-of-Staff to prepare a comprehensive report for consideration by the Army Executive and the Army Council. The IRA's Director of Publicity was asked to compile a report on the attitude of the Army and a senior Sinn Féin member was asked to carry out a similar assessment in that organisation. At a senior leadership meeting, convened to consider the assessments, the Army representative gave a comprehensive report detailing views from every department of the Army which indicated overwhelming opposition to any move by Sinn Féin to bring forward a paper on potential modalities for decommissioning.

The report from the Sinn Féin official was the opposite. There was no breakdown of views from specific cumainn, comhairle ceantair, comhairle cúige or the ruling Ard Comhairle. The Army representative

60 At section 4. e) it stated: 'All personnel and all armaments, equipment and other resources of Óglaigh na hÉireann shall be at the disposal of and subject to the Army Authority, to be employed and utilised as the Army Authority shall direct.' At section 6 i and ii it stated that the Army Council would: 'Maintain the organisational integrity and cohesion of Óglaigh na hÉireann until the objectives have been achieved, and maintain the political and military strengths and capabilities of Óglaigh na hÉireann until the objectives have been achieved.'

challenged the Sinn Féin official, saying it was insulting that such a slipshod report had been offered on such a serious question. A senior Sinn Féin figure intervened, stating that he thought that what the report was saying was... The Army representative replied through the chair: 'Is it his report or your report?' The Sinn Féin man understood exactly what was being asked. He was asked to retake his seat and did so without protest, knowing that to do otherwise would force him to show his hand. The same individual was never prepared to move ahead of the posse.

The report was submitted for consideration by the Army Authority in early September and by September 29th a statement was issued by the IRA stating: 'There is no possibility of disarmament except as part of a negotiated settlement. The demand for an IRA handover of weapons is ludicrous.' The months leading up to December would see an increased tempo. At the beginning of October the Army Council made a decision in principle that the ceasefire would end and that military action would be taken. That decision was conveyed to a select body of senior Army personnel at a meeting convened at the end of October. During October and November George Mitchell, the American appointed by the two governments to oversee decommissioning, sought to bring the two governments and the parties to accept a 'twin-track approach' in which decommissioning and talks would proceed in parallel. On November 2nd Labour MP Jeremy Corbyn made a proposal in the British House of Commons saying: 'That this house, recognising that the Irish peace process is in imminent danger of collapse, calls on the Prime Minister to announce a definite date for the start of all-party talks without preconditions.' The Dublin and London governments agreed to Mitchell's 'twin-track' approach on the eve of Bill Clinton's visit to Ireland on November 30th. Clinton in his public pronouncements pleaded with all sides to accept the 'twin-track'approach. Clinton's appeal was too little too late for the IRA. On December 8th the IRA issued a statement saying: 'There is no question of Óglaigh na hÉireann meeting the ludicrous demand for a surrender of IRA weapons either through the front or back doors.' Ten days after that statement a Sinn Féin delegation, comprising Pat Doherty, Rita O'Hare, Lucilita Bhreathnach, Gerry Adams and Martin McGuinness were in Dublin presenting Sinn Féin's modalities paper to the International Body on Arms Decommissioning. The document was a Sinn Féin response to the British government paper of May 1995, which suggested three possibilities regarding decommissioning:

'1, direct transfer to the authorities, North or South, for subsequent destruction; 2, depositing arms for recovery and destruction by the authorities; 3, the destruction of arms by those possessing them.'

Sinn Féin's response was made public on January 10th 1996. The party dismissed the first two possibilities but said: 'As part of a peace settlement, the disposal of arms by those in possession of them is a method which may find acceptance. This is a decision for those who have the arms.' In relation to the actuality of decommissioning Sinn Féin said it understood that 'the independent third party concept is one which may find acceptance'. The nod was as good as a wink to a blind horse. I thought that a double deception had been achieved. It remained to be seen who the ultimate victims of the deception would be. On January 22nd the International Body on Arms Decommissioning published a report. It was clear there was major choreography being orchestrated by someone.

Inside the IRA patience was stretched beyond breaking point. The Army Council was hamstrung and things would need to be brought to a head. The IRA had already decided that this phase of the 'peace process' was finished and arrangements for ending it were well in train. Regardless of the Army's ostensible position, the Sinn Féin paper, the Downing Street Declaration, the Frameworks Document and the Mitchell Principles were all still on the table and would frame any process in the future.

The ending of the ceasefire caught the British government completely unaware. The Dublin government had been given a heads up when an IRA representative contacted a senior Dublin civil servant in the early hours of Friday February 9th to inform him that the ceasefire would end imminently and that he should contact the Taoiseach immediately. At 5.30 p.m. RTÉ received an accredited and code-worded statement from the IRA which said that the ceasefire would end at 6 p.m. It wasn't broadcast until 6.58 p.m. because a journalist who had been advised to be on stand-by for an important statement from the IRA wasn't available. Three minutes after RTÉ broadcast the IRA statement a huge bomb ripped through the South Quay in London's Dockland. A 90 minute warning had been given through several media sources, but the British authorities had failed to clear the area and as a consequence two people were to lose their lives, despite having been told by police to leave the area at 6.48 p.m. Inan Bashir (29) and John Jeffries (31) died instantly when the 3,000lb bomb ripped through the Canary Wharf Tower. It would cost the British Exchequer £250m.

An IRA statement declared:

> The cessation presented an historic challenge for everyone and the IRA commends the leaderships of nationalist Ireland at home and abroad. They rose to the challenge. The British Prime Minister did not. Instead of embracing the peace process, the British government acted in bad faith with Mr Major and the unionist leaders squandering this unprecedented opportunity to resolve the conflict... The blame for the failure, thus far, of the Irish peace process lies squarely with John Major and his government.

On February 18th, IRA Volunteer Edward O'Brien, a 21 year-old from Gorey in County Wexford, died at Aldwych in London's West End, when a bomb he was carrying exploded prematurely. He was the first republican to lose his life since the ending of the ceasefire. A second Volunteer was also to lose his life on September 23rd that year. Diarmuid O'Neill (27), the son of Cork natives, who had grown up in England, was shot dead when Metropolitan Police officers stormed his flat in Hammersmith with stun grenades and tear gas. He answered their calls to come out with his hands up. He was shot with arms raised wearing only his underwear as soon as he appeared at his front door. He was shot six times and was denied medical attention for 25 minutes by which time he had died from his wounds. He was to be the last IRA Volunteer to die in the conflict. He is buried in Timoleague Cemetery in West Cork.

On February 28th John Major announced that he would not be seeking IRA decommissioning prior to talks commencing. Major and Bruton announced that all-party talks would commence in June. On June 5th the IRA stated: 'Let us nail completely the position on decommissioning. The IRA will not be decommissioning its weapons through either the front or back doors.' I was of the strong opinion by mid 1996 that the Movement was dangerously close to splitting. There were very fundamental questions which weren't being properly addressed. The paper on the constitutionality of decommissioning, prepared in September 1995, had never been properly discussed. Even though the IRA was saying that decommissioning was a non-starter, it was clear that Sinn Féin had been given dispensation to offer its own take on the issue at a meeting with the decommissioning body in December 1995 and a subsequent paper released by the party in January 1996. Myself and others felt that the IRA constitution had been violated and I also felt that the flawed peace process would be back on track sooner or later, despite the collapse of the 1994 ceasefire. I firmly believed that any settlement which would come from this flawed process would be completely contrary to the genuine long-term interests of everyone on the island of Ireland. I believed this because unionists were not even considering the root causes of the conflict. They were also being reassured of their position and veto over democratic change by the British and Irish governments, both of whom subscribed to the utterly preposterous position that the conflict was the sole responsibility of republicans. The framework of any political settlement was already set in stone and Sinn Féin hadn't the political strength to sufficiently influence matters.

An IRA convention was imperative if a serious split in the Army was to be avoided and if comprehensive discussion was to take place on the way forward. I understood the reluctance of the leadership to call a convention. There were at least three senior figures who were completely wedded to militarism. These individuals could exploit frustrations and low morale to advance their nihilistic agenda. I also understood that we were in a Catch 22 position and needed to address our difficulties with creativity, imagination and courage if we were to find an agreed and viable way forward. The convention came early in November. I happened to spend the entire night before the convention with three comrades for whom I had the highest respect. We, like many others, were debating exactly where we were. One thing we all agreed on was that the Movement was in serious danger of splitting. We were also agreed that none of us would do anything to contribute to such an outcome. Two of my comrades told me they thought anyone leaving the Movement would be making a serious mistake as they would be left without any influence over affairs. The other held his cards close to his chest.

The paper on constitutionality wasn't tabled at the convention and those implacably opposed to the prevailing strategy didn't fully reveal their hand. New members were appointed to the Army Council, bringing opponents of the strategy into the leadership, where they would be bound by collegiate responsibility. A new Chief-of-Staff was appointed and the role of the Army Executive was strengthened. It was however made clear that Sinn Féin would be given Army Council approval to pursue all-party talks. The convention also committed the Army to producing a comprehensive political and military strategy for pursuing the struggle. The convention was neither decisive nor definitive. There were too many questions left in abeyance and it was clear that much more soul searching would be needed to bring the Army to a unified position, if indeed that was possible.

By this stage I was seriously reflecting on where things stood. I was almost certain that it would be impossible for me to continue as things were at this point. The process was flawed and would, in my opinion, end up with a dysfunctional internal settlement. Under such a settlement, a resuscitated Stormont parliament would ensure the balkanisation of society and would bring about the creation of a self-reinforcing dynamic where each political block would be forced to reassure their respective bases that they wouldn't allow the other to prevail.

The death of my mother

I had a terrible and draining year in 1996 as regards my involvement with the Movement, but in my personal life it was to be truly awful. On July 10th, the day of my parents' wedding anniversary, I visited my mother in hospital. She was due to receive the results of a post-breast cancer assessment. She had been clear for the previous six months and was hoping for the final sign-off from the doctors. Myself and my father were with her when I noticed the consultant and oncologist making their way towards us. I didn't know why, but I got the clear impression that they were bearing bad news. I left the bed and intercepted them at the nurses' station. They informed me that they could only give information to the patient but indicated that all was not well. I asked them to delay speaking to my mother. They said they would come back in 30 minutes. I returned to the bed and asked my father to come for a quick cup of tea. At the top of the ward I pretended to have forgotten something and went back to my mother to tell her that things weren't what she was expecting and that I was going to prepare daddy for the bad news. He clearly didn't appreciate how serious things were.

All three of us were back at the bed when the doctors returned. Basically they told my mother that she had stage four cancer in her bones and in her kidney and that they would not be able to offer her anything other than palliative care. I spoke to the oncologist about an urgent referral to the regional cancer unit. He informed me that due to the Twelfth holidays she couldn't get an appointment for two weeks. I was furious and told the oncologist that it was ridiculous that a patient couldn't be prescribed proper medicine because a crowd of silly old men wanted to prance about in Orange sashes. I wouldn't let it go until he prescribed emergency pain relief while she waited on her appointment and assessment.

On the day of my mother's death Chrissie's sister Anne Marie married my old comrade Jimmy McMullan. I spoke to Chrissie that morning and told her I thought the end was near. I asked her to go ahead to the wedding and not to let our kids know how bad things were. Just after 9 p.m. my mother passed away. I left immediately, having organised for the family doctor to certify the death. On my way out the door I met neighbour Teresa Spence who'd come to the door to tell my mother that she'd won the parish lottery. She'd done the lottery every week and never won a penny but she won it in death. What an irony! I rang Chrissie telling her the news and asking that she not tell anyone. I went to the wedding and spent a few hours there pretending that nothing had happened. I told Chrissie that I was going back to the wake house and would see her first thing in the morning, when we could tell the children together.

My mother died on August 30th. She was 65 years-of-age. Our world was turned upside down. The entire episode was so painful and personal that I can't fully describe it adequately. Although I was heartbroken I couldn't cry for my mother's loss. Tears just wouldn't come.

As a family we didn't handle the loss well. Grief was tearing us apart and there was tension and disagreement during the wake. It didn't help that politics got mixed up with the whole thing.

When I reached my mother's house I was numb with grief. I spent the night talking with my sister Carol who had flown home from holiday in Spain. My youngest brothers Mick and Eamonn sat with us chatting. The four of us were close to each other throughout the wake. I don't remember too much standing out during the wake, which lasted until the burial on September 3rd. One thing that I do remember was a confrontation I had with my father. He was drinking heavily. He'd made a habit of it since he'd retired. I challenged him, telling him he should sober up and act the role of a father and take control of things. He exploded at me telling me to mind my manners. 'You understand nothing', he said. 'That's my right hand and over 40 years of my life lying in that box below the window. Now get out of my sight.' Another thing that stands out vividly is the nine white roses that our uncle Stanley Hill brought to my mother. She was in a coma by this stage but Stanley bent close to her and said very tenderly: 'Rosie there's a wee rose for each of your babies. We had some great times, didn't we love?' The petals fell from the roses bit by bit and the last petal fell at 8 p.m. on Friday August 30th, an hour before my mother passed away. Strange little things like that happen in life and they grab our attention.

Throughout the wake the house was crowded with neighbours and friends calling to share stories, pass on condolences and pay their respects. We heard tales about our mother which we'd never known and we celebrated her life. An Irish wake is a wonderful and healing ritual. Timmy, the then boyfriend of Chrissie's sister Bernie, was home for Anne Marie's wedding and he found the whole thing intriguing. Chrissie was a source of great comfort and advice for me at what was a very trying time. She told me to remember that I had lost my mother and didn't want to lose any of my family through estrangement. Things were very strained between myself and my sisters Pauline, Collette, Theresa and Martine and with my brother Rab. We locked horns constantly. Myself and Pauline had been inseparable but during these trying days we were anything but. Pauline had adopted a controlling role and was constantly telling everyone else what to do. I had already, in consultation with my father, bought a grave near the gates of the City Cemetery, which would make it easy for him, in light of his failing health, to visit the grave. I had also arranged for the family doctor to certify the death quickly and for the undertaker to prepare the corpse and have it back in the house as soon as was possible. Pauline announced that she had decided that my brother Rab would take care of all the funeral arrangements. This caused me great annoyance as I, the eldest son, had assumed that I would fulfil that role. I spoke briefly to Rab telling him that I wanted to recite a poem at the graveside and then avoided him and my four sisters as best I could. I was angry and I deeply regret that we as a family didn't handle our grief better. It took a number of years for the rift to heal. Time, as they say, heals most things.

My mother had a great send-off. I bade her farewell with the words of Máire Mhac an tSaoi, a daughter of Belfast man, Sean MacEntee, former Adjutant of the Belfast Brigade IRA and the last survivor of the first Dáil Éireann, who died in 1965. I recited her poem 'Caoineadh' which captured how I felt at the time.

> A tearful voice on the wind and a grey spread of sky, she most beautiful has been left in her narrow constricting grave, alone. The soft breeze will blow westwards, leaves will bloom on branch, seasons will turn and the sun will rise, in the sky stars will trace their constant path; from the earth above her, from her soft breast and her gentle body, through the pleasant day and through tears of dew, from the sod upwards, grass will grow – but never again shall proper music be composed nor soft laments; the heart loses strength, and the sharp mind loses its edge.

My mother was gone, I was heartsore and would miss her terribly. Things would never be the same again. Challenges lay ahead but as always we would need to face and overcome them.

Another ceasefire and another parting of the ways

John Major had finally run his race by early 1997 and on May 1st he went to the polls. His party suffered their worst defeat since 1906, ending 18 years of unbroken Tory misrule. 'New Labour', or the reconfigured Tories, as I viewed them, were swept into power on a landslide. The obsequious and oleaginous Tony Blair was at the helm. I felt Blair was the most dishonest politician ever to lead the Labour Party, until Keir Starmer came along. By June Bertie Ahern, another politician who had lots of questions to answer, was leading a coalition government. The obnoxious and virulently anti-republican Mary Harney of the Progressive Democrats was Tánaiste. Sinn Féin retained its sole Dáil seat in Cavan/Monaghan and registered a negligible 0.60 percent vote increase. I had been directed to manage the election campaign in west Belfast. Adams won the seat back from Joe Hendron of the SDLP. He gained 25,662 votes, an increase of 8,836 on his 1992 performance. Adams let it be known in the wake of the election that he thought all-party talks could proceed if there was a willingness in Westminster, a clear hint that another ceasefire could be forthcoming from the IRA if conditions allowed.

Sinn Féin's vote in the Six Counties rose to its highest position with 127,000 votes, a 16 percent share. The party also saw the election of Martin McGuinness in Mid-Ulster, where he ousted Willie McCrea of the DUP. Unionists would never hold the seat again. The SDLP also had a good election with John Hume, Eddie McGrady and Seamus Mallon all Westminster-bound with a vote share of 24.1 percent. By May 13th Blair had signalled that he was willing to move quickly to talks. He sent an aide-memoire to the republican leadership outlining his thoughts on the way forward. This would become a bone of contention between the IRA Army Council and the Army Executive at a later point. On May 21st, in the local council elections, Sinn Féin gained a further 23 seats. Party strategists were clearly pleased with the way things were shaping up. On June 25th a 'Document on Decommissioning' was released on behalf of London and Dublin for the 'guidance' of those wishing to participate in all-party talks.

The IRA continued in the early part of the year with a series of armed actions. On February 12th an IRA sniper claimed the life of the last British soldier, Lance Bombardier Stephen Restorick (23) from Underwood in Notts, to be killed in its campaign. Later his parents, John and Rita, would become strong advocates for the peace process in Ireland, despite fierce criticism. On June 16th the IRA killed the last RUC men to die in the conflict. Roland Graham (34) and David Johnston (30) were shot dead outside Lurgan RUC station in County Armagh. There were also gun, rocket and bomb attacks in the Six Counties and bombings in England.

The worst riots in the North since the 1980s took place between July 6th and July 11th. The riots began when the British Army and RUC forced an Orange march down the nationalist Garvaghy Road in Portadown. The memory of Ian Paisley and David Trimble's triumphant dance down the same road in 1995 was still very fresh in people's memories and the riots in nationalist areas were of a ferocity not seen in a long time. Loyalists were still killing Catholics with impunity. On May 8th a gang of loyalists in Portadown had stamped 25 year-old Robert Hamill to death in front of armed RUC men who failed to intervene. On July 15th loyalists killed 18 year-old Catholic Bernadette Martin at Aghalee as she slept in a bed at her boyfriend's house. Her killer would say he had committed the murder as a birthday present for loyalist serial killer, Billy Wright. Then on July 24th loyalists in south Down kidnapped and tortured a 16 year-old Catholic boy, James Morgan, and dumped his mutilated body into an animal pit where it was found the following day.

Despite all the continuing horrors, it was clear that the IRA was moving inexorably towards a renewed ceasefire. I was struggling with my own position and was putting myself through mental hell as I wrestled with the decision as to whether or not I would remain in the Movement. Basically it appeared to me that there were three major questions: (1) The Mitchell Principles and related issues about the breaking of the IRA constitution (2) The lack of clarity and in some cases honesty of the leadership and the low morale of the Army as a result; and (3) the Army Council exceeding its powers as defined in the constitution. Aside from these internal matters, I was also deeply concerned about the flawed nature of the proposed talks process. I strongly felt that any process flowing from the Downing Street Declaration and the Frameworks Document would lead to a false peace where the root causes of the conflict would be unaddressed and where dishonesty and pretence would be ingrained in the entire process. I was convinced that Sinn Féin was not only entering all-party talks on this basis, but firmly felt that they would enter a power-sharing Stormont with the unionist veto unchanged and completely intact. Despite all the public posturing of Sinn Féin, I was certain that this was the road the party was set to travel.

The only thing that surprised me was that many astute people, some more astute than me, seemed to be buying into that process. Many did later arrive at the same conclusion as I did as the process unfolded. They would leave the Movement as individuals, just as I intended doing. Between 1998 and 2007 a large proportion of the IRA's frontline soldiers resigned from the Movement. However no significant opposition ever emerged to challenge Sinn Féin. There were of course the militarists, who were in an entirely different position. They would delude themselves that armed struggle could be successfully re-employed. They also hoodwinked themselves and others into thinking that an effective military campaign could be waged against continued British rule in Ireland. They were, in my opinion, simply condemning young people to prison while they rested on their reputations as serious revolutionaries without ever having to devise serious and effective strategies. Some who were drawn towards the militarists did so from much baser motivations. Others simply wanted to be the 'big fish in the little pool'. What unified all the militarists and the disgruntled was their deep contempt for former comrades. They ended up much more disparaging of fellow republicans than they were of the unionists or the British. They despised Sinn Féin's leading politicians and had a visceral hatred towards certain individuals. It was and remains a total tragedy.

1997 was a political disaster in my view. Republicans were on the cusp of underwriting an internal settlement which would, I felt, give unionism a new lease of life despite its unreconstructed supremacism and racism. Unionists were, and remain, filled with 'planter' guilt and a siege mentality similar to that of the white supremacists in South Africa. They were and are a fearful tribe who can only display their fear as hatred for Untermensch, which has always been the disloyal nationalist community since the inception of the Orange statelet. When they eventually began to share power with republicans they made the Irish language community the scapegoat and turned their hatred on all things Gaelic as they couldn't castigate their partners in government too stridently.

I was convinced we had entered a new era. I was very much in favour of a ceasefire. Armed struggle had run its course. It would be counter-revolutionary and morally indefensible, in my opinion, to continue using a tactic which was without merit. Republicans had developed struggle to the point where we could devise a comprehensive non-armed strategy to attain our objectives. Our challenge was to have a mature and reasoned debate on how we carried the struggle forward. We had brought the

Orange statelet to a point where it was unsustainable going forward and needed to bring about conditions where the fundamental causes of the conflict could be honestly addressed. I believed that the IRA should have called for a dumping of arms and should have instructed all members of the Movement to use peaceful revolutionary political actions to complete the unfinished business. The Hume/Adams process, the basis for the 1994 ceasefire, was dead in the water. It had been nullified by the actions of the Dublin government, which was now clearly on a joint enterprise with the London government and other parties to contain and politically render republicans impotent. Republicans were in check, a situation delivered by Albert Reynolds, who had abandoned Hume/Adams and climbed into bed with John Major.

I was reflecting on the 30 years of struggle and the suffering, heartache and grief which had been visited on all sides. I still held to the oath I had taken as a youth. However I wasn't going to allow anything to prevent me making a decision in an honest way and in clear conscience. I was convinced that the British were engaged in a strategy of atrophication of the revolutionary forces of republicanism through protracted negotiations.[61] I had first heard of this strategy from people in Managua in 1992 and again from Pepé José Mujica when I met him in Montivedeo in Uruguay in 1995. Pepé is still an inspiration to me. He was one of the leaders of the Tupamaros, named after Túpac Amaru, the last survivor of the Inca Royal House, who was beheaded in 1574 on the orders of the Spanish conquistador Martín García Oñez de Loyola.[62] Pepé served 12 years in prison but ended up as President of Uruguay, a role which he performed with great skill, dignity and humility from 2010 until 2015.

Back in Ireland I had shared my misgivings with other comrades who I felt held the same opinion as myself. I knew that four senior figures were already planning to leave and form another military organisation if they failed in their attempts to change the direction of the leadership. I agreed largely with their assessment of where we were at, but vehemently opposed their conclusion. I wasn't giving any succour to

---

61 A process where the state indicates it will begin peace negotiations and lulls the revolutionary forces into a ceasefire. The offer of genuine peace talks is little more than a ruse. Once in talks the state drags the process out until the point where the revolutionary forces are so depleted that they are incapable of resuming struggle even if they wish to do so.

62 Movimiento de Liberación Nacional, National Liberation Movement, a Marxist group which fought a struggle in Uruguay from the 1960s until the 1980s. They ended up in power as part of 'El Frente Amplio', a broad left to centre coalition which ruled Uruguay from 2005 to 2020. José Mujica ended up as President.

people who were going to engage in a militarist misadventure, which was unjustifiable and which would only lead back to the position we were already in. One only needs to look at where the militarist rump are now to see that they were devoid of any real strategy. All they have succeeded in doing is filling the prisons and causing unnecessary pain and suffering. Our community is left as a result with a rag bag alphabet soup of minor groups which split again and again. It is also as plain as the nose on your face that they are heavily penetrated and indeed in some cases under the control of British intelligence forces.

Other senior people were also very uncomfortable with the situation we had reached by 1997. I know some shared the doubts that I myself felt. They were, however, going to remain loyal to the leadership and would remain within the Movement. As one of them told me and as he would repeat in public at a later date: 'I would prefer that we were somewhere else, but we are not, and that is it, as far as I am concerned. Revolutionaries have to be pragmatic – wish lists are for Christmas.' I could understand exactly where he was coming from. However I had no desire to engage in the fallacy that Hume/Adams could be resurrected and I certainly had no desire whatsoever to be dragged into a sham peace process which would see the IRA used as a bargaining chip and would eventually see it brought to an end on other people's terms. I felt the IRA should dump arms and issue a clear statement that they had done so, that the armed struggle was over and that they had ordered all Volunteers to continue with peaceful revolutionary activity in pursuit of the IRA's revolutionary objectives as outlined in the constitution. Sinn Féin could go its own way but the Movement shouldn't allow the party to act as proxies for the IRA. I wasn't naive either. I knew there was a serious danger of the IRA splitting and turning inwards and that would have been a disaster. Room for manoeuvre was very limited. My faith in the leadership was almost gone. Worse still I felt that there were those who were engaged in dishonesty. Sophistry and constructive ambiguity was rife and there were those engaged in Jesuitical arguments, seeking to justify the nullification of those elements of the constitution which didn't suit their agenda.

The IRA announced a renewed ceasefire on July 19th 1997. On September 9th Sinn Féin signed up to the Mitchell Principles. My mind was made up. The constitution of the IRA had been violated, as far as I was concerned. I knew that a huge effort was underway to have a second IRA convention called. I would wait to see how that played out. The Army Executive was pressing very hard for an emergency convention to be held. It was called in October.

Two days after Sinn Féin signed up to the Mitchell Principles, we as a family had great cause for celebration; our fourth child was born. Fionnghuala was born as bald as a coot, although with her long blond hair today, you wouldn't think so. She was a very pleasant child and she filled my life with hope at a time when hope was in short supply. She is a great adult and has graduated university with a teaching degree in Irish. Fionnghuala was only a few weeks old when the IRA gathered for the convention. The chairperson of the Army Executive, who has since passed away, gave a measured speech which addressed the difficulties and concerns as they appeared to the Executive. These included a failure to properly implement the integrated political/military strategy promised at the 1996 convention, the exceeding of powers by the Army Council, the failure of the Army Council to take direction on constitutional matters from the Executive and the violation of the constitution of the Army. I agreed with most of the points made. The militarists, however, overplayed their hand. A senior woman Volunteer made a fatal mistake when she failed to address the issues at hand and instead launched into an emotive appeal based on her dead brother's sacrifice during the struggle, which she asked delegates not to betray. A delegate from General Headquarters asked her to give way, which she did. The chair of the convention invited the delegate to address the convention. He first of all challenged the woman delegate in strong terms telling her: 'How dare you wave your brother's bones below our noses. We have all buried too many comrades to be swayed by emotion.' He went on to appeal to delegates to deliberate on the issues before the convention on their merits. He asked that things be weighed and decided through logic and the force of sensible argument, and that it be done in non-emotive terms. The previous delegate had lost the argument before she started. The convention ended with new faces on the Army Council, including some who would have remained critics had they not been tied to collective responsibility. A new Executive was also elected and the new Chief-of-Staff's position was strengthened. The move towards talks was all but irreversible. For me there was only one decision left to make.

By October 1997, 28 years after I joined the Republican Movement, I was on the verge of resigning. I was almost 40 years-of-age and had no idea what I would do with the rest of my life. It was a time of great uncertainty for me and one of very deep emotion. I was, however, resolute in my decision. My time in the Republican Movement was at an end. The night before I went to convey my decision to the person I needed to convey my resignation to, I sat alone and listened to three songs: 'Limerick's Lament' by Seán Ó Sé, Toirdhealbhach Ó Cearbhalláin's 'Farewell to Music' and 'The Time Has Come' by Christy Moore. I was heartbroken. I was at a very low ebb. But I was certain that remaining a member of the Republican Movement was impossible for me. I was totally comfortable and convinced that I was doing the right thing. I would do nothing which would split the Movement. Others left the Movement at the same time as me but they were leaving to form the Real IRA. They were wrong. I was going home, hard as that was.

There were those who pleaded with me to stay but I was having none of it. My mind was settled and I had not arrived at my decision without long and very careful thought. I left one former comrade who spent a few hours trying to change my mind with the words that I didn't know if he were the worst or the best judge of character I had ever met. I parted with him saying: 'I'm not judging anyone. History will do that on us all in the fullness of time. In my opinion personalities are unimportant; we all end up in the same place, dead and buried'. I told him that there was every chance that he was right and I was wrong, but assured him that he didn't need to concern himself with me as I was going home and would steer clear of any public criticism. I never fell out with anyone and bear no grudges or ill-will. I remain on very friendly terms with the majority of those with whom I spent my years in the struggle. I am certain that they too made their decisions in clear conscience and followed the path they did in what they thought were the best interests of the struggle. It was simply a case of me not agreeing with them. The people who I felt most frustrated with were the ones who claimed to be the only legitimate republicans and who ended up with hatred for those with whom they didn't agree on political or strategic questions. It is a stupid and nonsensical position. Those who oppose republican objectives were, and are, the common opponents for us all. It's sad that people find it so difficult to differentiate people from their politics.

A new era, a new beginning

I left the Republican Movement on Thursday October 16th 1997. I was 39 years-of-age. My wife was 32 and we had four children, the youngest just over one month old. I couldn't remain idle and so I applied for a job as director of the West Belfast Traders' Association. I was interviewed on October 29th and by Monday November 3rd I had started in that post. I had never been employed in this capacity before but I knew I would do my best. I had one big advantage in that I had never had a public profile as a republican and was therefore able to move into the world of work as someone without public baggage. Éamonn McPeake was chairperson; his deputy was Gerry Crawford. I grew to be very fond of both men. Gerry was a born businessman, as were his family. Michael, a true gentleman, ran the SPAR at the top of the Whiterock Road; David ran the shop at the bottom of Ladybrooke. Ann and Una were the backbone of Michael's operation. I proposed to Éamonn and Gerry that we should reach out to the other traders' associations in the city so as to be more effective in our external dealings. Working in this field I met others who were just as passionate about progressing their own areas. I met Arthur Carnaghan from the east of the city. He was an Evangelical Christian attached to the Iron Hall Mission at Thorndyke Street and Templemore Avenue. He was a decent man and I got on well with him, although I found his frequent religious references a bit strange. I also met two others from the Shankill – Jackie Phillips, who I was very fond of and his sidekick Sam Glenn, who I never got to know well. I haven't seen Jackie for many years now, but I occasionally see his name and he remains active in his local community.

I wasn't able to develop a love for the nature of the work itself and was doing it primarily to earn a wage. I never was, and still remain largely disinterested in money other than as a means to pay the bills. I was interested in community development and as a result I joined the West Belfast Economic Forum. Ruth Taillon, was the Forum's employee and director and among the committee members I served alongside were Mike Tomlinson, Bill Rolston, Bill Jeffries, Gerry Doherty and others. The Forum did excellent research and development work on questions of equality, justice and rights. I would also work with Bill Rolston in Féile an Phobail on the debates' committee. A visit was organised by the Forum in 1998 to England and Bill Jeffries, Gerry Doherty and myself were chosen to attend. Although I didn't mention it to the others, I was happy to go on the trip to see if I would have any difficulties getting into England. At Manchester Airport, a member of the police stepped forward and said to me: 'Will you fill out a disembarkation card sir?' I asked him what it was and he said: 'Don't worry sir, just fill in your name. You can use that strange Irish one or just write Jake Jackson.'

They detained me and brought me to a police base within the airport. They held me for more than five hours. I refused to even engage with them and spoke not a word while detained. One of them was constantly harping on about how well he knew Belfast and how he had watched me putting my children onto their school bus at the top of the Whiterock Road. He clearly knew the area well. He was full of cocky English bravado. He told me how his mother, who apparently knew nothing about politics, would watch the news on TV and would say ask him about the personalities. 'She thinks that Martin McGuinness is put forward by Adams who watches him from the background. She's very innocent and gullible,' he said, 'but what I want to know is do you or your father-in-law watch Gerry Kelly watching Adams watching McGuinness?' He continued non-stop with the same patter. The flatterer walked me out from the police office to a door which led into the airport's main concourse, when I was being released. At the door he caught me by the arm and said: 'The next time I'm standing at Shepherd's Lane (a local laneway across from the Whiterock shops) I'll introduce myself to you and maybe we can grab a coffee and have a chat.' As I stepped onto the concourse I gripped him hard by the elbow and whispered: 'Make sure you're packing and have back-up or you'll find it a costly exercise to confront me in Belfast.' I never laid eyes on him again.

I made my way to Sheffield where I met up with Gerry and Bill Jeffries. We made useful contacts and learned quite a lot from those we met. Many of those in South Yorkshire who we spent time with were associated with the political and economic innovations which earned the area the title of the 'People's Socialist Republic of South Yorkshire' during the 1980s.

Back home, the Good Friday Agreement was signed-off on April 10th, 1998, Two referenda followed on May 22nd, North and South. In the South it passed with a majority of 94 percent and in the North with a majority of 71.2 percent. I voted against it as I had no desire to see a return of Stormont rule. The soap opera had a little road to travel still and George Mitchell would have to be wheeled back in to cook up some more fudge to help get the show on the road. It would take until the end of 1999 before the IRA agreed with Mitchell's new twin-track approach and appointed a representative to liaise with the International Commission on Decommissioning. This body would be engaged in their work until 2010. Those serving on it were former Canadian General John de Chastelain, Finnish Brigadier Tauno Nieminen and US ambassador, Donald Johnson, who was replaced in 1999 by American General

Andrew Sens. Others who would play a role in the decommissioning saga were the South African multi-millionaire Cyril Ramaphosa, South African President since 2018 and the former Finnish Prime Minister Martti Ahtisaari. They were appointed international inspectors in 2000 but it was a wasted effort as David Trimble brought Stormont down in July 2001. In August the IRA agreed modalities for decommissioning.

Following huge international pressure asserted following the attacks on New York on September 11th 2001 the IRA came under renewed and fierce pressure to decommission arms and it was by then only a matter of when, and not if, they would decommission. 'Not a Bullet, Not an Ounce' was rhetoric from the past. Others were eventually appointed to act as witnesses to decommissioning. Father Alec Reid, the Clonard Redemptorist, and key figure in the Hume/Adams talks, and the Methodist Moderator Harold Good, would perform this role, first in Ireland and then later in Euskal Herria. It would be 2005 before the saga would end. However on July 28th, as I sat on my holidays in Spain I watched my comrade Séanna Breathnach reading out an IRA statement declaring that the IRA armed struggle was over. Amongst other things he said:

> The leadership of Óglaigh na hÉireann has formally ordered an end to the armed campaign...The IRA leadership has also authorised our representative to engage with the IICD, to complete the process to verifiably put its arms beyond use in a way which will further enhance confidence and to conclude this as quickly as possible.

Chrissie and I were sitting at dinner with Jude Whyte and his partner Mary Savage. Jude's cousin, a member of the Garda and a friend of his who was a Fine Gael councillor were also present. We were discussing the statement when I got a phone call from Séanna asking if I'd seen the statement. I told him I had and told him where I was and with whom I was dining. I asked if he would say a few words to the Fine Gael man. At the end of dinner the Fine Gael man sang 'Sean South of Garryowen' and in the spirit of the things I sang 'The Ballad of Michael Collins'.

We hadn't our share of dark days to seek in Ireland. But if we thought back in 1998 that dark days were behind us, the militarists who had departed after the 1997 convention had other ideas. From January to August 1998 they planted nine bombs in counties Armagh, Tyrone and Fermanagh. They also mortar-bombed RUC and British Army bases. On May 1st, Special Branch in the South shot dead one of the militarists as he embarked on an armed robbery in County Wicklow. He was Rónán McLaughlin (28) from Dublin. I had known his mother. I thought it a tragedy that he had died given that there was no chance of the militarists mounting an effective armed campaign. Those days were gone but it was clear that not everyone thought so.

In August 1998 Chrissie had brought me to the penthouse suite at Barrow House in County Kerry to celebrate my 40th birthday. It was a place I'd always loved but never imagined I'd spend a fortnight there. It was a classical Big House, sitting on the edge of Barrow Bay facing towards Fenit Pier and Fenit Island. The weather was glorious and we sat on my birthday drinking a bottle of Cuban Rum which I had brought back from Cuba in the mid-1990s. It was a wonderful day and the weather during our stay was between 19 and 24 degrees Celsius. We decided that we would eat a special meal on the Saturday before we went home. We invited our friends Marie and Martin Ferris to join us at the Oyster Tavern at Spa. We reached the Oyster shortly after 5 p.m. and a friend of ours, Áine Lynch, who worked there, told us that there were reports of a huge explosion in Omagh, County Tyrone. We were barely seated at our table when Martin got a phone call telling him that a neighbour had lost a leg in the Omagh blast. She had gone for a day's shopping. A 38 minute warning had been given by those who planted the bomb saying it was situated at Market Street. The RUC evacuated people towards the bomb rather than away from it. Regardless of what happened, or of the intentions of those behind the attack, or indeed the prior knowledge that Britain's dark forces had of the attack, the result was indisputable. The bomb exploded shortly after 3 p.m. and tore apart the main shopping street in Omagh. In total 29 people, including a mother pregnant with twins, died, with more than 200 people injured.

Three days later, the militarists said they regretted the loss of life and that it hadn't been their intention to harm anyone. They also announced that they had suspended all armed actions. Members of the IRA visited the homes of 50 militarists and warned them that there would be severe consequences if they continued to misuse materials illegally seized from the IRA. On September 7th 1998 the militarists declared a ceasefire but they would resume actions at a later date and under different guises.

Back in the heart of the Irish language community

I had a stroke of luck, or so I thought at the time, when I was asked to join Club Eachtra, an Irish Medium Youth Club in the Upper Springfield area at the end of 1998. The club was located adjacent to the site of the new Irish Medium School, Bunscoil an tSléibhe Dhuibh.

There had been a previous attempt to set up a school but difficulties saw it postponed for a number of years. By 1998 however it was going from strength to strength and is today a centre of excellence for primary teaching practice throughout the North.

I took enthusiastically to my new role and was keen to start up community gardening, bee-keeping and other activities to broaden the club's appeal and to integrate it more fully into the local community. It soon became apparent that there were problems. I began to probe what appeared to me to be irregularities. I was quickly frozen out and denied access to staff computers. I raised concerns and asked a respected outside Irish language activist to investigate. After much to-ing and fro-ing I decided that I would leave my new post to take up a role I'd been offered with Gaeloiliúint, a training and support organisation for the Irish Medium education sector. Here I would focus on the Éarlamh (Patron) scheme, which had been started years before by Séamus MacSeáin. Club Eachtra, thankfully collapsed under a cloud within a year of my leaving. In truth it was a good thing that it did, as in the years ahead a number of energetic and visionary young women would bring Irish Medium youth work to new heights and a much healthier place. At the time of writing the Upper Springfield is the regional leader in the development of Irish Medium youth provision.

Séamus MacSeáin was one of the founders of the Shaws Road Gaeltacht, Bunscoil Phobail Feirste, Cultúrlann and Meánscoil, later known as Coláiste Feirste. I have always admired both Séamus and his wife Brighid, Seán MacSeáin and his wife Máire and Caitlín Mistéil and her late husband Joe. These Irish language pioneers laid down so much of the foundation for Belfast's burgeoning Irish language community. They set in-train a series of developments which have left Belfast as the most Gaelic-friendly city in Ireland. Their simple motto was 'Don't say it, do it' as opposed to that of the sideline brigade, who live by the maxim 'don't do it, say it'.

The biggest development of all in 1998 was, of course, the signing of the Good Friday Agreement. It was to see the conclusion of an international treaty between London and Dublin known as the British/Irish Treaty, which established *inter alia* the constitutional status of the North, the establishment of inter-government relations, and the removal of Dublin's territorial claim over the North and the British government of Ireland Act of 1920, which had established partition and the north/south and east/west arrangements including the North South Ministerial

Council and Cross Border Cooperation Bodies and a British Irish Council. The second pillar was the signing-off on an agreement between the eight Northern political parties and the two governments on internal functions of the northern statelet. Elections to the Stormont Assembly took place on June 25th 1998. The British/Irish Agreement establishing the Stormont Assembly didn't come into effect until December 2nd 1999.

The Agreement was, in my view, fatally flawed from the outset and bequeathed us a balkanised, sectarian state, where the underlying, self-reinforcing dynamic is one of mutual distrust, where the main parties on either side must constantly reassure their respective bases that 'the other' will not be allowed to prevail. The DUP opposed it from the outset, as did Jeffrey Donaldson and Arlene Foster, who eventually jumped ship from David Trimble's UUP. Trimble himself and the UUP had major difficulties with it. Trimble in response to Jeffrey Donaldson's complaints about Martin McGuinness' suitability as a minister in 2000, said:

> I deplore the playing on emotion that's going on and the attempt to use certain individuals as scarecrows. There is, however, a real point here. It was obvious – looking not just at ministers or assemblymen, but looking at Sinn Féin as a whole – that, as far as democratic politics are concerned, they're not housetrained yet. They need to be housetrained and it is the experience of being in democratic politics which will housetrain them.

This was a breath-taking statement from the man who waltzed triumphantly down the Garvaghy Road past residents who had just been beaten off their own streets by the British Army and RUC to allow Trimble his victory jig. He had a cheek to criticise anyone about democracy, having started out his political career in the extremist Vanguard Unionist Party in the company of Bill Craig, the Rev Martin Smyth, Austin Ardill and others who later populated the fascist wing of the UUP.[63]

Trimble, the man who famously said 'there's a life after politics' got his baronetcy from Tory Prime Minister, David Cameron in 2006 and a year later he resigned from the UUP and joined the Conservative Party. He now sits in the British House of Lords as Baron Trimble of

---

63 Vanguard was established in 1972. Its leader Bill Craig was a former Minister of Home Affairs in the old Stormont, one-party regime. He described Vanguard's role at a rally in Ormeau Park, Belfast on March 18th saying: 'We must build up the dossiers on the men and women who are a menace to this country, because one day, ladies and gentlemen, if the politicians fail, it will be our duty to liquidate the enemy.' In October 1972 he addressed the Conservative Monday Club at Westminster saying: 'We are prepared to come out and shoot and kill. I am prepared to come out and shoot and kill, let's put the bluff aside. I am prepared to kill, and those behind me will have my full support.'

Lisnagarvey. Speaking on the 20th anniversary of the Good Friday Agreement he said: 'The one thing that would provoke loyalist paramilitaries is the present Irish government saying silly things about the border and the constitutional issue.'

The first Stormont Assembly with 108 members was convened on December 2nd 1998, on the same day as the establishment of six cross-border bodies. Those appointed to the Assembly were the successful candidates elected at the June 25th election of 1998. There were 28 members of Trimble's UUP, 24 from John Hume's SDLP, 20 from Paisley's DUP and 18 from Gerry Adams' Sinn Féin. Six seats went to John Alderdice's Alliance Party, five to maverick unionist Robert McCartney's United Kingdom Unionist Party, three to independent unionists and a pair each to the UVF-linked Progressive Unionist Party and the Women's Coalition led by Monica McWilliams.

Hume refused to enter the Assembly, given his less than cordial relationship with Trimble, and passed the baton to his deputy Séamus Mallon. Trimble was appointed First Minister and Mallon Deputy First Minister. There was no great chemistry between this pair either and they would spend long periods without even speaking to each other. Mallon, wearing his rose-tinted spectacles, would later laud this as a 'Golden Era' of co-operation when he was at his favourite pastime of castigating Sinn Féin. The Assembly suffered four suspensions including that of January 2017. Martin McGuinness resigned, forcing Arlene Foster from office, the most popular move by Sinn Féin since the calling of the IRA ceasefire. The latest 'Brexit' collapse caused by DUP in the wake of Sinn Féin's s 2022 election victory should be its last.

The voting pattern for Sinn Féin in its stronghold of west Belfast tells its own tale. There was a huge drop of 9,451 in the Sinn Féin vote in the constituency during the years in which the party sought to appease an unreconstructed unionism to keep the show on the road. Many republicans and nationalists had become increasingly annoyed at the unending insults flung at them by unionists. Despite everything Sinn Féin did, from attending British military commemorations to shaking the hands of British royals, unionists just continually slapped them in the face. Ian Paisley, Peter Robinson, Arlene Foster and Edwin Poots all dished out the insults. In a debate in 2015 Edwin Poots told Alex Maskey of Sinn Féin: 'We do business with you because it is in the interest of Northern Ireland that we have peace in Northern Ireland. We hold our noses and do business with you.' Sinn Féin's west Belfast vote is always a good barometer of Nationalist feelings. In 1997 the party had 25,662 votes. Four years into the Assembly in 2011 that had fallen to 16,211 votes. During 2016 it was crystal clear that nationalism was thoroughly disenchanted with the Assembly. Sinn Féin consulted its base and the leadership was taken aback at the depth of antipathy. Foster, the dour DUP leader, was the most despised leader of unionism since James Craig and her final 'crocodile' insult and Paul Givan's removal of meagre Gaeltacht grants from teenagers proved the last straw. When McGuinness pulled the Assembly down it was clear the move was popular with republicans and nationalists. Five months later Sinn Féin secured 27,107 votes in west Belfast.

When the cross-border bodies were established alongside the first Assembly, an old comrade Ted Howell approached me. Ted was a good Gaeilgeoir and a man whose political nous I respected. He wanted to know if I would be prepared to accept a nomination from Sinn Féin to sit on Foras na Gaeilge, the all-island Irish language body. I agreed on the condition that I would have independence of action. I agreed to report back in writing and verbally to Séanna Breathnach and to meet with anyone tasked by Sinn Féin with matters relating to the Irish language.

Appointments to the body were on a party-nomination basis with 16 members appointed in total, eight from the southern parties and eight from the northern parties. In the North, the SDLP appointed the chair, Maighréad Uí Mháirtín, alongside Liam Corey from Antrim, Anne Craig from Derry city and Patsy McGlone from Tyrone. The unionists appointed Aodán Mac Póilín (RIP) from Belfast and Gordon McCoy from Saintfield. Sinn Féin appointed Cionnaith Ó Suilleabháin from Cork and myself. From the South the appointees were Treasa Ní Ailpín, Bríd Uí Néill, Leachlain Ó Catháin, Maolsheachlainn Ó Caollaí, Pádraig Ó Duibhir, Séamus Ó Tonnaigh (RIP), Jacqueline Nic Fhearghusa and Liam Ó Cuinneagáin. There would be four changes during my tenure. Caitríona Ní Cheallaigh replaced Máighréad Nic Seagháin, Gearóid Ó hÉara replaced Cionnaith Ó Suilleabháin, Jacqueline Nic Fhearghusa replaced Liam Ó Cuinneagáin and Diarmuid Ó Murchú came in to replace Séamus Ó Tonnaigh who died on January 16th 2001.

I knew all the northern appointees personally with the exception of Maighréad Uí Mháirtín (Ní Herron) and Anne Craig. Maighréad's husband, Mícheál Ó Máirtín, had been my Irish lecturer in Queen's University in the 1980s and I also knew some of Maighréad's brothers and sisters from the Lámh Dhearg GAA club in Belfast. I became very fond of Maighréad. I had faith in her; she was a committed Gael and always acted according to her word in all her dealings with me. I knew both the unionists' appointees. I had a great respect for Gordon McCoy. On a personal level I got on really well with Aodán Mac Póilín and enjoyed his company. He was a very interesting man in many ways, but I could never agree with his politics. From the southern appointees I knew only Cionnaith Ó Suilleabháin, Jacqueline Nic Fhearghusa and Liam Ó Cuinneagáin. The best ever chief executive was Joe Mac Donncha from Galway. I remained very friendly with Joe until his untimely death on May 20th 2016. The major, and ongoing, problem with Foras na Gaeilge was the failure to have its annual budget benchmarked against similar semi-state bodies such as the Arts Council. I made the case for bench-marking repeatedly, believing it was the only way we could satisfactorily discharge our duties towards the Irish language. It never happened. £13.9m was made available to Foras in 1999. That would only increase to £18.16m by the time my appointment to the board expired eight years later. In real terms, the budget for dispersal dropped significantly with expanded responsibilities and increased staffing levels.

Another problem was that Foras na Gaeilge was one of two bodies tied together as the Language Body, the other being the Ulster Scots Agency. Consolidated accounts needed to be produced and with the Ulster Scots Body, this was always very challenging. The audit report from the Chief Regulator of Tax noted in 2003 in relation to the Ulster Scots Agency: 'The internal audit report of 2001 noted that there was barely an internal regulatory system in place.' By April the Internal Audit Unit had produced a handbook of regulations and protocols which instructed the agency how to carry out mandatory regulatory functions. The chair of the Board of Ulster Scots, Lord Laird, in the first nine months of the board's operation spent, amongst other items, £120, £260, £272.50, £125 and £240 on taxis. And although the board's remit was confined to Ireland, under Laird's chairpersonship, very significant sums of money were spent on trips to America, Canada and that famous hotbed of Ulster Scots activity, Viareggio in Italy.

On the Italian job, in February 2001, Laird and other board members were joined by members of Orange flute bands for the trip. The trip saw up to 40 of Ulster's finest Scots leave the North's shores in the biggest

Ulster Scots exodus since the Eagle Wing's failed journey of 1636.[64] On the American jaunt, two months later, Laird authorised the spending of a whopping £50,000 and was joined by the acting chief executive as well as a number of board members and five Orange 'musicians'. Laird defended his use of taxis for security reasons: 'Am I going to turn up somewhere, get out of a car and walk half a mile to a function wearing a kilt? That would be drawing attention to me.'

At the first meeting of the Language Body held in Dublin, or 'The Blak Hale' as the Ulster Scots Agency papers described it, all the Ulster Scots attendees had to wear earphones as the working language of the board was Irish. The chair, Maighréad Uí Mháirtín, invited people to make some introductory remarks. I, in my turn said: 'Am mair nor hairtfelt sonsie tae bae here fur the forgetherin o tha boord.' (I am more than happy to be here for the meeting of the Board.) 'My earset doesn't appear to be working properly,' said Lord Laird. The chair explained that I was speaking in Ulster Scots. 'I thank the gentleman for his kind words,' said Laird, 'but I unfortunately only promote Ulster Scots. I don't speak it.' The first line of Rabbie Burns' 'Ode to a Haggis' came to mind: 'Fair fa' your honest, sonsie face, Great chieftain o the puddin' race!' I miss Laird, who died in 2018. I had asked him a number of times to be consistent and use either Ulster Scots in his chosen name or English. 'Lord Lord' or 'Laird Laird' would have had a better ring to it than the hybrid he chose to use.

---

64 The 'Eagle Wing' was a ship bound for America with Presbyterian Planters. It departed in 1636 but turned back because 'adverse weather' was interpreted by one of the reverends on board as a sign from God to give up. The Rev John Livingstone wrote: 'But if ever the Lord spoke His winds and dispensation, it was made evident to us that it was not His will that we should go to New England'.

Chapter 9

The first decade of the new millenium

'Take life as you find it.' (Seanfhocal Uladh 458 Tír Chonaill)

End of a generation

Having reached 72 years-of-age my father was to pass away on June 9th 1999. He had been in ill-health and this had deteriorated badly following my mother's death. His spirit was still strong but he had lost some of his vitality. We began taking turns to stay with him. I spent two nights a week with him and one weekend in every three. Following my experience during my mother's final days I was determined that no one would be ordering me to do anything other than what I saw fit to do. Some of my sisters attempted to lay down all sorts of rules for whoever was taking care of Gerry. I informed them straight out that I would decide, in conjunction with my father, exactly how things would go when I was in his home. He had too much of a fondness for alcohol, and when money was scarce and drink was wanted, he would get up to all the tricks of the day to procure a drop of the pure stuff. I'm not castigating him, simply telling it as it was. I would take him in his wheelchair to his local drinking club and would leave him there with instructions for the barman to ring me when he'd had his fill. I would then return and take him home to get him to bed. At times he would ask me to read to him, a task I always loved. We had never enjoyed the greatest of relationships but in his final year, listening to him telling me more about himself, I got to understand my father a lot better. He hadn't really known his own father, who had died when he was very young. He clearly loved my mother. He thought she was the best thing that had ever happened to him and missed her sorely.

My father had been a self-taught man with very keen native intelligence. He was cultured in his own way. He was Marxist in his thinking and had an abiding dislike for the clergy and for capitalism in general. We had a lot, perhaps too much, in common in our personalities and that affected how we related to each other. I loved him but I could never feel the same affection towards him as I'd had for my mother. He was oxygen dependent in his last years and in his final months it got progressively worse. He was taken into hospital for the final time in May 1999. In his final days we were pestered by my sister Theresa, who was waiting on a neighbour, Martin Flynn, delivering Padre Pio's glove, which allegedly had miraculous properties.[65] One day myself and Rab were outside eating a sandwich beside the statue of the British Queen Victoria, which stands in the grounds of the hospital. I noticed a fingerless mitten sitting on a windowsill and wrapped it in the cling film from my sandwich. On going back to the ward I gave it to Theresa without comment. She blessed herself and placed it on my father's chest. I don't know about my father but we certainly felt relief with Theresa now settled down.

On June 7th my father asked me to speak with him alone. He told me he wanted to die at home but that the doctors wouldn't permit it as the levels of oxygen he required couldn't be administered outside of hospital. He asked me if I would carry him from the hospital and drive him home to die if he were to discharge himself. I told him I would. He sent for the others and told them of his decision. After much anguish and argument, the doctors assented to his request. The following day he was sent him home in an ambulance with the clear message that he would die from a lack of oxygen. I sat with him through his final night and was to be relieved next morning by Carol. He struggled for every breath. It was torturous to watch him bathed in sweat and fighting for every breath but stoically facing death. I felt a great pride in him choosing to face death on his own terms and in the room he and mammy

---

[65] Padre Pio, now Saint Pio of Pietrelcina, was born Francesco Forgione in the town of Piertrelcina in 1887. He gained the name Pio when he joined the Order of Friars Minor Capuchin. Throughout his life he exhibited the stigmata. A cult grew up around him and his mittens were sought for their supposed miraculous properties. He died in 1968 aged 81 and was made a saint in 2002.

had shared as husband and wife. At around 3 a.m. he asked me to fetch him a glass of whiskey. He took one small sip and I set it on the shelf beside his bed. Carol arrived at 4 a.m. and I left to buy Belfast baps for our breakfast. When I returned from the bakery he had passed away. I gave him a kiss and covered the glass of whiskey with cling film. Carol and I then started phoning all our siblings. My father's wake was much more comforting than my mother's had been. There wasn't the same tension and everyone made sure not to do or say anything to upset each other. Theresa spent the first day of the wake reciting the 'miracle' of how Padre Pio's glove had brought him such relief. I eventually took her aside and explained that it was the 'Miracle of Padre Primark'. She told me what I'd done was a sin. 'Believe me Theresa,' I said, 'it's not the first and probably won't be the last.'

    We were now looking down a generation and not upwards at the one above us. We, the children of Gerry Jackson and Rosie McNally, were the generation which our own offspring now looked up towards. On the day of the funeral I fetched the remnants of his last glass of whiskey and we all took a sip. Before the coffin was closed we placed his last half-empty bottle of whiskey beside him. We accompanied him on his last journey and laid him to rest beside his beloved Rosie. I would need to lay his ghost to rest in my own time. There had been huge changes in our lives but his own life had also been witness to many changes. When my father was born in 1927 Éamon De Valera was leading Fianna Fáil into Leinster House. Kevin Higgins, the Free Sate Minister of Justice, was gunned down by the anti-Treaty IRA. Countess Markievicz had died at 59 years of age. In the North, the Parliamentary Act of Titles had changed the name the United Kingdom of Great Britain and Ireland to the United Kingdom of Great Britain and Northern Ireland. The statelet of Northern Ireland had its existence confirmed. All talk of border change and the promised Border Commission was gone. The Free State was officially born.

    By the time of my father's death Gerry Adams and Martin McGuinness were, like De Valera in 1927, taking their party into a partitionist assembly for the first time. The Good Friday Agreement was alive but not fully implemented. In 2022 it still hasn't been fully implemented and that's despite us having had in the interim the Hillsborough Agreement, the Saint Andrew's Agreement, The Fresh Start Agreement and the Stormont House Agreement of February 2017 which was agreed or not agreed, as the case may be. We also have, for good measure, the take it or leave it Simon Coveney and Julian Smyth 'New Decade – New Approach'.

We have agreements coming out of our ears but there is precious little agreement. There's even less implementation. I am a simple man and must confess to being even less clear today than I was back in 1993 when the republican peace initiative was scuppered by the signing of the Downing Street Declaration. The more things become clear the more obscure they become, in the topsy turvy land of Ireland's six north-eastern counties with a pretend up-and-down parliament for a pretend state.

New Millennium, new job and new baby

I had a very busy year in 1999 but the following year would be even busier. Máirtín Ó Muilleoir approached me at the end of 1999 and asked me if I'd be willing to take on the role of Deputy Editor of the *Andersonstown News*, with responsibility for setting up its new Monday publication. I told him I would consider it. I informed him just before Christmas that I would take on the job, provided the world didn't end on December 31st 1999 as many were predicting. Máirtín's offer was a big challenge, which could have been made much worse had the millennium bug wreaked its prophesied havoc. Thankfully, the dire warnings were as far off the mark as were the warnings from the evangelic zealot in Cornmarket who had been telling me all my life that 'the end is nigh'.

Myself, Sports Editor John Martin, photographer Mal McCann and Newry journalist Seánín Graham made up the Monday team. John would end up as hurling correspondent for *Gaelic Life*, while Mal and Seánín would both end up at the *Irish News*. Back in 2000 we were all in each other's company from 8 a.m. until 11 p.m. and many times much later. Seánín was a wonderful worker and a great colleague who put her whole effort into her work. I was heartbroken for her when management ended her contract one month before she was due to be made permanent. In hindsight she was done a favour as she went on to make herself a solid career as Health Correspondent at the *Irish News*. I know her termination from the *Andersonstown News* left its mark on her but she prevailed and became stronger.

Chrissie was pregnant with our latest child when I began work at the *Andersonstown News*. She went into labour on February 15th. The birth was a nightmare. Chrissie had always had natural births, but this one was a complicated affair. Chrissie and the baby, whom we named Tiarnán, were very lucky to survive when an emergency section was required. I will never forget the wave of pure joy and relief that swept through me when I heard the baby cry and heard one of the medics tell Chrissie that she and the baby boy would both be fine. Tiarnán was born on a Tuesday and in his case Tuesday's Child was certainly full of grace.

Three days later I had to return to work and get Chrissie's mum to tend to her and the baby and the other kids, who were, two, seven, 12 and 13 years-of-age. I had to work late every night. I have to admit that it put us under more stress than even that which we'd experienced during the worst of the conflict. Chrissie had little respect for my employers and I could fully appreciate how she felt. I continued working for the *Andersonstown News* until Christmas 2003. I would also spend periods editing *Lá*, the Irish language paper, which had been bought by the Andersonstown News Group. I made some very good friends during my time there: John Martin and John Ferris as well as Maria McCourt, Thomas McMullan and Barry McCaffrey from the *North Belfast News*. The friendship lasts right up to the present. I was also very fond of Shelly Loughran, Brónach Ní Tuama, Bríd McIlhatton, Kevin McCabe, Kieran Sloan and Anthony Neeson. In 2003, I was informed that the time I spent attending meetings of Foras na Gaeilge would be deducted from my annual holiday allowance, which would leave me with only seven days holidays each year. It made up my mind for me that I would leave the place as soon as an opportunity allowed. The final straw for me was the decision by management to place advertisements for the Police Service of Northern Ireland (PSNI) in the Irish language paper. I applied for a job as director at Forbairt Feirste, an Irish language development agency. I started in post in January 2004. It was a challenging and rewarding job and I remain employed there at the time of writing. I am very grateful that I was given the opportunity and the privilege of being associated with Forbairt on behalf of Belfast's Irish language community.

St Andrews and the interim Assembly

By 2006 it was clear for all to see that the Stormont soap opera was going to be given a new lease of life. Aside from all the to-ing, fro-ing and arguing it was clear that the local parties were stretching themselves to find a formula which would allow for the resurrection of the institutions. The London and Dublin governments were also letting it be known that salaries and finance would cease if the parties failed to get the show on the road again. On Thursday April 6th, Blair and Ahern arrived in Belfast and unveiled their plan for restoration. Under the proposals there would be an interim Assembly established by May 15th. The pantomime would run until October 11th when the governments and the parties spent three days in St Andrew's in Fife at a cost of £390,000. It was obvious that whoever paid the piper would call the tune. I could hear the fife and drum in the background as Ian Paisley stepped up to the plate with Martin McGuinness. Paisley couldn't hide his grin, having finally reached the place he always wanted to be. He was the cock crowing on the dung heap which was the Six Counties. Unfortunately the old arch-bigot would be turned into a hero of the peace. It was repugnant.

I remember the day Paisley retired from politics. I was in the Cultúrlann having lunch when Áine Ní Gallchóir from TG4 came in looking for views on his retirement. Initially I refused to give an interview but was finally overcome with so much anger that I agreed to speak. She asked how I felt about Paisley's departure from politics: 'It's 40 years and 4,000 deaths too late,' I said.

On Friday October 13th 2006 I was hosting a celebratory dinner for Belfast's Irish language community in Belfast City Hall. There were 450 guests in what was the largest ever Irish language celebration to be held in the former bastion of unionism. Forbairt had prepared a booklet and a series of information stands to mark the occasion. The city's DUP deputy mayor, Ruth Patterson, gave the welcoming address, including a few lines in Irish that I had drafted for her. During the event I took a call from a senior Sinn Féin official telling me that an Irish language act would be part of the deal which was about to be done at St Andrew's. I also learned that Martin McGuinness and Ian Paisley were flown home on a private jet together. Paisley to celebrate his 50th wedding anniversary and McGuinness for some other purpose. The same caterers were serving at both Paisley's and our dinner.

The interim Assembly established as a result of St Andrew's was to begin sitting on November 24th. There was a little drama or pantomime when Michael Stone, the UDA killer who had attacked the funerals of the Gibraltar Three[66], turned up armed with grenades. Stone burst through the revolving doors, brandishing a weapon but was seized and disarmed by a female security guard who was on her first day of duty. She proceeded to thump Stone over the head with his own weapon.

---

66 IRA Volunteers, Dan McCann, Mairead Farrell and Seán Savage, who were gunned down in an SAS ambush in Gibraltar in 1988.

Stone initially claimed he was there to kill Gerry Adams and Martin McGuinness but later claimed it was an artistic performance. The recovery of eight bombs in the grounds of Stormont undermined that story and the judge at his trial gave him 16 years in prison.

At a special Sinn Féin Ard Fheis in Dublin on January 28th 2007, 90 percent of the delegates gave their endorsement to Sinn Féin's acceptance of the policing proposals contained in the St Andrew's Agreement. At the Assembly election on March 7th, the DUP gained 36 seats, Sinn Féin 28, the UUP 18, the SDLP 16 and Alliance seven. This was the first time Sinn Féin had gained more seats than the SDLP. It was the beginning of the SDLP's inexorable decline, which was to continue on the watches of Margaret Ritchie and Alastair McDonnell and which continues under Colum Eastwood who at least reclaimed Derry from Sinn Féin. Stormont reconvened on May 8th and at the end of May Sinn Féin took its seats on the Policing Board. Paisley and Martin McGuinness headed up Stormont with Conor Murphy, Caitríona Ruane, Michelle Gildernew and Gerry Kelly being appointed as Sinn Féin ministers. Paisley appointed Arlene Foster, Peter Robinson, Nigel Dodds, Ian Paisley Jnr and Edwin Poots. Neither Paisley Snr nor his son lasted too long. Paisley Jnr left under a cloud in February, having become embroiled in a planning scandal involving DUP funder Seymour Sweeney. Paisley Snr announced the following month that he would resign as both First Minister and leader of the DUP. By January 2008 he had also been hounded out of the leadership of the Free Presbyterian Church. The Free Presbyterians are a religious sect with less than 10,000 adherents in Ireland, yet they wield an inflated influence in unionist politics. A little known off-shoot of this sect is the Caleb Foundation, an ultra-conservative, Christian fundamentalist lobby group founded in 1998. It is close to many DUP politicians including Edwin Poots, Nelson McCausland, Diane Dodds, Gregory Campbell, Paul Givan, Mervyn Storey and Stephen Moutray. Supporters are also said to include Jim Allister and Sammy Morrison from the TUV. Its current chair is Wallace Thompson, a former senior civil servant and long-term DUP member who served as ministerial advisor to Nigel Dodds. His secretary at the Foundation until 2012 was David McConaghie, who stepped down after being caught placing a camera in the female toilets at DUP MP David Simpson's offices.

As part of that new Assembly we had to work under the successive authorities of DUP ministers Edwin Poots, Gregory Campbell and

Nelson McCausland. This would later be taken over by Sinn Fein's Carál Ní Chuilín of Sinn Féin but eventually it would revert to the DUP when Paul Givan became minister. We weren't afforded a meeting with any of these ministers, apart from Carál Ní Chuilín, who was very supportive of what we were trying to do. The other four offered only varying degrees of disrespect for Irish speakers. Givan's crass removal of a minor £50,000 Gaeltacht Bursary Scheme for teenagers was one of the actions which eventually brought all of nationalism to a position of total antipathy to Stormont. People were fed up with the Sinn Féin appeasement of unionism. The strength of feeling eventually forced Sinn Féin to scupper Stormont, a move which I was convinced they didn't want to make.

Chapter 10

Toward the three score and beyond

'When the work of the best leaders is finished the people will say "we did it ourselves".' Lao Tzu (601–circa 531 BCE)

Life's too short for peeling chestnuts

The end of the first decade of the 21st century saw me in my 50s. I felt no differently in my head than I had done when I was in my 20s, but my body was telling me a different story. I was afflicted with Ulcerative Colitis. I was unwilling to submit to surgery so my consultant tried a variety of treatments. To make matters worse, I found out that I was an insulin dependent diabetic. I ended up on immuno-supressants, which left me open to a whole array of illnesses. Over a number of years I would contract Clostridium Difficile, Campylobacteriosos, Norovirus and Salmonella. I spent a lot of time in hospitals but was able to read a huge amount of books which I wouldn't otherwise have gotten the chance to do. Every dark cloud has a silver lining.

I became very friendly with my consultant surgeon. Terry Irwin is an interesting man. He was secretary and later President of the Travelling Surgical Society of Britain and Ireland, an organisation in which his father Sinclair had also performed a prominent role.[67] Sinclair was a

---

67 A group of surgeons from the British Army Medical Corp, established in 1924 to learn from differing medical techniques and to broaden their perspectives. The Society undertakes a field trip once a year.

former member of the Royal Army Medical Corps and a keen rugby player, having won caps for Queen's University, Ulster and Ireland. His grandfather Samuel had also been a surgeon and an Ulster Unionist MP from 1948 until his death in 1961. When Terry and his wife Jenny were organising a visit to Ireland for the society in 2012, Terry asked if I would organise a dinner and cultural talk for them in Cultúrlann. He explained that many of the members were ex-British Army surgeons and wondered if it would be a problem to have them in Cultúrlann. I explained that Cultúrlann had an open door policy and prided itself on welcoming people from all backgrounds. That was thanks to its founders, Áine Nic Gearailt, Séamas Mac Seáin, Gearóid Ó Cairealláin, Eoghan Ó Néill, and others, who had taken possession of an old Presbyterian church on the Falls Road and turned it into one of the finest cultural centres in Ireland. The dinner and talk went extremely well and I was outside taking some air when I met a former military surgeon who told me that he had last been outside Cultúrlann in the 1980s when it had been a derelict building. He had been applying a tourniquet to a wounded soldier and was taking heavy fire from the IRA in nearby Shiels Street. He expressed his delight with how the place had been transformed. I agreed wholeheartedly with him and shared his wish that the dark days were now behind us for good.

I developed a great respect for Terry from the first day we met. He was leading a team of medical students around the ward and was being shown around by a ward sister. She had introduced me as 'this patient'. Terry rebuked her: 'The patient is Mr MacSiacais. Kindly introduce him properly.' The nurse refused to say my name. I realised that Terry was uncomfortable and I reassured him that it didn't matter to me. Terry and I would be poles apart on our politics but both of us realised that our common humanity was much more important than politics or cultural background. I bore the nurse no personal ill-will; in fact I pitied her, as ignorance can be a terrible burden. Such insults have been borne by Irish people ever since the inception of the sectarian northern statelet. Much had been borne in sullen silence but with the rise of the post-civil rights generation it would be suffered no more. Thankfully today's generation refuse to tolerate insults and discrimination and will ensure that the sectarian nonsense will be confined to the dustbin of history, where it always belonged. The ignorant, and those too ready to offer insult to others, are unfortunately still in our midst. We still, in the 21st century, have to listen to so-called leaders calling us crocodiles and leprechauns and spouting nonsense like 'curry my yoghurt' (a play on the Irish phrase 'go raibh maith agat' meaning thank you), but their days are numbered.

Thespian life

I was always interested in drama. In the early 1980s drama began to come to west Belfast with increasing frequency. Peter Sheridan's 'Diary of a Hunger Strike' was one such welcome production. By the end of the 1980s we were becoming spoilt for choice. Gearóid Ó Cairealláin and Aisteoirí Aon Dráma were providing productions in Irish and then along came Pam Brighton, Marie Jones and Shane Connaughton with DubbelJoint Theatre Company. Later still we would have Toby McMahon and the Clonard Players, JustUs Theatre Company, Aisling Ghéar, Kabosh and Brassneck Theatre Company.

Aisteoirí Aon Dráma always struggled for money. They performed miracles and provided the best of entertainment first in the Cluain Ard Club and later in Cultúrlann. There were always lots of professional actors with fluency in Irish, notably Frances Quinn, Noel Magee, Tony Devlin and Niall Cusack. I had the pleasure of acting alongside all four during my stint as an amateur thespian. I acted in various plays including 'The Polite Burglar', 'The Feast of St Michael', 'Dumbwaiter' and 'Oh Rahjerum!' The last play saw me enter the stage in a stylish red dress and red stilettos as Jane Birkin and Serge Gainsbourg's song 'Je t'aime' played in the background. A chance not all of us get! The formation of Foras na Gaeilge in 1999 provided a source of funding for Irish language drama, thanks in large part to the unstinting support of Deirdre Davitt who championed the cause.

My wife Chrissie played a huge role in the formation of the JustUs Theatre Company. She was working as Community Development officer for Féile an Phobail and was asked to do something for International Women's Day. Rather than just going with the usual, Chrissie decided to produce a play showing the experiences of the wives of IRA prisoners. She brought together Christine Poland, Maureen McGuinness, Sue Ramsey, Máighréad Uí Adhmaill, Donna McGarry, Anne Marie Adams, Brenda Murphy and Bridie McMahon (RIP). Others would join later. With help from the formidable Pam Brighton and using only their own resources and what they could beg, steal or borrow, they staged 'Just a Prisoner's Wife'. It was a brilliant and timely production, giving hugely humorous but highly political insight into the women who sustained much of the struggle and held families and communities together in the face of wholesale imprisonment. The drama had to do multiple runs and was also brought into the Portlaoise and Long Kesh prisons, where I believe everyone had a ball. They went on to stage 'Murphy's Law', 'Ordinary People' and 'Binlids', a powerful depiction of life in west Belfast during the conflict which made its way eventually to New York. JustUs was an amazing initiative which gave impetus to a new flowering of writing, acting and production experience to more than a few women who went on to have very successful careers in drama. I am very proud of my wife's role in it all.

I feel indebted to those pioneers who helped develop what is now a very lively local industry in entertainment. It would be remiss of me not to mention the huge work that is also ongoing in this field in Irish Medium schools. The students of Coláiste Feirste did me a great personal favour when we decided to open Beechmount House to the public in 2015. The building is the oldest existing house in Belfast, built in the 1750s. The students told the story of the house's 260 year history. In set pieces, with direction from Máire Mhic an Bhaird and costume design from Roland Spottiswoode, the students brought to life each of the periods of occupancy in the company of relatives of all the previous owners, who had been traced by local historian and Gaeltacht pioneer Brighid Mhic Sheáin.

The status quo ante, revisited

A huge change came about in the funding prospects for Irish language groups based in the Six Counties with the establishment of Foras na Gaeilge and its motto: 'A New Era For Irish'. The development of this project saw some money finding its way northwards for the first time. Of course the lion's share continued to be given to the Southern-based groups: Cumann na bhFiann, Conradh na Gaeilge, Oireachtas na Gaeilge, Glór na nGael, Gael Linn and Gaelscoileanna. In April 2008 Foras na Gaeilge began a review of core funding. Its main aim was to make cutbacks. Foras sought to achieve these cuts by establishing schemes which a group or groups would be invited to apply for. These would cover all the areas which were in fact the statutory obligations of Foras itself. I saw it as an attempt to cull groups critical of Foras and to franchise out the work of Foras. If that were the case, I asked at various meetings, then what was the point of Foras na Gaeilge existing. I suggested that the review was looking in the wrong direction and should in fact focus on the efficacy and effectiveness of Foras na Gaeilge itself.

That, of course, was never going to happen, in my opinion. Comhdháil Náisiúnta na Gaeilge and Forbairt Feirste tried very hard to ensure that all the groups worked together and sought to ensure the review delivered beneficial results. We managed to draft two documents supported by all groups entitled: 'Towards an agreed vision' and 'The Irish language voluntary sector – preparing for the future together'. It was obvious to me, and being reported back to me, that certain key figures were meeting in secret with Foras and were working to ensure that any available water would be used to turn their own mill wheels. Only Comhdháil Náisiúnta na Gaeilge was culled in the 26 Counties. However in the North, Forbairt Feirste, Altram, Pobal and Iontaobhas Ultach were all axed. Only Raidió Fáilte survived in the Six Counties because of the differing broadcasting regimes north and south, which ensured northern radio provision.

The process was dragged out until June 2013. As Pól Ó Muirí, the *Irish Times* Irish columnist, noted: 'The mills of God grind very slow, but its even slower in the case of the mills of Foras na Gaeilge.' During 2011 it was clear where things were headed. Forbairt had begun working closely with officials in DCAL to ensure that the progress made in the Gaeltacht Quarter wouldn't be damaged by Foras returning to the status quo ante. Forbairt was working closely with three Stormont ministers to convene a second development conference on the Gaeltacht Quarter. We succeeded in having Clive Dutton re-employed to review what progress had been achieved since 2004 and to make recommendations for actions going forward. We had the full support of Culture Minister Carál Ní Chuilín. Dutton produced his 'Big Gaeltacht Quarter Plan 2013–2033'. This was unveiled on September 20th at a conference in Coláiste Feirste along with a Gaeltacht Quarter Charter, which was signed by Stormont ministers, Carál Ní Chuilín (Culture), John O'Dowd (Education) and Mark H Durkan (Social Development) and the Mayor of Belfast, Máirtín Ó Muilleor, as well as by 200 attendees at the conference.

Dutton recommended that Forbairt Feirste be funded directly by the Department of Culture and that a joint secretariat between Forbairt and departmental officials be formed to oversee the implementation of his plan. It was a good start and under the direction of the departmental Deputy Secretary, Arthur Scott, good progress was made. Arthur appointed Damien Rae as the civil servant to handle day to day issues with myself. We became friends and Damien was quick to grasp opportunities where possible. I worked with a variety of civil servants from then on and some stood out, particularly Ian Maye, who hailed from the Village, a tight-knit working class loyalist area of Belfast. Seán Mistéil and I were at Ian's mother Sadie's funeral on July 28th and I made an arrangement to see him when he returned to work. On August 5th I got a call from Ian's colleague, Joanna McConway, telling me that Ian had unexpectedly passed away. Seán and I sadly had to make a second trip to Saint Simon's Church of Ireland on the Donegal Road.

Acht na Gaeilge: questions of identity and practicality

The question of an Irish Language Act for the Six Counties has been a bone of contention since 2003. There have been pickets, campaigns, political stand-offs and marches for more than 18 years. It was the advocacy group Pobal, led by English immigrant, Janet Muller, which was behind all the original work and responsible for the hard slog which made the issue a red line for nationalists. I admired all the work Janet did and her passion for the issue. I also felt sorry for Janet when others sidelined her and stole her clothes.

Janet had built up international support and brought in outside expertise for drafting legislative recommendations. Her most ardent collaborators were Wilson McLeod and Robert Dunbar from Edinburgh University, Fernand de Varennes from the Université de Moncton in Canada, Colin Williams from Chaerdydd University and the former Six Counties Ombudsman Maurice Hayes. Her work was vindicated with the signing of the Saint Andrew's Agreement when the British stated: 'The Government will introduce an Irish Language Act reflecting on the experience of Wales and Ireland and work with the incoming Executive to enhance and protect the development of the Irish Language.' A public consultation in December 2006 found 93 percent in favour of Irish language legislation. However from the outset it was clear that the British would leave the question to be dealt with by the flawed Stormont Assembly where it was sure to become mired in bickering. The British failed to introduce the legislation which everyone thought had been promised. Instead they left it to Ian Paisley, Peter Robinson, Arlene Foster and later Edwin Poots, all of whom have scant regard and even less respect for Irish. Poots, the then 'Kulture Minister', ordered a second consultation; in the event an increased majority supported legislation. The unionists said point-blank they would never give legal protections to Irish speakers and that was to be the tune from successive 'Culture' ministers – Poots, Gregory Campbell, Nelson McCausland and later Paul Givan. Pobal never gave up, but in the Foras na Gaeilge tilt against Six County-based Irish groups, Pobal was to lose its funding and the advocacy role was given to Conradh na Gaeilge. Conradh was much more astute in its approach. From 2014 onwards it organised 'independent' groups and campaigns but ensured that Conradh na Gaeilge personnel were the public face and spokespersons for every one. There were always two approaches to legislation, one which sought to keep the focus on organisational-based campaigning and the other which sought a broad based independent campaign. The first approach stressed a rights' based act and definitive legal protections for an exhaustive list of rights. The other sought general recognition for the Irish identity and general protections for Irish speakers' rights. I supported the second approach. In my view, the act would never be more than a symbolic recognition of Irish identity. It would be a fool's errand to put so much energy into pursuing legislation in the belief that any real or practical change would come from it. In 2022, after 16 years of wrangling, we still await the introduction of the promised Irish Language Act.

Mainstreaming the Gaeltacht Quarter

I began working in Forbairt Feirste in 2004; nine years later we were forging ahead with plans for the Gaeltacht Quarter at the level of the joint secretariat, which had been established in October 2013. We endeavoured, between the ministerial Gaeltacht Quarter conferences of 2013 and 2015, to ensure the project was included in the programme for government. We succeeded in securing that objective. We also focussed on creating a list of priority actions which would be implemented from the 'Big Gaeltacht Plan'. The programme for implementation totalled £50m over a 10 year period. Those aims achieved to date include the purchase of Cultúrlann, the Raidió Fáilte capital build, the building of Áras na bhFál, the funding of Gael Chúrsaí and phase one of the Ard na bhFeá development, including the Béal na bhFeá handball facilities and the Spórtlann na hÉireann facilities. Still to be completed are the Spás Díon – Irish Archive building, the Teach Ard na bhFeá development, the phase two Spórtlann hurling facilities and the Crannóg na bhFeá, housing and tourism development. To date £24.7m has been secured and the outstanding £25.3m is being actively pursued. On October 23rd 2015, in front of an audience of 200 delegates in Coláiste

Feirste, ministers Carál Ní Chuilín and John O'Dowd reiterated their commitment to the development of the Gaeltacht Quarter.

Minister Ní Chuilín said: 'Belfast's Gaeltacht Quarter continues to provide social, cultural and economic benefit to our entire community. There is much more than can still be achieved.'

It was a welcome endorsement of the work which had been ongoing for 15 years. It was clear that the Gaeltacht Quarter was gaining traction among politicians and opinion makers. At the same time, many unionist politicians remained to be convinced of the worth of the initiative. In 2015 Arlene Foster was elected leader of the DUP. On December 10th I wrote to her congratulating her and asking that she bring a DUP delegation to the Gaeltacht Quarter to 'appraise your party of the work being done and to seize the opportunity to advance our mutual objective of ensuring no cold places for anyone in society'.

It wasn't the last letter I would send to Arlene Foster. I have yet to receive as much as an acknowledgement. I also wrote in similar terms to her successor, Edwin Poots, on June 1st 2021 and to his nominee for First Minister Paul Givan. My latest invitation to DUP leader Jeffrey Donaldson has still not been accepted.

The majority of unionist politicians unfortunately remain as hostile to Irish as their forbears have been since the creation of the Northern statelet. I was certain that the Stormont Assembly would remain as unstable as it had been since 2013, when Peter Robinson torpedoed the institutions with his infamous 'Letter from America' putting paid to the hopes of a Peace and Reconciliation Centre at Long Kesh. I felt that the damage to the DUP/Sinn Féin rapprochement would be irreparable. Despite all the efforts and the hope of a new beginning with McGuinness and Foster it was clear that the ship was badly holed below the waterline and that sooner or later it would sink. Questions of identity, respect and the honouring of previously agreed deals would remain like an albatross around the neck of the dysfunctional set up. This had been the same since the Stormont Assembly first saw the light of day back in 1999. In my opinion political unionism and its various leaders had never genuinely engaged in the process other than as a means to advance a discourse which held republicans solely responsible for all that had gone wrong. 'House training', the 'wearing of sackcloth and ashes' and the 'holding of noses' were the only ways in which unionism would deal with Sinn Féin. They remained comfortable and convinced, not without reason, that the British government would always have their backs, irrespective of how they behaved. At an intellectual level, unionists understood that the dynamic and the demographics had changed but emotionally they couldn't deal with the corollary. Peter Robinson understood where things were headed by 2012 when he warned that unionism needed to engage and win support from nationalists. The first decade of the new millennium would see an end of the unionist majority, but there were still plenty of 'King Canutes' who convinced themselves that they could hold back the tide.

By 2013 Conradh na Gaeilge in the South had started the 'Dearg le Fearg' campaign in response to ongoing issues surrounding the Irish language. On February 2014 they brought more than 10,000 people onto the streets of Dublin. Soon they would try to replicate this in the North where they had new people employed under the Foras na Gaeilge funding scheme. They began building alliances with certain people and began a two-pronged strategy: firstly to campaign for additional resources for Irish which would of course be channelled through the six national organisations, and secondly campaigning for an Irish Language Act. They would replace Pobal, which had campaigned on this issue since 2004. Forbairt Feirste remained outside of all the manoeuvring and acted only on those issues with which we were in agreement. I counselled others to be cautious of Conradh's approach. Sadly there were individuals who bought into it as a result of self-interest and even acted with the Dublin-based vested interest groups, often against the interests of their fellow Belfast Gaels. I believe they did this because they saw opportunities for themselves. I wasn't totally surprised but I was hurt by the selfish actions of some people in particular in whom I had invested a lot of time and trust.

Forbairt Feirste continued to focus on securing resources for demonstrable need within the Belfast Irish community, seeking to build the infrastructure of the Gaeltacht Quarter and address key developments for social, economic and educational capacity building. We were aiming, as best we could, to build a strong infrastructure and basic resources so that future generations could continue to drive forward the work of ensuring social profit, significant job creation and income earning opportunities which would ensure sustainability going forward. During 2015 and 2016 we succeeded in securing commitments for a further £9m investment. However there was a lot of prevarication and delay and I sensed that all wasn't going well. The political atmosphere was growing increasingly toxic. In 2016, I started a project named Áras an tSonais (the tranquil place). A cousin of Chrissie's, Kerry Grady, had put me in touch with a Welsh stonemason and I had him travel to Ireland where he built a replica of an ancient Irish corbelled stone beehive hut in partnership with the students of Coláiste Feirste. It was to mark our ancient roots and was completed before the building work got underway to deliver a state-of-the-art 21st Century school for Belfast's Irish community. The project, which had 20 tonne of stone donated by White Mountain Quarries, also involved the shipping of slate from the Welsh Gaeltacht to underline our common Celtic heritage. It was a huge undertaking and also marked the introduction of bee-keeping and honey production to the school site. When Tom Griffiths from Llwyngwril had completed his work, I invited Waylon Gary White Deer, an elder of the Choctaw people, to preside at the official opening. Unfortunately I was hospitalised the week before the opening. I am reliably informed that they got on just fine in my absence.

Chapter 11

Differing discourses

'It's little that's not some help.' (Seanfhocal Uladh 849 Tír Chonaill)

2016 – Fresh Start or false dawn?

There was no way silk could be put on the mad goat of an Assembly at Stormont. The emperor had no clothes and the time to call it was fast approaching. Elsewhere in Ireland another crowd were also without clothes in the spring of 2016. That was the Irish Naturist Association, who organised a nudist picnic at the beach in Curraghcloe, County Wexford. The Gardaí threatened to arrest them. If both the Assembly and the Curraghcloe crew were without clothing, it was a different case with the new DUP leader, Arlene Foster, who was fond of dressing in the empire colours and who loved sporting an outsized British Crown on her lapel. There had been a brief hope that she might prove to be a breath of fresh air. It was soon clear she was nothing more than a dyed-in-the-wool frontier unionist. She became more acerbic with time. It was clear she was not the leader unionism needed in light of the changing dynamics and demographics.

Other seeds were sprouting to undermine Stormont's shaky foundations and the long-term survival of the union with Britain. Those seeds were Foster's hugely controversial Renewable Heat Initiative scheme, her total disdain for Irish speakers and her party's championing of Brexit. She and her party sided with British nationalism and the right wing European Research Group (ERG) in the deluded belief that the arch Tories would be more than fair-weather friends. The question of the Irish language, although the least important, would prove to be the straw that broke the camel's back. An ailing Martin McGuinness forced Arlene Foster from office in 2017 making specific reference to this issue. In the South the general election of February 26th delivered the 32nd Dáil. Fine Gael secured 49 seats, Fianna Fáil 44, Sinn Féin 23 and Labour seven seats. Labour had suffered a loss of 30 seats, leaving them just one ahead of Solidarity/People Before Profit. The remaining seats went to smaller parties and independents. The 32nd Dáil lasted longer than anyone expected, thanks to Micheál Martin's decision to prop up the Fine Gael minority government. But things would become even more grim for the big establishment parties in the 33rd Dáil elected on February 8th 2020. Sinn Féin won 37 seats, Fianna Fáil 37 and Fine Gael 35. Labour and PBP both lost one seat and the Green Party secured 12. It was a nightmare scenario for the establishment. It was June 27th before the Civil War enemy parties cobbled together a government with rotating taoisigh and cabinet ministers. Fine Gael's Leo Varadkar and Fianna Fail's Micheál Martin are the embodiment of neo-liberals in the classic style of Margaret Thatcher.

For me personally 2016 would prove to be a horrendous year. During Christmas 2015 I felt inexplicably out of sorts. I couldn't understand what was ailing me. At the end of January I arrived for work but simply sat outside my office incapable of entering the building. I was in a stupor, unable to motivate myself and feeling an anxiety I'd never experienced before. I made my way to my mother's grave and sat there for hours, questioning myself. Over a number of weeks I became progressively worse. I wouldn't see anyone and hid upstairs at home. I lost my appetite, stopped sleeping and showering. I was haunted by thoughts of suicide. I was in turmoil and in hell. It was as if someone else had taken possession of my body. I was living day to day, in reality hour to hour. I still find it difficult to adequately describe the awfulness of my condition. I was in a bitter and bottomless pit. Negative thoughts were swirling around me like a whirlpool, pulling me deeper into darkness and despair. I was in a bleak place, unable to reach anyone. Others, despite their best efforts, were unable to reach me. I felt like curling up into a ball and quietly dying. The anguish and the suffering were overwhelming. Somehow, behind the maelstrom of negativity and thoughts of self-harm, a voice of reason somewhere in the recesses of my mind reminded me that I was thinking illogically. When I managed to sleep for any length of time my waking thought was why I hadn't just died in my sleep. Chrissie told me I was depressed and should seek help. I eventually went to see my doctor, who prescribed pills and arranged an emergency appointment with a counsellor for me. This got me through the immediate crisis of suicidal thoughts, but I still felt rudderless. I felt I was wading through treacle. My emotions were topsy turvy and constantly fighting with each other. My mind was my enemy. I felt alone, afraid, desolate, empty and ashamed. It was as though I was a ghost person, doing all the basic tasks to get through the day. I was surviving but not living. I was a stranger to myself and unable to read or focus. Without my family and close friends I couldn't have clawed my way back from the depths to which I had sank. I discontinued counselling as I feared it could become a cul-de-sac. Chrissie was a tower of strength for me. After a while I was able to go out walking with an old friend and gradually I recovered the will to live. Seán Mistéil, Pilib Ó Ruanaidh, Pádraig Ó Maolchraoibhe and a few others were a huge help to me.

By May I felt that I was suffering from a heavy flu. I was hot and cold by turns and was beset by cold night sweats. I was exhausted. Over a number of days things got progressively worse. I finally consented to go to hospital where my temperature was recorded at 42 degrees. I was hospitalised for six weeks and was told that I had suffered an unidentified viral infection. I continued to try my best to work but I was functioning well below par. My daughter Orliath was a constant source of advice and by September she had given me the name of a private counsellor. I reasoned that if I was paying for counselling I would avoid this issue becoming a cul-de-sac and so I contacted Jarlath Benson. I began a series of counselling sessions which commenced on September 13th 2016 and lasted until January 24th 2018.

On first meeting Jarlath I felt he was someone I could work with. He had a great sense of presence, an immediacy and a depth which I found reassuring and calming. His counselling suite was perfect for me, an old mill with thick solid walls coming down with books. In the upper room a large window looked out over a pond where ducks and swans swam. It felt safe and secure. However I was still very unsettled in myself and was embarking on a long and painful journey. Jarlath explained to me that I was making the journey of the Italian poet, Dante Alighieri. I would journey down through purgatory to hell before setting my feet on a path to whatever paradise I could find. It took time and patience. I shed many tears along the way and for the first time I began to actually feel the emotions and wounds that I had 'securely' locked away in their mental compartments. I would recite some experience to Jarlath and he would stop me at some point to ask: 'And how did you feel about that?' I would nearly always respond: 'That's how it was. It was normal.' He would explain that it wasn't normal. Gradually I began to see that my life, like so many others, had been anything but normal. My doctor explained to me that I was suffering Post Traumatic Stress.

Thanks to Jarlath I eventually emerged from the nightmare. Beyond depression I found myself much more comfortable in my own skin. I was much calmer and thanks to certain insights and small coping mechanisms Jarlath equipped me to live with my condition. In our early sessions he gave me insights: feelings aren't facts, there are many complex and sometimes competing elements to our being. I needed to relive and lay to rest painful experiences during our session. I learned that we are multi-layered and complex beings. Jarlath gave me useful ways to regain and retain peace. He explained that I should view the central voice in my internal conversation as a conductor who, from all the discordant sounds, could bring a harmonious symphony. If any voice got too noisy or was causing disharmony, the conductor needed to ensure it was brought back into sync. The ammunition to fight the flight to the hamster wheel and a harmonious inner dialogue were necessary for the attainment of peace. I need not be the best at anything, which was the eternal bane of my life. Now I simply try to do my best. Jarlath taught me perspective and humility. I always understood that I was no better than anyone else and that no one was better than me. I gained a simple lesson out of this, which I paid dearly for, and that was that none of us is really very important. Life will go on without us. The only really important things are integrity, health and the love of family and friends. Hope is always there and the only thing in life which can't be fixed is death.

By the end of the year things were looking bleak at Stormont. Amidst the already swirling scandals, the new opposition parties were raising a storm over the dispersal of a £20m Strategic Investment Fund, £1.7m of which had found its way into the coffers of Charter NI, a group associated with the UDA. The SDLP branded it as a slush fund and alleged funding was doled out to favoured community groups. The scandal of the £400m spent on the RHI project hung over Stormont like the sword of Damocles. The establishment was hanging by a thread as the other political parties pushed for a vote of no confidence in Arlene Foster, which she lost. Martin McGuinness made an impassioned plea for her to temporarily stand aside. However with supreme arrogance she dismissed any such notion of stepping aside. Sinn Féin began consulting its base and was taken aback by the depth of antipathy to Stormont. To drive the last nail into Stormont's coffin Paul Givan withdrew a minor £50,000 fund available for underprivileged children to attend Gaeltacht courses. He tweeted the news out two days before Christmas adding: 'Happy Christmas to you'. Gerry Adams described him as an ignoramus. It was the latest insult of many. The perceived pettiness and vindictiveness caused huge anger across the nationalist community.

On January 9th McGuinness announced that he was resigning, finally forcing Foster from office. In his resignation letter McGuinness spoke of stretching republicans further than he thought possible. He said that he had pursued his strategy for 10 difficult and testing years.

> At times I have challenged republicans and nationalists in my determination to reach out to our unionist neighbours. It is a source of deep personal frustration that those efforts have not always been reciprocated by unionist leaders. At times they have been met with outright rejection.

He laid the blame for the fall of Stormont squarely at the door of the DUP.

The equality, mutual respect and all-Ireland approaches enshrined in the Good Friday Agreement have never been fully embraced by the DUP. Apart from the negative attitude to nationalism and to the Irish identity and culture, there has been a shameful disrespect towards many other sections of our community. Women, the LGBT community and ethnic minorities have all felt this prejudice. And for those who wish to live their lives through the medium of Irish, elements in the DUP have exhibited the most crude and crass bigotry. The days of appeasement of unreconstructed unionism were over.

End of the status quo ante

It was clear when Martin McGuinness appeared at Stormont to inform Foster of his decision to resign that he was a very ill man. I had known from conversations with friends that he was seriously ill, but I was still shocked when I saw him on television. Within a fortnight of his resignation it was announced that the veteran republican would not stand in the election of March 2nd. By March 21st Martin McGuinness was dead. He was aged just 66.

I first met Martin McGuinness in Crumlin Road Gaol in 1975 but would get to know him better after my release from jail in the 1980s. We had disagreed on many things. I always viewed him as a Catholic nationalist, but he was at the heart of the republican struggle from the beginning. He was a key figure in the leadership for 40 years. He gave his life to the cause. I felt immensely sad for his family and especially his soul-mate Bernie from whom he was snatched at the point where they might have got to spend more time together. I was among the thousands who proudly attended his funeral. There was speculation about Arlene Foster's attendance. In the end she did the right thing. It was clear that McGuinness was a folk hero in his native Derry. He was widely loved within the republican family. Those who suffered at the hands of republicans had a different view. That was understandable. To their credit, most political opponents gave his family the space to grieve with dignity.

New leaders were taking up the reins of Sinn Féin by 2018. Michelle Ó'Neill had replaced Martin McGuinness as deputy leader and Mary Lou McDonald, who had joined the party in 1998 after having been a member of Fianna Fáil, had become the new president. It is still much too soon to assess where the new leadership will take the party. It is clear however, with the departure through death of Brian Keenan, Kevin McKenna, Joe Cahill and Martin McGuinness and the retirement from front-line activism of Pat Doherty, Martin Ferris and Gerry Adams, that an era has ended.

The status quo had ended, both within Sinn Féin and Stormont. In total 90 MLAs had been elected in 2017 but they wouldn't take their seats until January 2020, when British Secretary of State Julian Smith and Dublin Foreign Affairs Minister Simon Coveney, bounced the local parties back into Stormont with a take it or leave it deal, known as New Decade New Approach (NDNA). The DUP lost 1.1 percent of the vote share, ending up with 28 seats. Sinn Féin increased its vote share by 3.9 percent gaining 27 seats. Only 1,168 votes separated the two biggest parties. The SDLP managed to secure 12 seats and the UUP continued its decline holding on to 10 seats. Alliance returned a respectable eight seats on an increased vote share of 9.1 percent.

June saw an election to Westminster, when the SDLP and UUP lost all their representatives to the English parliament. Sinn Féin and the DUP both gained seats and votes to leave them with 10 and seven seats respectively. The DUP was cock-a-hoop, holding the balance of power with Theresa May's government. However the party seriously overplayed its hand. As a consequence, the DUP left itself in a post-Brexit pickle which engendered an existential crisis for unionism and the Union.

Even though the MLAs had been elected to Stormont, ordinary nationalists had no desire to see the assembly revived. Sinn Féin understood the mood. Danny Morrison had been out of the Sinn Féin mainstream for a long time, but there were many, myself included, who believed that the Sinn Féin leadership used him regularly to fly kites and test positions that the party couldn't or wouldn't. In 2013, when Peter Robinson sent his infamous 'Letter from America', Danny wrote on Eamonn Mallie's blog: 'I hope I am wrong but I suspect that the Assembly could collapse. If unionists are thinking this cannot happen, they should think again.' After the fall of Stormont in 2017, Danny wrote in the *Irish News*: 'It appeared to me, even at that stage, (after Christmas 2016) that Sinn Féin was still trying to preserve things but I believe the base had shifted.' Danny was right. There was no more stomach for Stormont among the republican base, even if the leadership was content to keep the thing afloat. During the election Foster made clear there would be no Irish Language Act saying, 'If you feed a crocodile, it will keep coming back for more.' The anger even among soft nationalists was palpable.

Brexit brought the national question centre stage. On June 14th Leo Varadkar replaced the totally ineffectual Enda Kenny as leader of Fine Gael and taoiseach and Simon Coveney took over the Department of Foreign Affairs. Neither were any less anti-republican than their predecessors. In fairness they were to play a very good hand. In the Six Counties tensions were higher than at any time since the ceasefire. Unionists were constantly claiming there was a so-called cultural war being waged against them. The term had first been used by former convicted UVF gunman Billy Hutchinson back in 2013. Hutchinson served life for the 1974 murder of two Catholics, Michael Loughran (18) and Edward Morgan (27). They were among 95 innocent Catholics murdered that year. Hutchinson claimed in an interview in 2014 that the killings had prevented a united Ireland.

The turbulent year of 2017 was to end with the arrival of Storm Ophelia which wreaked havoc across Ireland and prevented former US president Bill Clinton from flying into the Six Counties where he had intended to persuade the local parties to get Stormont back up and running.

Dearg le Fearg and the deal that was or wasn't

Following the success of the Dearg le Fearg march in Dublin in 2013, it was decided that an independent group would be set up in the Six Counties to campaign for an Irish Language Act. The first meeting was held in Cumann Chluain Ard. I proposed to the meeting that no group should be allowed to hijack the campaign, which should remain broad-based and free from organisational self-interest. I also proposed that no spokesperson for the group should be aged over 30. The group adopted the name of Dream Dearg. By 2016 the group had come to prominence following repeated unionist insults and attacks. Unfortunately Conradh na Gaeilge ensured that its people were always organising and seen in the front line. They were also always acting as spokespersons for the group. Before long the youthful enthusiastic campaigning would be displaced as Conradh na Gaeilge made itself the sole spokespeople on the question of an Irish Language Act.

Dream Dearg's first demonstration in Belfast was a huge success. On January 12th, the morning of the march, the DUP's Paul Givan reinstated the Gaeltacht Bursaries, but the march went ahead. It was a popular demonstration that unionist racism and suppression wouldn't be tolerated. Stormont had been pulled down three days before the march, giving lie to later claims by some activists who convinced themselves that the Dream Dearg campaign had brought down Stormont.

There was a new and hugely uplifting energy with the campaign and I was delighted to see activists of all ages taking to the streets. I personally thought the demand for an Irish Language Act was ever only going to be symbolic. It wouldn't and won't deliver any real change but it was great to see people active. There was hope that, if handled right, the campaigning could lead to significant gains around real need.

I was coming out of my darkest period and was delighted to make my first public outing with my grandchildren to attend the 'Lá Dearg' day of action on April 12th. More than 10,000 people made their way to Belfast City Hall for a rally and carnival supporting Irish language rights. Thousands of activists gathered outside Cultúrlann in a happy, exuberant and carnival crowd. I saw no one who was Dearg le Fearg ('Red with Anger'). What I witnessed was a good-humoured crowd, united in their determination to show unrelenting positivity while beset by anti-Irish negativity. This issue would be central to any efforts at putting Stormont back together. Later in April crowds of young people converged on the headquarters of the Education Authority to overturn savage cuts to Irish Medium youth provision. I was delighted they succeeded.

The new year was to see talks at Stormont. But on February 9th Arlene Foster tweeted that it was all over. The text of the deal, which the DUP pulled back from at the last moment, was published by local journalists Brian Rowan and Eamonn Mallie. Sinn Féin had got precious little on the Irish language, marriage equality or on a Bill of Rights. Later when I was interviewed on television I described the deal as a 'mess of pottage'. The DUP did us a favour scuppering it. The substance would be repackaged in 2020 and sold as the 'New Decade New Approach' deal, foisted on the parties by the British and Irish governments. I wrote a piece for Eamonn Mallie's blog stating that unionist hegemony was always based on the premise and the promise that they would forever resist nationalist encroachment. They did such a good job of making the Irish speaking community the new bogeyman that they left themselves with no wriggle room. From 1998 onward, unionists increasingly placed their focus on the Irish speaking community. They poured their anti-nationalist bile on Irish speakers as they could no longer vent their spleen so vociferously against their new Sinn Féin partners in government. The DUP elevated their cultural war against all things Irish or Gaelic. Paul Givan's Christmas present was the straw that broke the camel's back. Even nationalists who would have no truck with Sinn Féin were outraged. Unionism needs honest and proper leadership, which takes account of new realities, instead of selling a dream of the return to the 'good old days'. They need leadership which will secure their future on the island of Ireland in a way which is to their benefit and the benefit of all who live here. I've seen nothing in the interim from the DUP which would suggest such leadership is going to emerge, but we live in hope and die in despair.

Chapter 12

Life beyond the nightmare

'Moderation is good.' (Seanfhocail Uladh 693 Tír Chonaill)

Pax Americana and the pursuit of empire

The jihadist attack on New York's Twin Towers in 2001 was a defining moment in recent history which had a huge political impact. The attack has been analysed to the point where I for one am exhausted with it. I'll not add to it all, other than to say that it provided Western neo-liberal hawks with the excuse they needed to mould the world in their own image. North America and their puppets unleashed a carnival of war, horror and destruction which cost the lives of millions and the displacement of millions from Afghanistan to Iraq, Libya to Syria and Sudan to Yemen.

George Bush Junior's 'Operation Enduring Freedom', abetted by Tony Blair, cost 170,000 lives in Afghanistan. In neighbouring Iraq more than 655,000 were butchered in 'Operation Iraqi Freedom' and all that flowed from it. The world is still paying for the destabilisation of the region. In the civil war in Libya, fomented by the Americans, British and French more than 25,000 perished and 4,000 people remain missing. A once thriving and prosperous country has been reduced to chaos. In Syria the story is worse still; 470,000 have perished with more than 12 percent of the population having been injured. More than five million citizens, from a population of 22 million, have been turned into refugees, while 13.5 million have been reduced to dependency on international aid. In the Republic of Yemen and in Sudan the Americans and their puppets in the medieval Kingdom of Saudi Arabia have spent billions buying arms to fuel a war which has plunged the region into famine and claimed the lives of 230,000 people. Tragedy has also beset Myanmar. The vast majority of the war materials being used in all these conflicts emanate directly or indirectly from North America and Britain. These same pair of 'rogue nations' are also responsible for supporting and arming the Zionist war machine which is engaged in the wholesale slaughter of Palestinians.

Outside of their reprehensible role in warmongering and destabilisation, the British have also deeply unsettled their former unionist allies in the Six Counties with Brexit and its consequent protocol. Their contempt for international law and international treaties into which they had freely entered is staggering. All this, in the pursuit of a return to the glory days of the empire which are never coming back. That they wish for such a return is an indication of how little they really regret the wholesale slaughter and misery they brought to Africa, India, Ireland and elsewhere. You could be forgiven for thinking that these rogues have put the world on a journey to hell in a handcart. World politics is in as bad a state as it was with the rise of fascism in the 1930s. The right wing is gathering strength and Trumpism, while it lasted, distorted the mass media to such an extent that it was extremely difficult to believe anything we heard, watched or read. But as it says in Matthew 24:6: 'You will hear of wars and rumours of wars; but don't be alarmed, such things must happen, but the end is still to come.'

There were also moments of hope. I was privileged to be invited by friends in the Catalonian left party, Candidatura d'Unitat Poular, to observe the Catalonian referendum for freedom on October 1st 2017. I joined local people in the Sant district of Barcelona to secure a school from the threat of Spanish police occupation. The school was due to be used for voting. I stayed overnight in the school with friends and CUP activists, Gemma Garcia Fábrega and her partner, David Fernandez Ramos, in the company of hundreds of other freedom-loving citizens. The raw brutality unleashed by the Spanish Guardia Civil was awful to watch. I witnessed at first hand the horrendous attacks on peaceful voters. The spirit and courage of the Catalonian people was inspirational. Early on the morning of the referendum I watched two orderly lines of voters standing along the road to the polling station. A very elderly woman was brought in a wheelchair through the lines of people to cast the first vote. She had been a young girl during the fascist crushing of the Second Workers' Republic in 1931. Thousands greeted her with huge applause when she emerged from the polling station and gave a clenched-fist salute and said in a clear voice: 'Visca Catalunya,' 'Victory to Catalonia'. I had a lump in my throat as the crowd responded in one voice with the same battle cry.

The failed state reaches 100

It wasn't meant to be this way. Unionism had been all set to have its celebrations, bedecked in bunting with a jolly good knees up to mark the 100th anniversary of the 'Protestant state for the Protestant people'. Instead there have been back-room conspiracies, young loyalists rioting with the police and blood on the carpet at private DUP meetings. And, as if that all wasn't bad enough, we had the spectacle of the public slaying of Arlene Foster in the worst political assassination in DUP history. The removal of the previous two leaders, Ian Paisley and Peter Robinson, was made to have looked like a benign passing of the baton. Coronation without public acrimony had always been the DUP way. Any dirty linen was always washed strictly in private. Not so with the ditching of Arlene. Her sudden and very public dumping, the leadership contest which followed it, and the election and swift dumping of Edwin Poots was a very bruising and nasty affair. It was all a very far cry from the 2016 chanting of 'Arlene's on fire' at the DUP party conference at Shaws Bridge. Back then DUP members filled the stage in front of a banner proclaiming 'Strong Leadership for a Better Future' as the woman who was portrayed as their great hope danced on stage along with the rest for all she was worth.

Edwin Poots, whose father once called for the cutting of water and electricity supplies to nationalist areas, was to be the man who led the push on April 27th 2021. Arlene, who seemed taken completely by surprise, received news of a letter of no-confidence against her allegedly signed by 22 DUP elected representatives. She resigned the following day but has still to have sight of the letter which sent her packing. Poots then mercilessly wielded the knife, which had been sharpened ever since the introduction of the border in the Irish Sea. Unionism's crisis was out in the open and a bitterly divided DUP eventually elected Poots as their new leader when he defeated rival Jeffrey Donaldson by a margin of 19 to 17 votes. Poots' tenure of the top seat was short-lived and rival Donaldson must now seek to reunite a badly divided house.

Arlene had been held responsible for the worst own-goal in unionist history. The very Brexit, which she and her party had so keenly fought for, was to prove an existential threat to their floundering statelet. Their much lauded deal with Boris Johnson and their support for the European Research Group (ERG) had come back to bite them big time. Boris did as the Johnsons of this world had always done – he dumped the DUP who had wildly applauded him as the saviour of the Union, as soon as their usefulness to 'Project Boris' was over.

Unionism has never faced such a crisis and it is floundering in the face of it. Splits, recriminations, resignations and a deeply unsettled and potentially violent loyalism had turned what was supposed to have been a year of celebrations into a year of fear. The emergence of a Loyalist Community Council, which fronts, amongst others, the outlawed loyalist paramilitaries of the UDA, UVF and Red Hand Commando, has made its malign influence felt within all shades of unionism. Back in 1994 when the IRA declared a ceasefire, the then unionist leader James Molyneaux had described it as: 'The most destabilising event since partition and the worst thing to that has ever happened to us.' Now 27 years later, unionism faces another crossroads. The wasted years since that ceasefire have seen unionism avoiding having to deal with the underlying causes of conflict and operating like King Canute. They couldn't ever have realistically hoped to hold back the tides of change for ever. Change is now an imperative and rather than trying to shape their future on the island of their birth in a new partnership with their fellow citizens, they are thrashing about, threatening violence and burying their heads in the sand in the vain hope that things can go back to the way they were. Unionism is no longer the force it once was and, while it may be capable of fomenting unrest and instability, it has neither the strength nor the wherewithal to make good on its threats.

We may not like to admit it, but the sense of being an oppressed and maligned group is no less real for unionists and loyalists than it is for the white racist underclasses of England or the USA. Orangeism, like white supremacy, was possessed of all the political power, never mind that the working class white or orange privilege was more imagined than real. In the anachronistic Orange state, unionism, orangeism and loyalism had unlimited power to name and define all within the state in its own image. When the 'spectre' of sharing power with 'mere nationalists' looks like becoming inescapable is it any wonder that the empowerment of the 'lesser breeds' feels like oppression? Any recognition of rights for all takes on the character of 'concessions', 'betrayals' and an attack on 'our culture'.

For all the tragedy, heartache and slaughter which flowed from Britain's interference in Irish affairs, we remain one people on a very small island on the periphery of Europe. Surely in all our diversity we can enter into sensible dialogue without recourse to threats or a return to the violence which we all hope is a thing of the past.

We could all do worse in our current situation than to pledge, each and every one of us, that we will work to ensure no return to the violence of the past, no matter what. None of us possesses a crystal ball. Nor can we imagine what is possible in the time ahead. However one thing we can be sure of is that we will all continue to share this place that we all call home for the foreseeable future. No one can reasonably be asked or expected to abandon their culture but the creation of justice, peace, equality and mutual respect for each others' traditions is surely the aim of all sane people. No longer should we tolerate the disparaging of people's identity. No longer can we tolerate a hankering after supremacy of one over the other. For unionism there are two incontrovertible lessons from their history: one is that Britain will never have any relationship with them, other than one based on narrow British self-interest, and the second is that every time they have to return to the negotiating table their salami will always be sliced thinner.

The unionist dysfunctional statelet only lasted as long as it did because its sectarian monolith did what it had been designed to do. It kept nationalists out of power and ensured they would never have power. They ruled the place with an iron fist and ensured unionist supremacy, making sure that the croppies lay down. Their misrule ensured that the nationalist uprising which came in the late 1960s was always going to occur, sooner or later. That unionist monolith is now fractured beyond repair and won't ever be reconstructed. The 2022 Assembly election has put paid to any notion that unionism can revive its fortunes. Nationalism is in the ascendant. All is changed and changed utterly; it only remains for unionism to come to terms with the new era. Unionism in its centenary year is in a bad place. Four of the Six Counties now have nationalist majorities. The unionist bastion of Belfast now has a Sinn Féin majority and unionists have a precarious hold on only one of Belfast's parliamentary seats. Unionism is no longer a majority. It faces the prospect of a Sinn Féin First Minister at Stormont in the short term and also the possibility of Sinn Féin in government in Dublin. Unionism is without a vision and we must all hope against hope that a pragmatic leadership will eventually emerge. The tide of demographic change is not going to recede and nothing that unionism or loyalism can do will change that reality. We can have managed change and transition, or we can have chaos and further alienation and desperation among working class loyalists.

The future of the Six County link with Britain now rests solely on the will of the majority of people who live here. Calls for a referendum on Irish reunification have been given a massive boost by Brexit. Nationalism, with or without unionism, will remain heavily engaged in making sure that any such referendum will be planned for in detail and will be well managed.

The last word, at least for now

As I pen these final words, I am very conscious that I am now less than two years younger than my mother and my eldest sister when they died. Tomorrow is promised to none of us and that's the reason I am always delighted to welcome each new dawn. I've seen a bit of life. Some was bad, some was fair, some good and some wonderful. It takes all sorts to make life interesting. Variety is indeed the spice of life. I've attempted in the previous pages to give a flavour of my life; the black, white and grey. I really don't feel I have more than 60 years under my belt. It went very quickly. I, like all of you, have no idea what the future holds for me. I'll live until I die, be that next week, next year or in 20 years time. Life is fleeting and you only get the one. As the poet said in Psalm 39:

> My days are but a few breaths, my lifetime is as nothing. Everyone stands as a mere breath. Everyone goes about like a shadow. For nothing they are in turmoil; they heap up and do not know who will gather.

They say wisdom comes with age. I'm not so sure. I do know that our journey is often the destination in itself. Too many of us rush through our days which are all too precious. We miss out on simple pleasures which come from contact with nature. We miss out on the worth of the people we encounter from day to day. Love and life's wonders are like a rare and precious flower: you never know where you will find them and they often are found in the most unlikely of places. I was lucky to find and nurture the culture and the language of the Gael, that precious heritage which came down to us from the people who shaped this land of our birth. The wisdom and richness of our ancestors survived, despite the worst efforts of invaders who tried to stamp out all trace of Irishness. The Irish language and the values of the Gael have informed and enriched my way of living. I still firmly believe that 'the reconquest of Irish is the reconquest of Ireland and that the reconquest of Ireland is the reconquest of Irish', as Máirtín Ó Cadhain said.

I was 10 years old when Belfast's Irish pioneers began the Gaelic revolution in the city. We haven't seen the end of that revolution yet. It will last 100 years and more. I am very proud of all that has been achieved. There is, of course, a lot of talk about a re-unified Ireland and why wouldn't there be with everything so utterly changed in the Six Counties? I am convinced this will happen in my lifetime. But what shape will it take? Brexit has ensured that re-unification will be the eventual outcome and it is also, in my opinion, the true beginning of the full and complete end of the British empire. Britain will cease to be a world power, a process which has been ongoing since the end of the Second World War, in which it only played a peripheral role. I believe we will also live to see the end of the disunited kingdom itself. Brexit and the shenanigans of unionists have also made another thing certain. It has convinced nationalists of all hues that the six county statelet is unworkable and unsustainable. The beginning of the end for the Orange statelet began with the popular nationalist uprising of the late 1960s. The subsequent IRA campaign ensured it would never return. Brexit has kick started a real debate around the best way to shape and reunify Ireland. We need careful planning and measured debate as we move forward to ensure that we don't repeat the mistakes of the past. The people themselves must seize the initiative. Within our own organisations and spheres of influence we need to shape the dialogue so that we shape an Ireland which serves the genuine needs of all our people of whatever tradition, where the forces of conservatism, north and south, who have nothing but self-interest at heart, are marginalised. The debate is well under way. We need to seize the moment.

I'm convinced that our Gaelic revolution will not be driven forward by tokenistic campaigning but rather by Irish speakers taking resolute and self-confident actions which guarantee our future. Irish speakers need to be self-confident and self-reliant. We shouldn't be inciting anyone to anger. As Liz Saville Roberts from Plaid Cymru told us at the last Gaeltacht Quarter lecture before Covid, the Irish language and culture should provide people with an enjoyable experience. It should be full of joy and celebration and not a cause for anger or strife. We should be encouraging people to positive activism which identifies real need and then puts in place plans and strategies to meet that need. Let's all be part of the collective and let our mantra be: 'Don't say it, do it'.

In my own personal life I had to reach the depths so that I could reach for the heights. There is more understanding and more openness now around mental health and to anyone suffering with it, I hope you find the courage and help to face your challenges. That which doesn't kill us, strengthens us. In the final analysis, the only thing in life which has no cure or remedy is death. I began to write this memoir in 2018 and the process was cathartic. I hope you've enjoyed the read. It wasn't my intention to deliberately hurt or insult anyone in the writing of my story. This memoir is just a collection of reminiscences and reflections on those things which left an impression on me. I met many people on my journey who gave me hope, joy and inspiration, people who gave me insights into all that is best in the human spirit. I met others who had faults and weaknesses which led them on a different path. But it's never too late for change and maybe even some of those will straighten themselves out. Our common humanity is what binds us all together. Let's build on that. We can all, at times, be quick to judge and slow to forgive. Where there's life there's hope and where there's hope there's life. I came into this world, according to my mother, naked and empty-handed on a bathboard. I'll most likely go out the same way, though probably in a box and not on a bathboard. That is if I can't get permission to be disposed off in a recycling bin.

If I offended or upset anyone in these pages all I can say is: forgive me my trespasses as you so often and so readily forgive your own. Remember we are Gaels, as were our ancestors before us. We don't sleep, we simply rest from time to time. *Beirígí bua*.